# POLICE STREET POWERS AND CRIMINAL JUSTICE

Police Street Powers and Criminal Justice analyses the utilisation, regulation and legitimacy of police powers. Drawing upon six-years of ethnographic research in two police forces in England, this book uncovers the importance of time and place, supervision and monitoring, local policies and law. Covering a period when the police were under intense scrutiny and subject to austerity measures, the authors contend that the concept of police culture does not help us understand police discretion. They argue that change is a dominant feature of policing and identify fragmented responses to law and policy reform, varying between police stations, across different policing roles, and between senior and frontline ranks.

# Police Street Powers and Criminal Justice

*Regulation and Discretion in a Time of Change*

Geoff Pearson
and
Mike Rowe

·HART·

OXFORD · LONDON · NEW YORK · NEW DELHI · SYDNEY

HART PUBLISHING

Bloomsbury Publishing Plc

Kemp House, Chawley Park, Cumnor Hill, Oxford, OX2 9PH, UK

1385 Broadway, New York, NY 10018, USA

29 Earlsfort Terrace, Dublin 2, Ireland

HART PUBLISHING, the Hart/Stag logo, BLOOMSBURY and the Diana logo are
trademarks of Bloomsbury Publishing Plc

First published in Great Britain 2020

First published in hardback, 2020
Paperback edition, 2022

A catalogue record for this book is available from the British Library.

**Library of Congress Cataloging-in-Publication Data**

Names: Pearson, Geoffrey, author. | Rowe, Michael, 1967- author.

Title: Police street powers and criminal justice : regulation and discretion in a time of change /
Geoff Pearson and Mike Rowe.

Description: Oxford ; New York : Hart, [2020] | Includes bibliographical references and index.

Identifiers: LCCN 2020009203 (print) | LCCN 2020009204 (ebook) |
ISBN 9781509925377 (hardcover) | ISBN 9781509925384 (Epub)

Subjects: LCSH: Police—Great Britain. | Police power—Great Britain.

Classification: LCC HV8195.A2 P43 2020 (print) | LCC HV8195.A2 (ebook) |
DDC 363.2/30941—dc23

LC record available at https://lccn.loc.gov/2020009203

LC ebook record available at https://lccn.loc.gov/2020009204

ISBN: HB: 978-1-50992-537-7
PB: 978-1-50994-409-5
ePDF: 978-1-50992-539-1
ePub: 978-1-50992-538-4

Typeset by Compuscript Ltd, Shannon

To find out more about our authors and books visit www.hartpublishing.co.uk. Here you will find
extracts, author information, details of forthcoming events and the option to sign up for our newsletters.

# ACKNOWLEDGEMENTS

We must start by thanking our research participants, the many frontline police officers who volunteered to have an academic alongside them for the duration of their shift. It goes without saying that this work could not have been possible without them. In particular, some volunteers tolerated our presence and our questions on more occasions than it would be reasonable to have asked or expected. We hope we have done justice to them and have presented here something of their working world that they would recognise. Access to these volunteers would also not have been possible without a number of key contacts in both forces, who we would also like to thank. Ultimately both forces opened themselves up for scrutiny and criticism, which we appreciate is not always an easy thing to do. As with our volunteers, unfortunately we cannot name the key contacts at either force for reasons of anonymity.

Ethnographic work of this nature takes time, and we would like to thank those in our departments who have given us the freedom to spend so much time in the field, most notably Professor David Gadd and Professor Toby Seddon at The University of Manchester Law School. Over the six years of this project, we have also had some fellow travellers who have offered insights and assisted with some of the leg work. In this category, we would like to extend our gratitude to Dr Liz Turner and Lisa Weston, both at the University of Liverpool. Others have helped us to develop particular concepts that have been important for this book. In particular, thanks to Professor Ken Ehrensal, at the Kutztown University of Pennsylvania, who encouraged us to cast a critical eye over the knotty problem of 'police culture', and Dr Charmian Werren, at the University of Birmingham, who provided helpfully critical comments on the subject of 'ACAB'. We would also like to thank Dr Paul Quinton from the College of Policing for information and advice at various different stages of the research.

We have had further support, encouragement, and critique from participants at the Annual Ethnography Symposium. For most of the last six years, they have heard versions of parts of this work, sometimes only to hear a slight development on the same theme the following year. As an interdisciplinary audience and forum, the Symposium is a test-bed like no other. It is unfair to single one from amongst a community, but particular mention might be made of Professor John van Maanen, who has given valuable support to the Symposium and to our work from the start. We should also acknowledge contributions and questions from participants at the conferences of the Socio-Legal Studies Association and the European Society of Criminology, and the emerging Police Ethnographies annual symposium.

We would also like to express our appreciation to the team at Hart who undertook to publish this work: to one anonymous reviewer for their positive feedback (we now know who you are!), to Sinead Maloney, the editorial director who steered the proposal through, Bill Asquith, the senior commissioning editor, Sasha Jawed and Savannah Rado, our publishing assistants, and Maria Skrzypiec, the copy editor. We were also assisted in this work through the comments of two readers of early drafts, Christina Ashworth and Valerie Pearson. However, all errors are ours and ours alone! Finally, having spent many hours, days, and nights in the field, we should also acknowledge that this has entailed the passing of many caring and domestic duties onto two forbearing partners, Rachel Johnston and Christina Ashworth. We appreciate that dog walking, cat feeding, and school runs have been going on while we have been spending those long periods of time working alongside the frontline officers who are the focus for this book.

# CONTENTS

# ABBREVIATIONS

| | |
|---|---|
| ACAB | All Cops Are Bastards |
| ACPO | Association of Chief Police Officers (now NPCC) |
| ANPR | The Automatic Vehicle Number Plate Recognition system |
| APP | The College of Policing's Authorised Professional Practice guidance |
| ARV | Armed Response Vehicle |
| BOP | Breach of the Peace |
| BWC | Body-Worn Camera |
| BWV | Body-Worn Video (the footage taken from a Body-Worn Camera) |
| CPS | Crown Prosecution Service |
| Cuffing | The act of hiding a criminal offence that an officer is aware of |
| DASH | An electronic form that acts as a risk assessment tool for incidents of Domestic Abuse, Stalking and Harassment and Honour-based Violence |
| DVPN | Domestic Violence Protection Notice |
| EBP | Evidence-Based Policing |
| ECHR | The European Convention on Human Rights |
| GO WISELY | A mnemonic to assist officers remember how to conduct searches (Grounds; Object; Warrant; Identification; Station; Entitlement; Legislation; You) |
| HMICFRS | Her Majesty's Inspectorate of Constabulary and Fire & Rescue Services (formerly HMIC) |
| HRA 1998 | The Human Rights Act 1998 |
| MDT | A Mobile Data Terminal, built into a police vehicle |
| MDA | The Misuse of Drugs Act 1971 |
| NCRS | The National Crime Recording Standards |
| NDM | National Decision-Making Model |

| | |
|---|---|
| NFA | No Further Action: the decision not to charge or apply any other formal sanction against a suspect |
| NPCC | National Police Chief's Council (formerly ACPO) |
| OCG | Organised Crime Group |
| OSCO | Officer Seen Conditional Offer (essentially a ticket for a traffic offence) |
| PACE | The Police and Criminal Evidence Act 1984 |
| PAVA | A handheld incapacitant spray (Pelargonic Acid Vanillylamide) |
| PC | Police Constable |
| PCSO | Police and Community Support Officer |
| PEQF | Policing Education Qualifications Framework |
| PNB | An officer's Personal Notebook |
| PPO | Persistent Priority Offender |
| PPU | Prisoner Processing Unit |
| Q-Word | Quiet |
| Refs | A meal and rest break |
| STO | Specially Trained Officer, trained to deal with cases of sexual assault |
| Taser | The brand-name of a hand-held weapon which fires two small darts that send an electrical charge through the target to incapacitate them |
| TWOC | Taking (a motor vehicle) Without Consent |
| VA | Voluntary Attendance at a police station for interview (an alternative to arrest) |
| VRN | Vehicle Registration Number |

# TABLE OF CASES
# AND PRACTICE NOTES

# TABLE OF STATUTES, SECONDARY LEGISLATION, AND ECHR ARTICLES

# 1

---

# Introduction

---

## I. Framing the Debate

### A. 'All Cops are Bastards'

As the police van trundles along the deserted street of an English city in the early hours of the morning it passes by a railway arch featuring spray-painted graffiti reading 'ACAB'. The police officers in the van make no comment and, peering out from the passenger window, the researcher has neither the energy nor enthusiasm at this late stage in the shift to pull out their notepad and ask the research participant how it makes her feel. They are four letters you will see in graffiti all over Europe; an acronym that transcends language barriers and that can be encountered in many other forms, from social media messages, to music lyrics, even to film titles: *All Cops Are Bastards*.[1]

Although the acronym appears to have been established in popular culture, particularly in the punk, protest, and football scenes by the 1970s, its origins are unclear,[2] and it is also a phrase that has, to date, eluded the attention of academics or of the judiciary in the English courts.[3] This leaves open a number of interpretations of what 'All Cops Are Bastards' means. If we take the ordinary dictionary definition, a bastard is 'an obnoxious or despicable person', but the whole slogan may be used and understood in different ways by those expressing and hearing, reading, or witnessing the words. It could mean that every single police officer is 'an obnoxious and despicable person' who has chosen to join the police; in other words that they remain a bastard when off-duty or retired but that maybe the occupation of the police officer is particularly attractive to bastards. Alternatively, it could mean that normally pleasant individuals *become* bastards by virtue of some change brought about by membership of the police, be it through training

---

[1] Adapted from fieldnotes, Territorial Support, 2014.

[2] Also *All Coppers Are Bastards* (T Dalzell and T Victor (eds), *The New Partridge Dictionary of Slang and Unconventional English* (London, Routledge, 2015)).

[3] Although there are a number of reported cases elsewhere in the world where clothing, banners, and social-media messages with the acronym have led to arrests, convictions, and fines. Following *Harvey v Director of Public Prosecutions* [2011] All ER (D) 143, it is unlikely such a charge would be brought for this in England and Wales.

or being subsumed into the 'culture' of the police. A third way of interpreting the slogan is that the institution of the police *demands and requires* that the individual acts in this way; in other words *as individuals*, police officers are not all bastards, but that their duties and obligations require them to conduct actions in support and furtherance of a reprehensible and loathsome institution. Despite the problems inherent in the ACAB slogan, in introducing this volume, it serves a purpose because each of these interpretations finds echoes in some of the research literature on policing, on 'police culture', and police socialisation. We will pursue these interpretations a little further before reflecting on the purpose of this book.

Any one of these interpretations could account for the miscarriages of justice where officers have hidden exculpatory evidence or even manufactured inculpatory evidence to frame innocent people, often aided by an organisational system that makes independent investigation very difficult. Our research started shortly after the deaths of Mark Duggan and Ian Tomlinson, and the falsehoods spun by the Metropolitan Police Service about those events. The shadow of mass police violence at Orgreave, and catastrophic negligence at Hillsborough, still haunts the communities in the north of England where we conducted our fieldwork. Many readers will have also personally experienced what they perceived to be unfair or aggressive policing, and the statistics on arrest and stop and search continue to show that ethnic minorities are disproportionately the target of police powers by the predominantly-white police service. It is impossible to deny that there are some individual officers who are incompetent, lazy, dishonest, or even violent, or that historically the police service has on occasion been complicit in the misconduct of its officers, covering up misdeeds or leaking misleading information to the media in order to distract blame from themselves. Whatever its exact origins, and despite its numerous uses and interpretations, ACAB comes from a history of antagonism between some communities and the police which is usually not without foundation. There remains, for many communities, a continued problem with the legitimacy and representativeness of the police service which we do not seek to hide in these pages.

The elusive nature of ACAB also raises the importance of sense-making for our understanding of the police. Individual police officers will interpret the slogan differently and add weight to its meaning in relation to their role. Some may be personally offended, some may view it as not applying to them, while others may consider it legitimate comment on the past record of their institution. Some officers may simply not attribute much weight to it at all and, as we have seen from the vignette above, displays of the slogan may not lead to any response whatsoever. However, attacks on the police as an institution, or particular police operations, can result in officers responding in a very defensive manner. In 2018, the cosmetics firm 'Lush' launched a campaign highlighting the role of undercover police officers who infiltrated activist groups, which involved a number of women being misled into engaging in intimate relationships and even having children with men whom they believed were like-minded activists. The campaign included shop-window displays with slogans such as 'Paid to lie', and 'Police have crossed the line'.[4] Many officers active on social media interpreted this not only as an attack on a particularly dubious operation, or even the institution of the police, but as a personal attack on them and their role as a police officer, sparking a boycott of the company's products by many officers.[5]

We have chosen to focus on ACAB for the purposes of this introduction because, whichever of the meanings above is used, it appears to be based on two assumptions that we wish to challenge in this book. First, that there is a homogeneity to the police as an institution, a shared characteristic – whether pre-existing, taught, or culturally absorbed – of those who work as police officers. In other words, there is a shared workplace or vocational 'culture', or a shared organisational purpose that directs how officers behave. It suggests that regardless of their background, their views, their rank, or their role, a police officer cannot escape the reality that, while on duty at least, he or she is a bastard. Second, the slogan suggests that this shared characteristic, organisational 'culture', or occupational purpose, is a static given: the police have always been like this. This is how they are now, and this is how they are likely to remain. ACAB is offensive to many officers because, while they are likely to acknowledge the failings of the institution in the past, they are all too mindful of how the organisation has changed and how they, as individuals, would not engage in some of the extremes of 'despicable' behaviour engaged in by some of their predecessors.

Of course, cops *aren't* all obnoxious and despicable, and we should not need to spell out that this is not our major research finding. Neither could we reach the conclusion that the police as an institution were requiring officers to act in this manner; legislative protections for citizens, such as the Police and Criminal Evidence Act 1984 (PACE) and the Human Rights Act 1998 (HRA 1998), were placed front and centre in most training sessions we observed. Our research was geographically and temporally limited, so we cannot be sure that all *other* cops are not obnoxious or despicable. Neither can we deny with certainty that 'back in the day', all cops *were* bastards. But we believe these possibilities are highly unlikely. There is a wealth of evidence that indicates that police officers are not all the same, that generally they believe they are trying to do the right thing under difficult circumstances, and that most of their duties are valued by the public who, at the end of the day, democratically choose to fund them.[6] High-crime communities, we are told, often plead for more 'bobbies on the beat' to protect them, and politicians try to win elections by promising more police. We witness and hear stories of police officers finding lost children, breaking open cars to free overheated dogs,

---

[4] 'Cosmetic retailer Lush criticised by police over "spycops" ad campaign' *The Guardian* (1 June 2018).

[5] 'Lush "anti-spy cops" campaign criticised' *BBC* (1 June 2018) (www.bbc.co.uk/news/uk-44330078).

[6] R Reiner, *The Politics of the Police*, 4th edn (Oxford, Oxford University Press, 2014); P Waddington, *Policing Citizens: Authority and Rights* (London, UCL Press, 1999).

facing armed terrorists with only a baton, and informing relatives of those killed in traffic collisions with compassion and empathy. In the course of the fieldwork that forms the foundation of this book, we spent hundreds of hours accompanying officers as they safeguarded children, looked for missing dementia sufferers, sat listening to the stories of lonely pensioners, and broke into buildings to uncover suicides and sudden deaths, before having to break the news to relatives. We saw officers receiving abuse, threats, and assaults, and responding with restraint, and saw some of them sent to the verge of nervous breakdown by the pressures and stresses of their job. In contrast, while officers did not always follow law, policy, or accepted practice, deliberate or malicious abuses of power such as unlawful arrests, unnecessary use of force, or racial bias were, from our observations, exceptionally rare. When ACAB was sprayed on a railway bridge, or a poster claiming 'police have crossed the line' was displayed in a cosmetics shop window, we can recall McBarnet's claim that 'Front-men like the police become the "fall guys" of the legal system'.[7] In sum, it was impossible to conduct the research in the way that we did without feeling a huge amount of empathy towards our research participants and their colleagues in the role of police officer.

## B. 'Police Culture' and Individuality

ACAB gives the lie to a more fundamental myth: that police officers are *the same*. They go through the same training, dress the same, carry out the same tasks, and most importantly think the same. Many academic accounts of the police talk about 'police attitudes' or 'cop culture', probably most famously Reiner's focus on the 'core characteristics' of 'cop culture'.[8] A constant theme in this book, however, is that officers remain individuals. Training varies from force to force and from year to year, and even officers in the same classroom will interpret what they are taught differently. Further, police sense-making of their role, their powers, and the law and policy they are expected to follow diverges, with differences exacerbated by variation in their supervision. Once one takes the time to look, it becomes clear that police officers do not even dress the same, choosing different types of body armour, or jacket, or boots, choosing to take with them different technical gadgets or personal defence kit, and in some cases even sewing the word 'Police' onto a completely unauthorised item of clothing. Most fundamentally of all, they do not all think the same, or respond to the same incident in similar ways.

The concept of 'police culture' was integral to traditional studies on policing,[9] and some more recent projects also attest to its existence, albeit in an increasingly

---

[7] D McBarnet, *Conviction: The Law, the State and the Construction of Justice* (London, Palgrave MacMillan, 1981) 156.

[8] Reiner, *The Politics of the Police*.

[9] Eg J van Maanen, 'Police Socialization: A Longitudinal Examination of Job Attitudes in an Urban Police Department' (1975) 20 *Administrative Science Quarterly* 207; E Bittner, *Aspects of Police Work*

developed and nuanced manner.[10] However, to criticise the concept of a coherent and guiding 'police culture' is certainly not to take an academic step into the unknown. Numerous researchers of (largely English-speaking) police forces have noted the plurality of 'police cultures' or 'sub-cultures',[11] identified different 'styles' of,[12] or individual approaches to,[13] policing, emphasised its changing nature,[14] or downplayed the extent to which it determines how officers behave away from the canteen.[15] We do not intend to discuss in detail the existence or absence of 'cop culture' in this book, but some of our explanations for police officer understanding, interpretation, or behaviour are nuanced for the very reason that officers approach the job very differently and that this is not a result purely of the role that they are performing or the unit they are attached to. We will argue that you cannot understand police discretion through the lens of organisational or even occupational 'culture', but through a complex mesh of changing role-specific, individual, contextual, and supervisory factors.

## C. Police Change

*All Cops are Bastards* also fails to acknowledge another important feature of twenty-first century policing: organisational change. The ACAB slogan implies a static position, whereas during our period in the field, the police forces we were engaged with were continually undergoing change. These changes came from within and without the force. During our fieldwork, austerity politics led to public sector cuts that devastated police numbers. In one of the forces under observation in our research, a quarter of frontline staff were lost in five years. This led to dramatic changes to personnel and also to the structure and organisation of the forces. Command structures changed, shift patterns altered, roles were reformed,

---

(Boston, Northeastern University Press, 1990); S Holdaway, 'Constructing and Sustaining "Race" within the Police Workforce' (1997) 48 *British Journal of Sociology* 19; D Wilson et al, *What Everyone in Britain Should Know About the Police* (London, Blackstone, 2001); Reiner, *The Politics of the Police*; M Rowe, *Policing, Race and Racism* (Cullompton, Willan, 2004).

[10] Eg J Skolnick, 'Enduring Issues of Police Culture and Demographics' (2008) 18 *Policing and Society* 35; B Loftus, *Police Culture in a Changing World* (Oxford, Oxford University Press, 2009).

[11] J Chan, *Changing Police Culture: Policing in a Multicultural Society* (Cambridge, Cambridge University Press, 1997); S Herbert, 'Police Culture Reconsidered' (1998) 36 *Criminology* 343; L Westmarland, 'Police Cultures' in T Newburn (ed), *Handbook of Policing*, 2nd edn (Cullompton, Willan, 2008) 196; L Westmarland, 'Police Cultures' in T Newburn (ed), *Handbook of Policing*, 2nd edn (Cullompton, Willan, 2008) 253.

[12] R Grimshaw and T Jefferson, *Interpreting Police Work: Policy and Practice in Forms of Beat Policing* (London, Allen & Unwin, 1987).

[13] R Worden, 'Situational and Attitudinal Explanations of Police Behaviour: A Theoretical Reappraisal and Empirical Assessment' (1989) 23 *Law & Society Review* 667, 670.

[14] S Charman, *Police Socialisation, Identity and Culture: Becoming Blue* (London, Palgrave MacMillan, 2017).

[15] D Black, 'The Social Organization of Arrest' (1971) 23 *Stanford Law Review* 1087; P Waddington, 'Police (Canteen) Sub-culture. An Appreciation' (1998) 39 *British Journal of Criminology* 287.

specialised units were shut down or merged, and police stations and Custody Suites were closed. Neighbourhood officers became Response officers. Many others decided it was time to retire and try a new career.

At the same time, the police came under political pressure to reduce their use of stop and search, to move away from a target-driven approach to detections and arrests, to take domestic abuse allegations more seriously, and finally to increase the number of crimes recorded to satisfy the National Crime Recording Standard (NCRS). Combined with this were technological changes: the introduction of tablets, handheld devices, new databases and recording systems, and, possibly most dramatically of all, the roll-out of body-worn cameras. All of these developments took place in an ever-evolving organisational and legal landscape, with which officers were also expected to keep pace.

It started to become clear that, at frontline level at least, the police forces we were observing were neither resistant to change nor somehow conservative in outlook. Unsurprisingly, some officers struggled to keep up with the changes to law, policy, technology, and structure, and some officers were resistant to change. However, most engaged with it, or were forced to change their habits by supervisory pressures. In the case of body-worn cameras in particular, after a period of uncertainty and familiarisation, frontline officers almost uniformly embraced the roll-out. In short, from top-to-bottom the police service is in flux. The drawback is that this made our research incredibly difficult to conduct, as we spent much of our time trying to catch up with the most recent changes and trying to establish, between the different interpretations of new force policy, actually what the change was. The rapid and multi-faceted nature of this change, and the fact that it was implemented at different times and with varying interpretations of its form and importance by Inspectors and Sergeants (what we will call vertical fragmentation), exacerbated the differences in understanding and prioritisation between individual officers (horizontal fragmentation). Officers across different forces and different stations within the same force were often following conflicting versions of the same policy at the same time. Even within a particular station or a particular shift, officers would respond differently to change depending on whether they were available to attend a particular briefing or to complete a particular training package updating them on changes. Recently-delivered hardware or newly-installed software worked for some officers and not others. In short, change was experienced differently, and responded to differently, by officers.

## II. Focus and Remit of this Book

### A. Academic Field and Contribution

From the outset, we need to acknowledge the vast amount of literature that exists from various disciplines on the police service. Understanding the use of police powers has been the focus for social scientists for decades, and much of this work has utilised methods similar to our own. At times it felt like we were drowning in a sea of pre-existing research and that identifying an original contribution to this field was almost impossible. Ultimately much of what we found initially reflected the previous ethnographic studies of British, although less so North American, policing. While this reassured us of the quality of our own data, it was less useful in enabling us to make completely novel claims, and it took a considerable amount of time in the field, followed by subsequent desk-based analysis of our data, before we started to identify how our own position developed upon, and departed from, existing debates. Debates and positions have become exceptionally nuanced in the academic to-and-fro around key issues such as 'police culture' and police reform and, while we have attempted to give all due credit to previous studies, we acknowledge that there are many publications that we have not had space to cite. The backgrounds of the authors are in socio-legal studies and public admin-istration and management respectively, but this book inevitably also treads into the disciplines of criminology, sociology, anthropology, and police studies. While this breadth has brought some unfamiliar ideas to the discussions, it does also mean that, in places, we may omit references to literature that some readers will be expecting to see.

## B. The Research Participants

The focus of both our research and this book, is on 'frontline' police officers. By this we mean warranted officers who were engaged in active, physical, public-facing police work, which would include what has often previously been called 'beat work'[16] and is sometimes still referred to as 'patrol work'. It included Constables in the Special Constabulary[17] but not Police Community Support Officers (PCSOs) or civilian staff. The officers under observation were exclusively in uniform when out of the station (although some wore plain clothes on some operations), and almost always in uniform whilst in the station, unless signed off sick or injured. They were almost exclusively of the rank of Constable, although some observations and interviews were carried out with Sergeants and Inspectors, the former of which were increasingly performing desk-based jobs but would occasionally engage in public-facing policing away from the station. The role of Custody Sergeants was also a focus for our research. This is, therefore, an important limitation to this study. PCSOs and civilian staff play an increasingly important role in policing, with the former often filling gaps in diminishing Neighbourhood operations and playing a vital role in community relations and intelligence gathering. Further, the absence of senior officers in this study provides a second limitation: decisions of

---

[16] Grimshaw and Jefferson, *Interpreting Police Work.*
[17] The volunteer police force.

senior officers clearly play a fundamental role in influencing how frontline officers carry out their role and prioritise their shift.

Our research was carried out with an extensive range of different frontline police units and roles. The majority of our observations were carried out with Response and Neighbourhood officers. Response officers are those officers tasked with responding to reports of criminality, anti-social behaviour, risk to life, and suspicious activity that are usually reported to the police by members of the public through a telephone call to 999. These calls are managed in a police Radio Control Room, graded One, Two, Three or Four (Grade One requiring an emergency response), and communicated to officers working that shift via radio. Officers then essentially choose which calls to respond to, although sometimes they will be individually tasked to certain jobs. Neighbourhood officers are, in contrast, more proactive. They are responsible for a certain geographical area, identifying problems, developing intelligence, and seeking to resolve long-term sources of tension and dispute. They will engage with local councillors and community activists. Typically, Neighbourhood officers spend more time dealing with long-term and complex problems, although they may still respond to radio jobs and, as austerity reduced officer numbers, were regularly abstracted (reallocated to other duties) to stand guard at crime scenes or to assist with search warrants, for example. However, in contrast to the traditional view of the 'bobby on the beat', Neighbourhood officers spent little time on foot and most of the time in a marked patrol car or van.

In addition to these core policing roles, we also carried out extensive research with Territorial Support (proactive teams that include specialist drug and organised crime disruption units), Traffic, and Custody Sergeants in a number of Custody Suites. Finally, a smaller amount of time was spent doing research with a unit of Special Constables, Schools Officers, a Mental Health Triage team, a Dog Team, new recruit training, and officers carrying out event operations, including policing the city centre night-time weekend economy, and high-profile football matches. For these event operations, we typically 'shadowed' officers from the standard units who were occasionally tasked to join these operations. Reflecting the forces under study, volunteers were usually white, male, and with at least five years' experience. However, we also observed a number of female officers and some of our volunteers came from ethnic minority groups. In Chapter 5, we explain in detail the operation of the different roles and the structure of the typical shift.

All our participants were drawn from two police forces in six years between 2013 and 2019. We gained research access to Force A in 2013, having been approached by them to evaluate officers' use of discretion in their use of stop and search, and to Force B in 2016, having been approached by them to do the same work. For both forces, we undertook the research on the understanding that our observations would have a wider remit than just stop and search. The two police forces are in the north of England. Both are responsible for two major industrial cities and their surrounding suburbs, along with a large area of rural land surrounding them. The population served by these forces ranged from some of the most socially- and economically-deprived inner-city areas of the country through to isolated hamlets and farms, and also some of the richest suburbs in the country. This means that while we can be reasonably confident that our findings reflect practice elsewhere in the country, we cannot be sure that we can speak to the unique Metropolitan Police Service in London, nor would we claim that our findings will necessarily reflect the practice of policing outside of England and Wales.

## C. Police Discretion

The second feature of our research was that our focus was broadly on 'discretion' shown by frontline officers during the course of their shift. In Chapter 4 we dig down in more detail into the role of professional judgement, decision-making, and discretion, considering the role of policy, training, and occupational 'culture' in guiding the actions of frontline officers, and the pivotal role that discretion plays in terms of the application of the criminal law in practice. 'Police discretion' is a term often used uncritically but which potentially encapsulates a whole range of meanings and behaviour. Traditionally, in legal scholarship it was used in a narrow sense to mean the leeway granted by – and within – law, that officers possess to enforce the criminal law (or not) in any given situation. When faced with an offence being committed, discretion allows an officer a multitude of options. The officer may choose to take the first steps in deciding whether to charge the individual, either by arresting them or taking their details and asking for a voluntary attendance at the police station for an interview at a later date. Alternatively, they may have the power to enforce a street disposal, for example an on-the-spot fine. Finally, the officer may simply provide 'advice' to the suspect – essentially giving them an informal verbal warning or 'telling off'. Discretion can therefore be seen to be, 'the power to decide which rules apply to a given situation and whether or not to apply them.'[18] As we will see, discretion in this sense is absolutely essential for the police to function practically. However, it has also been argued that it poses a threat to the rule of law,[19] due process,[20] and other principles of equality, and can be a veil behind which discriminatory treatment of minorities or marginalised communities can take place; a cloak for prejudice.[21] As Chapters 6 and 7 will demonstrate, the force of the law typically comes down much harder on those who are not considered by officers to be 'decent folk'.

As we will explain later, our own use of discretion goes wider than an officer's freedom in terms of whether or not to take formal action in any given situation,

---

[18] R Ericson, *Reproducing Order: A Study of Police Patrol Work* (Toronto, University of Toronto Press, 1982) 11.

[19] J Skolnick, *Justice without Trial: Law Enforcement in Democratic Society*, 2nd edn (London, MacMillan, 1986).

[20] S Kadish, 'Legal Norm and Discretion in the Police and Sentencing Processes' (1961) 75 *Harvard Law Review* 904.

[21] Waddington, *Policing Citizens* 38–39.

and also includes more general decision-making processes engaged in by police which have received less attention in academic studies. The freedom that officers have during the course of the shift incorporates a wide range of opportunities to exercise professional judgement, for example in terms of which crimes to respond to, which streets to patrol, which members of the public to speak with, how to investigate alleged offences, when to switch on a body-worn camera, or when to run a red light in a Grade One response. It is equally important to understand why an officer would not prioritise responding to a particular type of offence, or an offence committed in a particular location, as it is to understand their actions when they arrive at the crime scene. Throughout our study, officers typically told us that their discretion was being curtailed. However, while the pressures, frame-works, and policies did appear to be increasingly onerous upon the freedom of officers (particularly with regard to crime recording), this wider decision-making authority remained fundamental to the office of Constable. We believe it is also essential to consider the wider contextual factors when we are investi-gating disproportionate use of police street powers against ethnic minorities and marginalised communities. Our research sought to develop an understanding of how officers utilised their discretion in the course of a shift. In this book we focus particularly on how this discretion impacted upon members of the public and the application of the criminal law.

## D.  Street Powers, Law, Policy, and Legitimacy

The central focus of this book, in terms of the utilisation of an officer's discretion, is on what we have called 'street powers'. The police, as an institution, have many powers that can be used in the pursuit of law and order, some of which can only be put in place by senior officers. For example, a section 60 stop and search order[22] can only be issued by an officer of the rank of Inspector or above, and anti-social behaviour dispersal notices can only be issued by a Superintendent or above.[23] While important, these 'office powers' are not the focus of this book, although we will come across occasions of their use at street level. The term 'street powers' refers instead to the powers that a frontline police officer possesses when they are away from the station, most obviously the coercive powers of stop and search, and of arrest. We also include in this, actions that an officer may take away from the station that are not formal or legal powers, but which operate in this way because of the imbalance of authority between police and members of the public. The most important of these was a request for a member of the public to 'stop and account'. However, our focus is not just limited to powers used in public spaces. For the

---

[22] Criminal Justice and Public Order Act 1994.
[23] Anti-Social Behaviour Act 2003, ss 30–36.

purposes of this book, 'street powers' also includes those used in private or quasi-private spaces, most usually houses to which officers have been called, but also pubs, clubs, schools, and sports facilities.

The discretion an officer has when applying the law is not the result of an absence of leadership or bureaucratic direction, but a legal power awarded to officers by the state.[24] The principle of constabulary independence and the rules and guidance contained in PACE provide that each officer 'has a legal right and duty to enforce the law as she sees fit, regardless even of the orders of her superior officers'.[25] The wording in PACE, section 1 (stop and search) and section 24 (arrest) states that the officer 'may' (rather than 'must') use their powers if certain objective criteria are satisfied, and key cases relating to abuse of power by individual officers, which we will consider in Chapters 6 and 7, tend to focus on the unlawful use of powers rather than the absence of their utilisation.

Much of the discussion in socio-legal studies, criminology, and sociology relating to coercive police powers, particularly surrounding issues of discrimination, has focused on the extent to which the police can be managed, controlled, or regulated to utilise their powers fairly and proportionately. A key weapon in the attempt to achieve this has been the law. PACE provides a check on the arbitrary or unfair use of police powers in two ways. First, it sets out that without satisfying certain objective criteria, police powers of stop and search, arrest, and detention will be unlawful. Second, through provisions such as section 76 and section 78, combined with the Codes of Practice, it provides for the exclusion of evidence from a criminal trial where evidence is unreliable, obtained by oppression, or was gathered in a way that would have an adverse effect on the fairness of the proceedings. Legal powers to regulate the behaviour of individual officers also arise from section 6 of the HRA 1998 which makes it unlawful for a public authority to act in a way that is incompatible with rights contained in the European Convention on Human Rights (ECHR), including for example the right to liberty (Article 5) and the right to privacy (Article 8). Along with traditional common law criteria, most notably the requirement to act 'reasonably', officers are now also required to consider whether actions they take which may infringe human rights are proportionate and necessary. These criteria and restrictions on police power should provide a 'substantial discipline on discretion'.[26] However as we will see in Chapter 3, there has been considerable disquiet about the way in which both PACE and the HRA 1998 have operated in terms of policing, and indeed in terms of whether legal rules are ever capable of protecting suspects' rights.[27] This book

---

[24] Grimsham and Jefferson, *Interpreting Police Work*.

[25] M McConville et al, *The Case for the Prosecution: Police Suspects and the Construction of Criminality* (London, Routledge, 1993) 2.

[26] P Neyroud and A Beckley, *Policing, Ethics and Human Rights* (Cullompton, Willan, 2001) 66.

[27] For example, D Dixon, *Law in Policing: Legal Regulation and Police Practices* (Oxford, Clarendon, 1997); A Sanders, 'Reconciling the Apparently Different Goals of Criminal Justice and Regulation: The "Freedom Perspective"' in H Quirk et al (eds), *Regulation and Criminal Justice: Innovations in Policy*

will revisit the debates about the effectiveness of PACE and the HRA 1998 in a new era of austerity policing and technological accountability.

In engaging with the debates about how police can or should be managed, regulated, or controlled, we will also be focusing on the importance of force policies and standards, as the Home Office, Her Majesty's Inspectorate of Constabulary and Fire & Rescue Services, and the College of Policing, along with constabulary senior management teams, attempt to improve standards and reduce complaints. Here we will be taking a broad view of 'policy', to include any order or guidance that frontline officers are expected to follow by a supervisory officer. In contrast to 'top-down' definitions of policy,[28] our focus will be on a supervisory model of policy, in which many different interpretations of the same top-down policy may be in play at the same time. We will also be considering the value of workplace conventions and practices, and the extent to which officers self-police the behaviour of their colleagues. Finally, we will be considering the other ways in which the discretion of frontline officers is curtailed or managed. In particular, Chapter 9 will focus on a number of relatively new developments: the camera phone (in the hands of members of the public), police body-worn cameras (BWCs) and video (BWV), and the NCRS. All these developments influence the way in which the officers interact with the public, utilise their coercive powers, and record incidents they encounter as crime. New systems and new technologies play a fundamental role in constructing the 'reality' of crime for society, altering the dynamics of accountability, and either supporting or undermining the legitimacy of the police as an institution.

The discretionary use of street powers by officers will be the focus of Chapter 6 (especially with regard to stop and account, stop checks, and stop searches) and Chapter 7 (arrest and detention). In Chapter 8 we will consider issues of the accountability that officers owe to the public and to their superiors, and whether increasing individual accountability can ever lead to the use of coercive street powers being seen as legitimate by 'over-policed' working class or ethnic minority communities. Chapter 9 will focus on the impact of new technology on frontline officers and how monitoring and NCRS have changed the ways in which officers use their discretion. Finally, in Chapter 10 we draw together our conclusions on the regulation of discretion, make a number of proposals for the reform of street powers, and identify key areas for future research.

## E.  Ethnography and Fieldwork

The final key feature of this book is its utilisation of empirical data gathered from a long-term ethnographic project with the two forces. There is a long history of

*and Research* (Cambridge, Cambridge University Press, 2011); C Harfield, 'Paradigm not Procedure: Current Challenges to Police Cultural Incorporation of Human Rights in England and Wales' (2009) 4 *The Journal of Law and Social Justice* 91, 104; M Lamb, 'A Culture of Human Rights: Transforming Policing in Northern Ireland' (2008) 2 *Policing* 386; McConville et al, *Case for the Prosecution*.

[28] Grimsham and Jefferson, *Interpreting Police Work*.

ethnographic research with police forces across the globe, and for good reason. Police forces are complex and ever-changing environments and gathering data on how frontline officers use their discretion and apply their street powers can be difficult to uncover, often 'resisting translation'[29] into accurate data from surveys or white-room interviews. Our ethnographic methodology relied upon observations of frontline volunteers for the duration of their shift, in conjunction with in-field conversation and semi-structured and unstructured interviews. Between 2013 and 2019, the authors were in the field for 163 shifts, accounting for over 1,500 hours of fieldwork. We worked out of 38 different police stations, and observed 78 different primary participants, making detailed fieldnotes in situ. In addition, the views of countless other officers who crossed the path of our participants during the course of our fieldwork were also taken into account when assessing the reliability of our data. As with all methods, ethnographic fieldwork brings with it a number of limitations, practical problems, and political and ethical issues. Nevertheless, we are confident that we were able to uncover empirical data that is reliable, rigorous, and will stand up to scrutiny.

The arguments in this book are all based upon this immersive fieldwork. In order to ground our arguments, and to give a flavour of twenty-first century policing in the north of England, we have written much of this book in the style of an ethnography – that is a descriptive account of the police under observation. We do not claim that the book is a comprehensive ethnography of the police forces in question. That would have proven impossible in a single monograph. Instead we have aimed to use ethnographic data to answer the key questions with regard to the regulation of street powers of modern-day frontline officers. Unless stated otherwise, vignettes presented in these pages are only examples of wider trends that we observed and are supported by other similar observations which could not be included in these pages for the sake of brevity. Unless findings were ubiquitous, examples of where they were observed have been included in the footnotes, including the officer's role and the month and year the observation was made. All officers, shifts, and stations have been anonymised, and we have taken care to hide the identity of the participating forces. In a few cases, where either an event was so unusual that the officer could be identified, or where the officer's actions fell so short of accepted practice, law, or force policy that there could be serious implications for them should they be identified, we have redacted further details. In the following chapter we turn to the utility, history, and challenges of ethnographic research and ethnography with the police.

---

[29] C Sellitz et al, *Research Methods in Social Relations* (London, Methien, 1965) 201–202.

# 2

# In Search of 'Police Culture':
# Ethnographic Approaches
# to Studying the Police

This chapter sets out our research approach and methodology, introducing the concepts of ethnography and ethnographic research and locating the methods within the field of study. It focuses particularly on the relationships between the police officers and the observers, problematising the researcher/participant divide and considering researcher influence on the field. This discussion also emphasises the importance of building relationships of trust over time. Our research has been conducted over six years, during which time we have – to varying extents – become embedded in some parts of the forces we are observing. This has further allowed for a long-term perspective on change rather than a snapshot of a point in time. But this chapter does more than deal with methodological concerns. It also looks to make a substantive point about the influence that ethnographic research has had on our understanding of the police and, in particular, on the development of the concept of 'police culture'.

## I. Ethnographic Research

### A. Ethnography as Methodology

Observation is the method most associated with ethnographic research, but to simply define ethnography as observation is, in our view, to misunderstand the versatility and value of the ethnographic approach. While the focus of this book is not the philosophy of knowledge, there is some purpose in understanding our perspective, not least because, as this chapter will illuminate, there are clear parallels between our work and the work of police officers. To understand our standpoint, it will perhaps be helpful to sketch out the origins of the project.

We were approached in 2012 to help one police force understand an ongoing problem and cause of community concern: the disproportionate use against young black men of powers to stop and search citizens. While the force was not confronting the levels of disproportionality evident at that time in London,[1] it remained a persistent feature both of practice and of comment. How might researchers help this police force understand the phenomenon? The assumption was that we would want access to data on stops and searches: the number carried out; the age and ethnicity of those searched; the grounds for a search; and the outcomes of the search. However, any review of the literature on stop and search reveals questions over the quality of such data and the controversies associated with its interpretation.[2] At the same time the data, where it did present reasons for concern, had nothing further to say about the causes, beyond there being apparent discrimination, or about how to effect change. In essence, there is no simple and uncontroversial way of describing the facts of this particular problem. To offer a real insight, we need to understand why officers act in the ways they do and how those actions amount to the picture that may be represented by statistics.[3] Interviewing or surveying police officers about their practices would reveal an edited version for external consumption (if ACAB communicates something of the perception of police officers in some communities, many officers have a similarly low opinion of social scientists). When interviewed, officers typically offer stories of successful searches, of the big drugs find or the knife hidden in a jacket. They are less forthcoming about those many searches that are unsuccessful or that go unrecorded. To understand what was happening, and why, requires a closer relationship with practitioners than such research approaches offer.

We need to understand how the use of a power, such as stop and search or arrest, fits into the work of a police officer. When does she consider the use of such powers, and what are the alternatives that might be available? What influences the construction of both the situations and the alternatives? What part does the officer's understanding of the law or force policy have to play? And what influence do public concerns about the use of such powers have on the considerations of officers? Answering these questions requires a familiarity with the detail and an empathy with the situations in which those officers find themselves. We need to be able to see the world, so far as that is possible, from the perspectives of those officers. Observing police officers was therefore the methodology we proposed.

We should at this point note that there is a difference between observation and ethnography. The latter term has been long fought over, with Atkinson and

---

[1] Home Office, *Police Powers and Procedures, England and Wales, Year Ending 31 March 2017* (2017) www.gov.uk/government/statistics/police-powers-and-procedures-england-and-wales-year-ending-31-march-2017.

[2] R Delsol, 'Effectiveness' in R Delsol and M Shiner (eds), *Stop and Search: Anatomy of a Police Power* (London, Palgrave Macmillan, 2015); B Bowling and C Phillips, 'Disproportionate and Discriminatory: Reviewing the Evidence on Police Stop and Search' (2007) 70 *The Modern Law Review* 936; B Bradford, *Stop and Search and Police Legitimacy* (London, Routledge, 2017); P Waddington et al, 'In Proportion: Race, and Police Stop and Search' (2004) 44 *British Journal of Criminology* 1.

[3] T Duster, 'Comparative Perspectives and Competing Explanations: Taking on the Newly Configured Reductionist Challenge to Sociology' (2006) 71 *American Sociological Review* 1.

Hammersley noting that, '[d]efinition of the term *ethnography* has been subject to controversy. For some it refers to a philosophical paradigm to which one makes a total commitment, for others it designates a method that one uses as and when appropriate'.[4] The etymology of the word points the debate in one way: an ethnography is a 'written representation of culture',[5] but increasingly we see the term being used to describe a research methodology itself, and sometimes nothing more discreet than an observational study analysed in a qualitative manner. The controversy about whether ethnography is a *process* of data gathering (a research method), or the *outcome* in terms of how the data is disseminated (a written account), is most neatly encapsulated in the 2011 debate between Tony Watson and John van Maanen,[6] with the latter suggesting that ethnography was the product of a *combination* of 'field-work', 'head-work', and 'text-work' (a position which seems to be shared by Paul Willis and Mats Trondman).[7]

We do not claim that this book is an ethnography of the police.[8] First, it is not written in the manner of 'thick description'[9] that is typical in orthodox ethnographies. Second, we have focused on a relatively small aspect of the police work observed, that of the use of police powers. As we will see below, in fact it is the *absence* of opportunities to utilise street powers that characterises most shifts. We do, however, claim that this book is *ethnographic*. First, the research methods employed are based on observation, long-term immersion in the field, and are firmly rooted in the interpretive paradigm of social research. We seek to 'make sense of the actions and intentions of people [and] make sense of their making sense of events'.[10] This book also looks to speak to the wider context in which decisions to utilise street powers are made, including the dynamics of the shift and of the police career. Second, we have presented our findings in a traditionally ethnographic manner, utilising fieldnotes, direct quotes, and vignettes to illustrate the interpretations and understandings of officers as they use their discretion over street powers and 'bridge between the experiences'[11] of the research participants and the readers.

---

[4] P Atkinson and M Hammersley, 'Ethnography and Participant Observation' in N Denzin and Y Lincold (eds), *Handbook of Qualitative Research* (Thousand Oaks, Sage, 1994).

[5] P Atkinson, *The Ethnographic Imagination: Textual Constructions of Reality* (London, Routledge, 1994); J van Maanen, *Tales of the Field: On Writing Ethnography* (Chicago, University of Chicago Press, 1988).

[6] T Watson, 'Ethnography, Reality, and Truth: The Vital Need for Studies of "How Things Work" in Organizations and Management' (2011) 48 *Journal of Management Studies* 202; J van Maanen, 'Ethnography as Work: Some Rules of Engagement' (2011) 48 *Journal of Management Studies*, 218.

[7] P Willis and M Trondman, 'Manifesto for Ethnography' (2000) 1 *Ethnography* 5.

[8] Although the authors hope to complete a monograph that will satisfy both sides of the 'what is ethnography?' debate in the future.

[9] C Geertz, *The Interpretation of Cultures* (London, Hutchinson, 1973; J Ryle, *Collected Papers Vol 1* (London, Hutchinson, 1971).

[10] D Ley, 'Interpretive Social Research in the Inner City' in J Eyles (ed), *Research in Human Geography: Introductions and Investigations* (Oxford, Blackwell, 1988) 121.

[11] G Pearson, 'Talking a Good Fight: Authenticity and Distance in the Ethnographer's Craft' in D Hobbs and T May (eds), *Interpreting the Field: Accounts of Ethnography* (Oxford, Clarendon, 1993) viii.

## B.  Ethnographies of Law, Policing, and 'Police Culture'

In employing this methodology, and presenting our work in this manner, we were hoping to build upon on a long tradition of ethnographies of, and ethnographic research of, the law and of police officers. Ethnography and research in and of the discipline of law may not appear obvious bed-fellows, and it has been argued that in contrast to other social science disciplines, ethnographic approaches have been under-used.[12] However, there is a long tradition of legal anthropology, particularly in comparative law,[13] and ethnographic methods and forms of delivery are increasingly used in leading law and society journals.[14] Moving away from its comparative roots, ethnographic approaches to law have focused on the operation and impact of law within developed Western societies[15] and ethnography plays a fundamental role in challenging legal positivism, investigating the social impact of legal procedures and contributing 'to the understanding of cultural hegemony, the construction of authoritative meanings, and processes by which these might be contested'.[16]

Ethnographic methods 'are useful tools for accessing the complex ways in which law, decision-making, and legal regulations are embedded in wider social processes',[17] and we concur with the view that 'deep and thick ethnography is one of the best routes we have in comprehending the complexity of law and legal processes in a changing society'.[18] It can be argued that illuminating and uncovering the way in which laws and legal procedures are applied in practice to social groups is ethnography's most powerful claim in terms of its relevance and veracity in legal scholarship. In contrast to the less 'ethnomethodologically-informed' modes of inquiry that dominate the legal discipline,[19] ethnography provides legal scholars with the potential to 'get at process',[20] and 'understand the relationship between law and society'.[21]

In contrast to their relative under-use in law, observational studies have been prominent in the study of police forces in the English-speaking world and,

---

[12] R Banakar and M Travers, *Theory and Method in Socio-legal Research* (London, Hart Publishing, 2005) 70.

[13] P Bohannan, 'Ethnography and Comparison in Legal Anthropology' in L Nader (ed), *Law in Culture and Society* (Chicago, Aldine, 1969).

[14] E Darian-Smith, 'Ethnographies of Law' in A Sarat (ed), *The Blackwell Companion to Law and Society* (Oxford, Blackwell, 2004).

[15] Darian-Smith, 'Ethnographies of Law'; R Kidder, 'Exploring Legal Culture in Law-Avoidance Societies' in J Starr and M Goodale (eds), *Practicing Ethnography in Law: New Dialogues, Enduring Methods* (Houndmills, Palgrave-MacMillan, 2002) 87.

[16] G Marcus and M Fischer, *Anthropology as Cultural Critique: An Experimental Monument in the Human Sciences* (Chicago, University of Chicago Press, 2014) 154.

[17] Starr and Goodale, *Practicing Ethnography in Law* 2.

[18] Starr and Goodale, *Practicing Ethnography in Law* 8

[19] S Burns (ed), *Ethnographies of Law and Social Control* (London, Elsevier, 2005) 1.

[20] L Nader, 'Moving On – Comprehending Anthropologies of Law' in Starr and Goodale, *Practicing Ethnography in Law* 190, 191.

[21] S Falk-Moore, *Law as Process: An Anthropological Approach* (London, Routledge, 1978) 255.

increasingly, elsewhere since the 1960s. The ethnographic work in the 1960s and 1970s of American social scientists, such Egon Bittner[22] and John van Maanen,[23] uncovered the gap between what we might expect police officers to do as 'law enforcers' and what they actually do. At the heart of this gap was the existence and operation of police 'discretion'. Most of the best analysis of the failures of previous attempts to regulate police powers and discretion in the UK have come from observational studies with officers.[24] In recent years, however, attention has tended to move away from the day-to-day of the front line and to focus upon specific practices or topics. Principal among these themes has been an interest in the knotty problem of 'police culture'.

The fascination with 'police culture' reflects the influence of anthropology in the practice of ethnographic research in this field. As ethnographers *par excellence*, anthropologists have prototypically been concerned with studying distinct peoples (*ethnos*) in remote locations. The traditional understanding of 'culture' was associated with language, customs, ceremonies, artefacts and beliefs that are alien to those of the anthropologist.[25] 'Culture' was seen as a stable and homogeneous entity that was to be *discovered* and *described* by the anthropologist, often with a colonial undertone that the 'culture' under study was in need of a process of Western civilisation.[26] Unsurprisingly then, the assumptions that underpinned early anthropological work have been much critiqued[27] and even lampooned.[28] Contemporary anthropologists, instead, are more likely to see 'culture' less as an entity to be studied and more as an ethnographic *product*: 'ethnography yields a product that is a translation (...) culture names the translation that ethnographers build for their audience'.[29] Therefore, 'culture' is increasingly understood as an artificial construction,[30] meaning different things to different people,[31] and unable

---

[22] E Bittner, 'The Police on Skid Row: A Study of Peacekeeping' (1967) 32 *American Sociological Review* 699; E Bittner, *Aspects of Police Work* (Boston, Northeastern University Press, 1990).

[23] J van Maanen, 'Beyond Account: The Personal Impact of Police Shootings' (1980) 452 *The Annals of the American Academy of Political and Social Science* 145.

[24] For example, S Holdaway, *Inside the British Police* (Oxford, Basil Blackwell, 1983); S Holdaway, 'Discovering Structure: Studies of the British Police Occupational Culture' in M Weatheritt (ed), *Police Research* (Aldershot, Avebury, 1989); M McConville et al, *The Case for the Prosecution: Police Suspects and the Construction of Criminality* (London, Routledge, 1993); D Dixon, *Law in Policing: Legal Regulation and Police Practices* (Oxford, Clarendon, 1997); S Choongh, 'Policing the Dross: A Social Disciplinary Model of Policing' (1998) 38 *The British Journal of Criminology* 623.

[25] These 'moments of incomprehension and unmet expectations' have been labelled 'rich points' (M Agar, 'Culture: Can You Take it Anywhere?' (2006) 5 *International Journal of Qualitative Methods* 1).

[26] Agar, 'Culture: Can You Take it Anywhere?'; R Rosaldo, *Culture and Trust: The Remaking of Social Analysis* (Boston, Beacon Press, 1989).

[27] G Marcus, *Ethnography through Thick and Thin* (Princeton, Princeton University Press, 1998); J Clifford and G Marcus, *Writing Culture: the Poetics and Politics of Ethnography* (Berkeley, University of California Press, 1986).

[28] H Miner, 'Body Ritual among the Nacirema' (1956) 58 *American Anthropologist* 503.

[29] Agar, 'Culture: Can You Take it Anywhere?' 6.

[30] Agar, 'Culture: Can You Take it Anywhere?' 8.

[31] R Brightman, 'Forget Culture: Replacement, Transcendence, Relexification' (1985) 10 *Cultural Anthropology* 509.

to explain or comprehend neither late twentieth century and twenty-first century differences in gender, religion, or nationality between those living and working in the same place,[32] nor the increasingly blurred physical borders between countries and regions.[33] 'Unstable in meaning and reference both synchronically and over time, the culture construct has exhibited exceptional liability',[34] argues Brightman. 'Culture', anthropology's 'longstanding darling', is 'increasingly embattled' and has started to disappear as a concept in anthropological discourse.[35] 'Culture's' day, in this discipline at least, may have come and gone.[36]

Elsewhere in the social sciences, however, 'culture' is more likely to be an object for study. This is particularly true for ethnographers, for whom the existence of shared understandings and behaviours assists in their descriptions of the people and places under observation.[37] While ethnographers generally aspire to empirically-driven description, unburdened by prejudices and prejudgement, they still have a tendency to look for commonalities in understanding and behaviour in the field they are describing, and these commonalities are still regularly couched in terms of 'culture'. Studies of the police reflect this wider practice, often relying upon ideas of 'culture' that have long been discarded by anthropologists as anything other than a method of translation. The idea of 'police culture' draws on the historical concept of 'culture' in seeking to understand how people become police officers. How do they come to adopt the beliefs and practices of the distinct community that is police officers, and particularly uniformed officers? Ethnographers observe training and other processes of socialisation into the 'culture'.[38] They ask what that 'culture' is and how it affects the work of officers.[39] They ask what has been the effect of efforts to change that 'culture'.[40] In such works, there is a tendency to assume both that 'police culture' exists[41] and that it affects, or even determines, the conduct of officers.

---

[32] Agar, 'Culture: Can You Take it Anywhere?'

[33] A Gupta and J Ferguson, 'Beyond "Culture": Space, Identity, and the Politics of Difference' (1992) 7 *Cultural Anthropology* 6.

[34] Brightman, 'Forget Culture' 539.

[35] Brightman, 'Forget Culture' 509.

[36] Agar, 'Culture: Can You Take it Anywhere?' 5.

[37] Though it should be noted that the idea of 'legal culture' has been critiqued (see R Cotterrell, *Law, Culture and Society: Legal Ideas in the Mirror of Social Theory* (Aldershor, Ashgate, 2006)).

[38] J van Maanen, 'Observations on the Making of Policemen' in P Manning and J van Maanen (eds), *Policing: a View from the Street* (Santa Monica, CA: Goodyear, 1978); N Fielding, *Joining Forces: Police Training, Socialization and Occupational Competence* (London, Routledge, 1988).

[39] WK Muir, *Police: Streetcorner Politicians* (Chicago, University of Chicago Press, 1977); JQ Wilson, *Varieties of Police Behaviour: The Management of Law and Order in Eight Communities* (Cambridge, MA, Harvard University Press, 1968); D Fassin, *Enforcing Order: An Ethnography of Urban Policing* (Cambridge, Polity, 2013).

[40] JB Chan, *Changing Police Culture: Policing in a Multicultural Society* (Cambridge, Cambridge University Press, 1997); B Loftus, *Police Culture in a Changing World* (Oxford, Oxford University Press, 2009).

[41] R Reiner, *The Politics of the Police*, 4th edn (Oxford, Oxford University Press, 2014).

The idea of 'police culture' has become more nuanced and layered in some studies[42] but, with a few notable exceptions,[43] the interest of ethnographies of the police in 'culture' has become a central focus just as its meaning in anthropology has been destabilised.

Our concern has been to tread carefully around the topic of 'police culture'. There is a tendency to give the term a status it does not warrant, not least because it is shorthand for a collection of ideas and problems. But our principal concern with understandings of 'police culture' is that they seem to explain everything, forming a convenient scapegoat for all failings in policing. The police use powers to stop and search or to arrest in a disproportionate way because there are deep-seated problems in their 'culture'. They are racist, or institutionally racist. They are macho. They are socially conservative. They learn this from the training academy and on the streets from their fellow officers. We must, therefore, change that 'culture'.[44] How we are to change something that is ill-defined is not clear. Moreover, this 'police culture' appears to exist only at the front line, on the street. Senior officers have, in some way, managed to cleanse themselves of any such influences.[45] The concept of institutional racism[46] does embrace the context, policies, and priorities within which officers operate and it is these wider influences that we also wish to understand. Police officers are neither automatons, programmed by 'police culture' or mechanically enforcing the law, nor free agents, able to choose at will and to exercise their individual prejudices. They are agents operating in an environment bounded by rules, constrained by policies and directed by supervisors. They have a limited resource. And they confront infinite varieties of situation, few of which fit simply into learned scenarios. These are the sorts of concerns that interest public policy and policy implementation scholars, and so we will draw significantly on this work.[47] We will return to and develop these themes in subsequent chapters but, at this stage, it will suffice to say that, despite any expectations we may have had when we began this research, we did not find the concept of 'police culture' useful either as a framework for understanding our observations or for explaining our field of research to the reader.

---

[42] S Charman, *Police Socialisation, Identity and Culture: Becoming Blue* (London, Palgrave Macmillam, 2017).

[43] M Bacon, *Taking Care of Business: Police Detectives, Drug Law Enforcement and Proactive Investigation* (Oxford, Clarendon, 2016); C Stott et al, 'Keeping the Peace: Social Identity, Procedural Justice and the Policing of Football Crowds' (2012) 52 *British Journal of Criminology* 381.

[44] Chan, *Changing Police Culture*.

[45] E Reuss-Ianni, *Two Cultures of Policing: Street Cops and Management Cops* (London, Transaction Books, 1983).

[46] W MacPherson, *The Stephen Lawrence Inquiry* (London, HM Stationery Office, 1999).

[47] M Lipsky, *Street-Level Bureaucracy: Dilemmas of the Individual in Public Services* (New York, Russell Sage, 1980); S Maynard-Moody and M Musheno, 'State Agent or Citizen Agent: Two Narratives of Discretion' (2000) 10 *Journal of Public Administration Research and Theory* 329.

# II. Fieldwork

We were conducting this research for nearly five years prior to commencing this monograph and continued during much of the drafting period. While there is a tradition of spending long periods in the field, this was not merely to 'tick a box' for ethnographic authenticity. We have committed to these hours for three key reasons. The first of these reasons is that it takes time to build a relationship with the officers we observe. The second reason is to verify our understanding of our observations. Finally, we spent time in the field in order to observe change over time, a feature which we argue is key to understanding the use of police street powers. In the next sections, we will explore each of these in turn and then introduce a brief discussion of ethical responsibilities.

## A. Building Trust

We were not 'flies on the wall'. Our role as observers was overt and all officers involved, directly or indirectly, had the right to refuse to collaborate with our work. In contrast with the days of colonial anthropology, and in keeping with contemporary developments in ethnography, we studied this field *with* our subjects rather than *on* them. In overt ethnographic projects such as ours, research *subjects* have become *participants*.[48] Members of the public could also refuse to allow us to enter their homes or to sit in during interviews under caution, although their consent may have on occasion been influenced by the authority of the officer asking for it on our behalf. We did not have Holdaway's luxury of being covert,[49] and not just because of ethical concerns (neither of us had the confidence or courage to be police officers). To get past a very public performance of 'good' or 'by the book' policing, we needed to establish ourselves as trustworthy, particularly given the levels of scepticism about academic (which is often understood to be liberal, idealistic, and pointless) discussions of the realities of policing. It is well-established that gaining such trust in fieldwork relations takes time.[50]

In the field we both experienced the sense that we were, to a certain extent, witnessing a performance put on for our benefit.

> During one encounter, officers stopped and searched a group of young men. As the search proceeds, one of the young men is being interviewed in the back of a police van. His mate, noticing me, asks who I am and what I am doing. When he is informed of my

---

[48] Marcus, *Ethnography through Thick and Thin*; Clifford and Marcus, *Writing Culture*.
[49] Holdaway, *Inside the British Police*.
[50] G Evans, 'Practising Participant Observation: An Anthropologist's Account' (2012) 1 *Journal of Organizational Ethnography* 96.

role, he laughs. 'That must be why they are being nice to me this time'. Later, a member of the public asks about me. When my purpose is explained, he says that that makes sense. 'I've never seen [Territorial Support] be so polite'.[51]

Similar to Souhami's 'feats of endurance',[52] we also both experienced the small tests and hurdles placed in our way as we met new officers, whether as volunteer research participants or as bystanders.

> Billy, a physically imposing and proactive Territorial Support officer in Maron, aggressively questioned the terms of our Participant Information Sheet and Consent Form. In particular, he wondered why we would report any serious criminal offences we might observe? 'Is that what you are looking for and expect to find?' He agreed to being observed but, during the course of that first shift, he and his partner, Timothy, locked me in the back of their police car for more than an hour while they conducted a search of an address. And, later still, while they locked up a detainee, they left me alone for more than an hour in a room adjoining a staff canteen. As other officers, unaware of my role, gathered for their meal breaks, they peered through the window into the room to see who the stranger was. This indignity was only amplified by the fact that the lights in the room went out if there was no motion for a period of minutes. At the end of the shift, I received a call from the Sergeant. 'How have you been treated?' To have complained or to have demanded some form of privileged treatment would have, then and there, ended the access.[53]

The following night, the same officers were much more amenable, and more than four years later, the Sergeant still laughs about it. Sometimes, fortune smiles on the ethnographer.

> On the very first observation with officers on patrol, Thomas was tasked by his Sergeant to make an arrest. Intelligence suggested that two men are engaged in a potentially violent dispute that might involve firearms (one of those involved is known as 'Pistol Pete'). Thomas has some information about known addresses and associates. During the course of the shift, he demonstrates what it is to be a good and proactive officer, following up the leads. As the evening draws in, he calls colleagues to an address as back-up. He believes the male he is to arrest is at the address and wants no mistakes. He proves right and he makes the arrest. But as he prepares what he needs to say at the Custody Suite when he presents his detainee, Thomas realises he has the wrong brother. It is his Sergeant's fault, but he looks across at me seated in the passenger seat next to him. His whole career collapses before his eyes as he imagines the reports that (I may write). But no such reports are forthcoming.[54]

> On the next observation with Thomas, a few days later, another officer asks what I saw during that first outing. Thomas laughs and says 'Unlawful entry, wrongful arrest!'[55]

[51] Territorial Support, Knapford, September 2015.
[52] A Shouhami, 'Constructing Tales of the Field: Uncovering the Culture of Fieldwork in Police Ethnography' (2019) *Policing and Society* 1.
[53] Neighbourhood, Maron, January 2015.
[54] Territorial Support, Brandham, November 2013.
[55] Territorial Support, Brandham, November 2013.

Six months later, Thomas introduces me to fellow officers. 'You can do anything in front of him. He won't drop you in it.'[56] While this vote of confidence did help to recruit further volunteers, it did misrepresent the ethical obligations placed upon us to report any serious offences we observed. This is a point to which we will return later in this chapter.

We should acknowledge that, however open the officers were with us, we were observing volunteers. Our participants were not a random cross-section of officers. They put themselves forward with the support of their immediate supervisors. They were, therefore, more likely to be deemed competent officers, whether in their own estimation or in that of their supervisors. But we were also observing their *fellow officers*. They were sometimes partnered with a second officer or in a van with two or three other officers. And they are always part of a team and coordinating their activities with other units from other stations. As we observed one officer, we encountered many others. These others were, doubtless, wary of our presence but, even in brief encounters, a small modicum of trust could be developed by, for example: putting pen and paper down; ostentatiously not taking notes when some off-colour comments were made; or not reacting to the scrutiny of officers.

We recognised a point in time, marked differently in each team, when we felt we were tolerated, even accepted. It is the shift when our accounts of an incident are sought – did it really happen the way the officer says? It is the briefing where the Sergeant jokes about the last time we observed with that team? It is the meal break at which officers make fun of the observer? Evans has likened the process of gaining access and trust to an apprenticeship or similar induction into a workplace or a trade.[57] Ethnographers move from the margins to become competent practitioners (or observers), and not just academics, as these relationships of trust are built.

## B. Verifying Our Understanding

However, time in the field is not simply about building trust. Much of what we observe is routine, even boring.[58] Many of the incidents are 'rubbish' jobs, ones that police officers believe more appropriate to social workers than to crime fighters, including domestic disputes, neighbour disputes, and reports of persons missing from care or from home. Such is the bread and butter of Response officers. Those officers tasked with a more proactive role, such as the Territorial Support and Traffic, will not normally deal with such routine work but will experience long

---

[56] Night-time Economy Team, Brandham, July 2014.
[57] Evans, 'Practising Participant Observation'; J Lave and E Wenger, *Situated Learning: Legitimate Peripheral Participation* (Cambridge, Cambridge University Press, 1991); E Wenger, *Communities of Practice: Learning, Meaning and Identity* (Cambridge, Cambridge University Press, 1999).
[58] Fassin, *Enforcing Order*.

hours of boredom, patrolling dark streets with no sign of movement at 4 o'clock in the morning. Sharing that time with them is, in itself, an important part of building a relationship with those officers. It also helps us to understand the thirst for action and excitement. Only an understanding of the dynamics of boredom and desire to see action can explain the presence of seven police cars at reports of a minor domestic dispute that has spilled out into the street on a warm summer afternoon.[59]

Time in the field also offers some reassurance that what we have observed and what we believe we understand is indeed 'true' or accurate. It is not just because long periods in the field allow the researcher to blend more into the background, thereby mitigating the amount that their presence changes the behaviour of the observed,[60] although this is undoubtedly true. But, like Evans' competent practitioners,[61] we learn by observing and by talking to practitioners. We may start with naïve questions, but over time we understand and can anticipate how scenarios will develop.

> During one shift, there was a second observer in the van. He was from the German police. As the German officer asks questions, I realise how much I have learnt. I am able to interpret the exchanges over the radio and could offer the same explanations as the police officers I am observing.[62]
>
> Observing a domestic violence call, I recognise a change in mood. The female complainant has raised the stakes, leaving officers with no choice but to arrest the male. I am in the back room with the male while the two officers are in the front room with the woman. As the situation changes, I quickly realise I am in the way and move past the two officers and out onto the street outside. Whatever happens, my presence will not help. As I pass the officers, one just simply nods an acknowledgement. In that moment, I both understood the situation as the officers saw it and very obviously that it was not for me to act or get in the way.[63]

These two brief moments may appear small, even insignificant. But they felt significant. We experience almost a physical sense of relief that we have understood, that our hours of observing have paid off. We can read the field and have achieved some level of competence. Like an artisan, it is not book knowledge but a more physical, even sensory, knowledge that we recognise.[64] This sense that we understand does not stand up to the more positivist tests of validity associated

---

[59] Response, Kirk Machan, July 2015.

[60] Sometimes referred to as the 'Hawthorne Effect' (for a critique of its use, see M Chiesa and S Hobbs, 'Making sense of social research: how useful is the Hawthorne Effect?' (2006) 38 *European Journal of Social Psychology* 67).

[61] Evans, 'Practising Participant Observation'.

[62] Territorial Support, Knapford, July 2015.

[63] Response, Westmarch, February 2018.

[64] P Atkinson, 'Ethnography and Craft Knowledge' (2013) XI *Qualitative Sociology Review* 56; R Sennett, *The Craftsman* (London, Penguin, 2008); M Rowe et al, 'Learning and Practicing Police Craft' (2016) 5 *Journal of Organizational Ethnography* 276.

with statistics. However, if our purpose is to try and see the world as police officers see it, that one nod means something quite important.

## C. Observing Change Over Time

Six years' observation allows for a sense of change over time. Researchers will too often seek to identify what is the case or what happens at a particular point in time. Like pinning a butterfly to a board in a display case, the image is vivid and accurate, but it gives no sense of movement. Police ethnographers develop particular understandings, of socialisation[65] or of 'police culture',[66] and explanatory frameworks, whether of types of police organisation[67] or police officer.[68] These frameworks endure and are a point of reference for studies many years later.[69] Do they still hold 'true' in a particular police unit in a particular police force in a particular country? They are codified and become received wisdom, appearing in textbooks almost as fact.[70] Even where time is a deliberate element of social science research, there is too often a simple and linear sense of time. Charman's work examines the changing beliefs of officers as they progress from trainee, through probation to become an experienced officer.[71] This does emphasise the process of becoming an officer, as represented in interviews, but it also presents that progression as a description of how it is, as static.

Observing officers in two police forces for six years unsettled any easy sense of certainty. For example, moving between shifts and between stations, we saw the many small differences as much as we could see any of the familiar signs of 'culture'. Sergeants played very different roles from one team to another.[72] Some would want to get out from behind a desk at any opportunity while others remained largely invisible in the field. Some were a source of advice and guidance while others could not be trusted to help. We noticed the ways in which some shifts came

---

[65] J van Maanen, 'Police Socialization: A Longitudinal Examination of Job Attitudes in an Urban Police Department' (1975) 20 *Administrative Science Quarterly* 207; N Fielding, *Joining Forces: Police Training, Socialization and Occupational Competence* (London, Routledge, 1988); D Cassan, 'Police Socialisation in France and in England: How do they Stand Towards the Community Policing Model?' (2010) 16 *Cahiers Politiestudies* 243.

[66] Holdaway, *Inside the British Police*; Loftus, *Police Culture in a Changing World*.

[67] Wilson, *Varieties of Police Behaviour*.

[68] Muir, *Police: Streetcorner Politicians*; Reuss-Ianni, *Two Cultures of Policing*.

[69] The easy points of reference for our work are, for example, WR LaFave, 'Police and Nonenforcement of the Law – Part I' (1962) *Wisconsin Law Review* 104; WR LaFave, 'Police and Nonenforcement of the Law – Part II' (1962) *Wisconsin Law Review* 179; Bittner, 'Police on Skid Row'.

[70] For example, we might argue that Reiner's model of police culture is presented as evidence of the thing it describes. And we would note that this model does not draw on primary research, but is built upon research presented by other scholars.

[71] Charman, *Police Socialisation, Identity and Culture*.

[72] AP Brief et al, 'Correlates of Supervisory Style Among Policemen' (1976) 3 *Journal of Criminal Justice and Behaviour* 263; RS Engel, 'The Supervisory Styles of Patrol Sergeants and Lieutenants' (2001) 29 *Journal of Criminal Justice* 341.

together, serious incidents permitting, for meal breaks to talk and joke, sometimes with their Sergeants and Inspectors,[73] while other shifts sat around an otherwise empty room, staring in silence at a television on the far side.[74] These patterns are disrupted by changes to rostering that, in the interests of efficiency, vary the hours officers work so that they no longer share a shift pattern with their colleagues. The 'canteen culture'[75] is a fragile one.

During our period in the field, both police forces underwent significant cuts to budgets and, therefore, to officer numbers. In detail, they responded differently, but each changed shift patterns, reorganised functions, and centralised activities in the name of efficiency. Our observations all too often commenced with a simple question: 'what has changed since I was last here?' Neighbourhood teams became thinner on the ground and covered larger areas. Response officers were centralised, in larger groups and in fewer locations, and responded by decentralising themselves, creating space at satellite stations with a desk and coffee-making facilities.[76] Neighbourhood and Territorial Support teams were depleted and tasked to jobs, such as warrants and searches, for more and more of their time. These changes all filtered down to affect what we observed. Where Response would have dealt with shoplifting in one force in 2014, by 2018 this was no longer an emergency matter but was handled centrally and scheduled for a slower turnaround. In the second force, burglaries were similarly downgraded, unless there was reason to believe the burglar was still in the vicinity. New technologies began to impinge on the work of officers at the same time. These included body-worn cameras (BWCs), tablets and other mobile devices, and new ways of monitoring officer duties and performance, to which subjects we will return in Chapter 9.

Some of the most significant changes during the course of our fieldwork (particularly relating to stop and search) have been the result of central government interventions, as mediated through law, through guidance, and through the College of Policing. In Chapter 6, we will discuss the introduction of the Best Use of Stop and Search Scheme[77] in more detail, but we observed that the way those changes were received was affected by a variety of factors. Those most frustrated by efforts to limit the use of powers were the proactive officers who used them far more than others. For Response officers, the changes scarcely impinged upon them, except in so far as they understood them to be an 'attack' on the police as a whole. The attitude of senior officers in each force further affected the way officers responded. In one, there was a tendency to resist the changes and to encourage

---

[73] Response, Kirk Machan, July 2015.

[74] Response, Ffarquhar Road, September 2015.

[75] M van Hulst, 'Storytelling at the Police Station: the Canteen Culture Revisited' (2013) 53 *British Journal of Criminology* 624; PAJ Waddington, 'Police (Canteen) Sub-culture: an Appreciation' (1999) 29 *British Journal of Criminology* 287.

[76] Response, Arlesdale Green, February 2018.

[77] Home Office/College of Policing, *Best Use of Stop and Search Scheme* (2014) assets. publishing.service.gov.uk/government/uploads/system/uploads/attachment_data/file/346922/Best_Use_of_Stop_and_Search_Scheme_v3.0_v2.pdf.

officers to continue to use the powers. In the other, the message was not mediated by senior officers in so clear a manner and the impact was more dramatic.

Our point about time is that we have observed change. We have not asked if things have changed since ethnographic work was last done in a police force. We have not tried to isolate a phenomenon that is static. With time, our early sense of understanding was destabilised as we compared our different observations and as we noted how patterns changed. With time, that uncertainty began to crystallise into a fresh sense of clarity, something that will hopefully emerge from this work. Perhaps we should note the prospect that more fieldwork and the inclusion of more police forces in our research might cause us to revisit what we write here. Normally, in longitudinal ethnographic research, we would expect to reach a point of saturation, where continued time in the field led to diminishing returns in terms of new data. However, change within the field meant that we never felt we were reaching a point approaching saturation.

## D.  Ethical Responsibilities and Relationships in the Field

The ethnographic approach is, as we have noted, more than simple observation. Ethnographers of the police do not observe officers from afar or as they appear in 'fly on the wall' documentaries. They sit next to them in the police station and in the patrol car, and stand alongside them in the street and in the queue for a coffee. They listen to their radio, observe their briefings, and try to stay awake with them in the early hours of the morning. With this access comes a series of challenges and responsibilities. Principal among these are our ethical responsibilities to the police force, to the officers we observe, and to the public we also observe.

Our prime ethical responsibility has been informed consent. Participant Information Sheets and Consent Forms were distributed to all those interested in participating. These detailed the nature of the research and what we intended to do with the data, in a format familiar to the officers. We promised our participants confidentiality and anonymity, both for the police forces and for the officers we observed. In this work, we have fictionalised the names of places (using two English literary sagas of the modern era) and have given each officer observed an identity from a selection of common names and nicknames. This is much as one might expect in any research of this nature.

However, the consent of those volunteering does not cover those other officers who we encountered during the shift. We have not required all officers to read the information sheets and give their informed consent. To have done so would have been impractical for us as researchers and would have hindered officers in the course of their duties. Instead, we took care to explain our research to all those we encountered. This might not occur immediately, in the heat of the moment at a scene for example. When circumstances allowed (eg while waiting at a scene, in the police car or van, over a coffee or meal break), we introduced ourselves and our work to as many as we could. This offered the additional possibility of identifying further volunteers. Where officers raised concerns or objections, we offered assurances about anonymity and our concern that no officer should be detrimentally affected by our work.

Having said that, we were also conscious that we have wider responsibilities.[78] In the fieldnote excerpt earlier in this chapter, Billy challenged the wording of our information sheet and specifically the way in which we spelled out our duty to speak out if we observed any illegal act committed by a participant. We have noted that, as volunteers, the officers we observed were likely to be officers considered by themselves or their superiors to be dependable. Nevertheless, there were occasions on which officers have stretched their interpretations of the law, using the 'Ways and Means Act',[79] ignored what they understood to be policies in a particular case, or simply made a mistake. To have reported all (or any) such incidents would have jeopardised the research. Understanding the ways officers interpreted the law and their responsibilities in practice was precisely the purpose of the research. We were not concerned to see that officers followed the law and force policies. However, should we see any act that appeared to be criminal and serious in nature, we also had some responsibilities to the police forces and to the public. We agreed to report this to the force through an independent senior officer. However, what might constitute a serious and/or criminal act was not tested in practice.

That we have not seen serious misconduct raises a question. Are we seeing the 'real' thing or just a sanitised version of policing? This question can haunt ethnographers. However, we have noted that, with time, we built a degree of trust with the majority of our participants. Furthermore, our research interest is in the ways in which apparently dependable police officers might still find themselves exercising powers in a disproportionate manner. What are the factors that direct their attention in particular ways and affect the decisions they then make? We were not, therefore, targeting so much the 'rotten apples' as the rest of the barrel. And our approach to our participants has then been much more open and collegial than a focus on poor conduct would allow.

We regularly offered to let officers read or listen to our fieldnotes, although usually this opportunity was declined. However, many of our fieldwork excerpts have been checked with officers in what has become an increasingly collaborative ethnography.[80] These offers and checks demonstrate a degree of transparency to officers, showing them what it is that we have paid attention to and made note of. In this way, consent is more informed than by the terse description of the aims of the research presented in our information sheets. Checks also assure us that we have understood the scene we observed and the ways in which the officers involved interpreted it. By showing our notes to other officers, in different stations

---

[78] J Ferdinand et al, 'A Different Kind of Ethics' (2007) 8 *Ethnography* 521.

[79] The 'Ways and Means Act' is a euphemism for whatever is expedient in a specific situation, particularly when it is not expressly permitted in rules, policy, or law (see Holdaway, *Inside the British Police*); P Waddington, *Policing Citizens: Authority and Rights* (London, UCL Press, 1999).

[80] Marcus, *Ethnography through Thick and Thin*.

or a different force, we are able to check that our representation of an incident is both credible to other officers and is anonymous.[81] Finally, these member checks demonstrated to officers that we had understood them and the dilemmas they faced. We were not there simply to judge their actions but to get as close as we can to seeing the world through their eyes.

## III.  Data and Analysis

In the field, much of what we do as ethnographers is familiar to police officers. They still carry their pocket notebooks and are expected to make contemporaneous handwritten notes about their actions and decisions. They write up such brief observations in greater detail at a later stage, generally during the same shift, but not always. They ask people to tell them what happened and to explain their decisions. In some respects, this went further.

> On my first day with the team, two officers take me on patrol in an unmarked car. They have no assigned jobs for the moment, and so they are out looking for faces they know, for intelligence about who is associating with whom, for trouble. But they are also showing me their patch, giving me the tour. As they drive from one housing estate to another, we are also moving through territories. Some of these are marked with graffiti on street corners, others are self-contained estates that need no marking. Callum tells of an old gang being challenged by two younger gangs. He talks of their cultures as different, as distinct. One gang prefers extreme violence, another guns. He talks of their feuds.[82]

These officers develop a detailed, almost anthropological picture of places and people over time. These pictures are a kind of collage, of information accumulated by other officers or by reports from members of the public. They are recorded in a file (now an electronic record) and connected to other files to form a bigger picture.[83] Mutsaers[84] has identified similarities with the work of anthropologists. They may come into contact with everyone but will tend to focus on the poor and underprivileged. They work in the unpredictable real world and not in offices or laboratories and, in that real world, they endeavour to 'go native' or undercover. Borneman and Masco draw similar parallels with spies and secret police, but their points hold for many more conventional law enforcement officers:

> Both involve looking, listening, eavesdropping, taking notes, recording conversations, snapping photos, and establishing trusted confidants. We call it participant-observation;

---

[81] Showing Spencer a draft article, he was convinced some of the fieldnotes were from observations we had conducted with him. They were not.

[82] Territorial Support, Devil's Back, July 2016.

[83] M O'Neil and B Loftus, 'Policing and the Surveillance of the Marginal: Everyday Contexts of Social Control' (2013) 17 *Theoretical Criminology* 437; JH Ratcliffe, *Intelligence-led Policing*, 2nd edn (London, Routledge, 2016).

[84] P Mutsaers, *A Public Anthropology of Policing: Law Enforcement and Migrants in the Netherlands* (Tilburg, Tilburg University, 2015) 1–2.

they call it spying. We seek informants; they seek informers. Both intend to understand and create a representation of someone else's reality. We craft these representations into an 'ethnography' based on personal encounters, autobiographies, events, ritual partici-pation, and lived experience; they craft them out of similar observational materials into an official file.[85]

Much of what these officers do and much of what interests them, then, is familiar to us as ethnographers. Mutsaers comments, almost in passing, that this is why 'street-level police experience is of such great value to the anthropological discipline'.[86] We would argue that the value is mutual.

However, we should note the differences too. The first key difference, as Borneman and Masco remark, is the purpose for which the notes and records are created and what we then do with them. Officers contribute small pieces of data to a much bigger picture and they work with very structured formats. As ethnogra-phers, we seek to make sense of a mass of notes accumulated over time in a much less structured manner. Indeed, the authors physically took notes in different ways. One took notes on a digital recording device in between incidents and during the shift. This then afforded the option to briefly interview officers about those inci-dents and to present verbatim transcripts, some of which appear in this work. The other recorded observations in a handheld notebook that could easily be put away in a jacket pocket. These scribbled (and often barely legible) notes were then typed up to form a record of each shift.

These initial notes, whether audio or written, were essentially prompts to the memory. We did not create a 'full' record of a shift, but noted those activities that seemed relevant at the time. We noted the contexts and situations that shaped the decisions officers made. However, we observed different things. We have remarked upon our different disciplinary backgrounds, one from socio-legal studies and the other from public administration and management. This clearly affected the things we paid attention to and the notes we took. For one, officers' understandings and use of the law were a key point of interest. For the other, processes of briefing, deployment, and management were the starting point. With time, we have shared our notes and began to develop some understanding of the points of interest to the other, but our different disciplinary backgrounds still tended to dominate our respective notes.

This process of sharing notes became the first step in our analysis. We each identified anomalies and puzzles from our observations, checking them with the other. We compared notes and stories, seeking to confirm or explain these puzzles. What we soon uncovered was the differences between officers. There is no one answer to many of the dilemmas and problems officers confront. But we also noted variations between roles, shifts, and even between police stations. As, from April 2016, we began to undertake research in our second police force,

---

[85] J Borneman and J Masco, 'Anthropology and the Security State' (2015) 117 *American Anthropologist* 781, 783.

[86] Mutsaers, *A Public Anthropology of Policing* 2.

these differences multiplied. At the same time, and lying behind or beneath these variations, we began to make sense of the shared understandings and frameworks. We also started to realise that the differences in our understandings of structure, policy, and work-practices were not simply the result of one or both of us failing to comprehend the field in front of us, but reflected the different interpretations of police work of different officers, and the effect of change upon the force, which did not occur in a uniform or consistent manner. Despite our frustrations at the time, the disparate jumble of beliefs, practices, and behaviour, and the apparent absence of an overarching 'culture', was to become our first concrete argument. There is a temptation to make this sound a more scientific process than it was.[87] Instead, we argue that the process of reading and rereading our notes, of checking, with each other and with our collaborators, and of continuing to observe over time, is a process of analysis. We have confidence in what we are going to say because we have had that nod from an experienced officer.

If the ways we take notes and perform our analysis are very different to the work of police officers, there is a second difference, and perhaps a more important one. As observers, we have no responsibility to act. We have occasionally found ourselves performing minor supporting roles, regularly guiding an officer to a destination by use of 'Google Maps' on our phones, identifying suspects, searching fields, tracking down cannabis farms by sense of smell, memorising or reading out vehicle number plates, or directing a torch-light beam underneath the seats of a car to assist a search. We have even been tasked with holding an officer's hat while they administer to a drunk,[88] moving traffic cones at a road traffic incident,[89] assisted in the bagging of stolen property,[90] and given statements on particular incidents.[91] But we have not been responsible for the decisions made and actions taken. In contrast, officers are. It is to the powers they exercise and the ways they are held accountable for their use that we now turn.

---

[87] Neither of us has used NVivo or any other form of analytical tool.
[88] Night-time Economy Team, Knapford, October 2015.
[89] Territorial Support, Brandham, February 2015.
[90] Response, Kirk Machan, July 2015.
[91] Territorial Support, Brandham, December 2013.

# 3

## Regulation and the Law

Although our research project covered a number of interlinked topics, controversies, and themes, the focus of the current book is specifically on street powers and the extent to which they can, or should, be subject to regulation or control. A considerable amount has already been written about the relationship between the police and the law, and this chapter will revisit these views before establishing how we intend to contribute to and move forward the debate. It will first provide an overview of what we believe is now a broad consensus about the relationship between the criminal law and the work of the police, drawing on research on police work going back to the supposed 'discovery' of police discretion by research with officers in the United States in the 1960s.[1] We will then focus on attempts by English judges and legislature to regulate police powers, most notably through the Police and Criminal Evidence Act 1984 (PACE), before moving on to the consider the role that human rights under the European Convention (ECHR) have played in restraining police officers in their position as agents of the state, particularly following the Human Rights Act 1998 (HRA 1998). The relative successes of these statutes are considered alongside the impact of non-statutory guidance, procedures, and policy – national, force-wide, and at a divisional and station level – on the use of police powers.

## I. The Relationship between Policing and the Law

The emergence of academic narratives of police discretion during the 1960s, and the increasing use of ethnographic methods to uncover how discretion was utilised, led to the development of what is now a broad consensus amongst policing academics that the police are not primarily 'law enforcers'. As Waddington points out, 'law enforcement is not what the police do nor what the public ask the police to do ... the police are not very effective crime-fighters'.[2] However, this contrasts with the public opinion of police work, the typical aims of officers

---

[1] W LaFave, *Arrest: The Decision to take a Suspect into Custody. The Report of the American Bar Foundation's Survey of the Administration of Criminal Justice in the United States* (Boston, Little Brown, 1965).

[2] P Waddington, *Policing Citizens: Authority and Rights* (London, UCL Press, 1999) 4–5.

when entering the police service[3] and their subsequent interpretation of what is 'real' police work,[4] most political and journalistic commentary on policing, and common law interpretations of the duties of the police.[5] This leads us to question: what is the relationship between the police and the law? While primarily this question has focused on the relationship between the police and the criminal law that officers have been tasked to uphold and enforce, there are also questions to be asked with regard to police obligations under civil law (particularly liability in tort) and, of course, the laws that regulate their duties and behaviour, from PACE to the reforms to the police service and the Police Act 1996 by the Police Reform and Social Responsibility Act 2011, which introduced Police and Crime Commissioners. Administrative law is also important, with the prospect of a judicial review hanging over the decision-making processes that create and apply force policy. Unsurprisingly, therefore, both civil and criminal law are considered to 'permeate' policing,[6] meaning that 'the discourse of law' should be 'the starting point for making sense of police work'.[7] As Reiner contends, the 'legal powers of the police are arguably their defining feature'.[8] There is, however, a certain risk of circular reasoning here; explaining the relationship of the police to the law by referring back to the legal basis under which the institution operates takes us only so far.

In England and Wales, the police constable has famously been referred to as a 'citizen in uniform', whose power only comes from the consent of those she is policing.[9] Reiner strongly disputes the former claim, calling the idea of the constable being no more than a citizen in uniform simply a myth.[10] Even if we only consider the legal underpinnings of the police service it is difficult to disagree. When the officer takes their oath and obtains their warrant card, common law has long dictated that their obligations in respect of the criminal law change dramatically from those of other citizens. Police officers are sworn to keep the peace and apprehend offenders,[11] whereas there is no general obligation on citizens to even report crimes they witness. While officers retain discretion and operational

---

[3] H Goldstein, *Policing a Free Society* (1977) University of Wisconsin Legal Studies Research Paper No 1349, 3 (with regard to policing in the United States); S Charman, *Police Socialisation, Identity and Culture: Becoming Blue* (London, Palgrave Macmillam, 2017).

[4] R Ericson, *Reproducing Order: A Study of Police Patrol Work* (Toronto, University of Toronto Press, 1982) 5–6.

[5] *Fisher v Oldham Corporation* [1930] 2 KB 364; *R v Commissioner of Police of the Metropolis, ex p Blackburn (No 1)* [1968] 2 QB 118.

[6] D Dixon. 'Changing Law, Changing Policing' in M Mitchell and J Casey (eds), *Police Management and Leadership* (Sydney, Federation Press, 2007) 23.

[7] R Grimshaw and T Jefferson, *Interpreting Police Work: Policy and Practice in Forms of Beat Policing* (London, Allen & Unwin, 1987) 274.

[8] Preface to L Skinns, *Police Powers and Citizen Rights: Discretionary Decision Making in Police Detention* (London, Routledge, 2019) xi.

[9] See the Home Office's interpretation of this at www.gov.uk/government/publications/policing-by-consent/definition-of-policing-by-consent.

[10] R Reiner, *The Politics of the Police*, 4th edn (Oxford, Oxford University Press, 2014) 207.

[11] *Fisher v Oldham Corporation* [1930] 2 KB 364.

freedom, this is not absolute. Each police force is tasked by the state to uphold the criminal law, and Chief Constables cannot abrogate this responsibility. Their duty is to enforce the law of the land, to detect crimes, and allow 'honest citizens' to 'go about their affairs in peace'.[12] Further, following the HRA 1998, the police service has a number of positive obligations enshrined in law: 'to safeguard the life and physical integrity of individuals known to be at risk', to 'investigate crime efficiently', and 'to ensure that individuals can enjoy their Convention rights'.[13] The legal obligations of the police are now mediated through the police and crime plans of the relevant Police and Crime Commissioner.[14] This obligation is passed down through the Chief Constable's 'direction and control' of her force and its officers.[15] Therefore, even when we are looking at the 'hole in the doughnut' that is police discretion,[16] we need to acknowledge the 'primary status of law as an objective and guide for the police', because, 'upholding the law not only forms a mandatory objective, it also legitimizes the powers of the police and authorizes their operational independence'.[17] However, while this is of course fundamentally important, it does not assist us in investigating how the criminal law is used in practice, or the effectiveness of the law in regulating policing behaviour.

It is well established that frontline officers spend only a proportion of their shift on duties that are directly connected with upholding the criminal law by investigating offences, apprehending criminals, and deterring potential offenders.[18] For Neighbourhood policing in particular, there is a 'massive tail of peripheral activities', which, combined with a preference for informal warnings for most offenders (which we will discuss in Chapter 7) indicates the 'relative absence of "legal" work' in this form of policing.[19] It should perhaps be no surprise that some scholars have suggested that officers 'seldom invoke the law' in police work.[20] However, when we interrogate this explanation of policing, we would first point out that there is not a clear dividing line between what is and is not 'criminal' according to the law. Certain incidents can be constructed as criminal or not, depending on the interpretation of the individual officer, or increasingly that of someone in the Radio Control Room. One of the points we will discuss in Chapter 9 relates to the fact that incidents which frontline officers would typically not have classified as criminal previously, are now classified as such by the National Crime Recording Standards. Nevertheless, there was a clear view amongst officers as to

---

[12] *R v Commissioner of Police of the Metropolis, ex p Blackburn (No 1)* [1968] 2 QB 118.

[13] K Starmer, *European Human Rights Law: The Human Rights Act 1998 and the European Convention on Human Rights* (London, Legal Action Group, 1989) 415–16.

[14] Police Reform and Social Responsibility Act 2011, s 8(2).

[15] Police Reform and Social Responsibility Act 2011, s 2(3).

[16] R Dworkin, *Taking Rights Seriously* (Cambridge, MA, Harvard University Press, 1977) 31.

[17] Grimshaw and Jefferson, *Interpreting Police Work* 278.

[18] R Ericson and K Haggerty, *Policing the Risk Society* (Oxford, Oxford University Press, 1997) 19.

[19] Grimshaw and Jefferson, *Interpreting Police Work* 165. Ericson and Haggerty refer to this as a largely non-criminal 'kaleidoscope of trouble' (*Policing the Risk Society* 19–20).

[20] Eg R Worden 'Situational and Attitudinal Explanations of Police Behavior: A Theoretical Reappraisal and Empirical Assessment' (1989) 23 *Law and Society Review* 667, 668.

what was *broadly* criminal and what was considered non-criminal 'social' work. From our observations, Neighbourhood policing certainly required officers to spend much of their time attempting to resolve sub-criminal disputes, preventing or deterring sub-criminal anti-social behaviour, reassuring vulnerable members of the community, and searching for missing persons. Officers in other policing roles (for example schools officers and mental health triage) spent significantly less time than Neighbourhood officers on upholding the criminal law. Across the service, officers increasingly saw their job as less about crime fighting and more about the welfare of vulnerable people. Our participants frequently complained that they spent so much time acting as 'social workers' that there was simply no time left for 'thief taking'.[21] During our time in the field, however, despite this commonly-held belief, we saw no evidence that focus on the 'social work' aspect of policing was increasing.

In both forces the cuts to police numbers had resulted in reorganisation and an increasing proportion of frontline officers performing Response roles. While Response officers were regularly tasked to non-criminal incidents (for example road traffic accidents, attempted or actual suicides, missing dementia sufferers, or runaway children), their predominant role was in responding to allegations of criminal activity (usually domestic violence, burglaries, stolen cars, or affrays). It was simply not the case for Response officers observed during our fieldwork that 'criminal law enforcement is merely an incidental and derivative part of police work'.[22] For Response officers, Grimshaw and Jefferson's claim that even pre-PACE, the law remained 'a focus of the officer's attention, *even if in a practical form*, rather than disappearing beneath subcultural norms' (emphasis added)[23] still appears to be accurate. Organised Crime Disruption units also typically remained focused on disrupting and gathering intelligence on organised crime, and Traffic officers spent most of their time monitoring and responding to (albeit usually minor) traffic offences. It is difficult, therefore, to generalise about the amount of time which frontline officers as a whole dedicate to investigating crime or deterring offenders. We should also be careful not to underestimate the amount of criminal law enforcement that officers do. We would agree with Herbert that, at least in the current environment, 'the law is typically underplayed as a determinant of police behaviour', and remains, 'a principal means by which officers regularly reach a definition of the situation'.[24] Further, we should also not assume that the priority of the law for most frontline officers is either temporally or geographically static, nor that any existing focus by officers in some roles on sub-legal disputes and welfare risks will survive the rigours of cuts to police numbers and resources.

---

[21] See also K Lumsden and A Black, 'Austerity Policing, Emotional Labour and Boundaries of Police Work: An Ethnography of a Police Force Control Room in England' (2018) 58 *British Journal of Criminology* 615.

[22] E Bittner, 'Florence Nightingale in Pursuit of Willie Sutton: A Theory of the Police' in H Jacob (ed), *The Potential for Reform of Criminal Justice* (Beverley Hills, CA, Sage, 1974).

[23] Grimshaw and Jefferson, *Interpreting Police Work* 110.

[24] S Herbert, 'Police Culture Reconsidered' (1998) 36 *Criminology* 343, 352.

Moreover, just because an officer identifies a criminal offence, apprehends a suspected offender, or arrives at the scene of a suspected crime following a 999 call, does not mean that they will enforce the law by way of formal action. There is a difference between an officer's focus on a criminal offence and setting the wheels of the wider criminal justice system into motion. It is in this common situation, where an officer is faced with a suspected criminal offender, that the relationship between the officer and the law is most interesting and contentious. First, of course, the officer needs to apply their understanding of the criminal law to the situation to determine whether they have the power to take formal action. Their understanding of the criminal law, however, is typically quite limited; officers cannot be expected to fully understand all the multitude of criminal offences that exist or the subtle differences in the way these offences are interpreted and developed in court. Officers possessed an understanding of the basic mens rea and actus reus of common offences (eg theft, threatening behaviour, assault and bodily harm) and also a keen understanding of areas of new or changed law that may have been brought to their attention in a recent briefing or training package (eg dangerous dogs legislation).[25] However, often officers asked colleagues (or even the observer) for advice, or were observed re-appraising their understanding of potential offences online following their decision in an individual case because they were unsure whether their interpretation of the law had been correct.

> Over two Late shifts, Response officers discussed one case in some detail. After an argument, a man threw a car manual in anger, striking his partner in the eye. She went to hospital and, while there, found out she was pregnant. This further means the medical staff cannot save her eye. Is this a s 47 [Offences Against the Persons Act Offence]? Or s 20? Or would it be s 18? Was there intent? They refer to the [Crown Prosecution Service] for a decision.[26]

Officers were also observed to regularly overlook potential offences or mistakenly apply the law. This is unsurprising; frontline officers are tasked to make decisions in which they were expected to apply an accurate understanding of often highly-complex laws as well as constantly-changing police procedure and policy, at the same time as remembering tactical priorities (eg the identity of wanted or dangerous offenders), and technical aspects of policing (eg with regard to portable technology, health and safety, and self-defence). Often these need to be split-second decisions and sometimes under enormous pressure and scrutiny from perpetrator, victim, and witnesses. To expect the police to always be able to understand and apply the right law at the right time is simply unrealistic. As Waddington neatly sums up, 'The police do not enforce the law because they cannot. Laws must be interpreted and that interpretation is always context specific. Therefore, discretion is unavoidable'.[27]

---

[25] Dixon criticises the teaching of the law to police officers and notes the lack of research in this area (D Dixon, *Law in Policing: Legal Regulation and Police Practices* (Oxford, Clarendon, 1997) 277–78).

[26] Response, Westmarch, February 2018.

[27] Waddington, *Policing Citizens* 63.

Moving on, even when the officer believes that an offence has been committed, and that the suspect before them has committed it, they still possess a wide range of discretion in terms of their response.[28] This can be called 'invocation discretion', drawing upon Goldstein's groundbreaking work in the 1950s and 60s.[29] At one extreme, they could make an arrest (if they determine they have a reason for this in addition to the suspected crime). Alternatively, they also have the power to require the suspect to voluntarily attend (VA) the police station at a later date to be inter- viewed under caution about the suspected crime. For some offences, officers will possess the power to give a formal warning that will go on their suspect's record (eg for cannabis possession) or impose a Fixed Penalty Notice (FPN) or traffic offence ticket. At the other end of the scale, the officer may choose to give 'verbal advice' (ie an informal warning or 'ticking off') or may simply turn a blind eye to the offence. It is in this wide space of alternative responses, often without the restraints of policy or supervision, that police discretion is at its most powerful and contentious. It is in this space that the relevance of the criminal law starts to fade, or becomes subsumed by a whole variety of non-legal considerations and pressures. Here the law stops being something that must be enforced or upheld and may instead become a 'resource'[30] to achieve the ends the officer wishes, or a 'control device' to impose order, assert authority, or acquire intelligence.[31]

It can in some cases become a tool to reproduce social control or authority 'by extracting deference and inflicting summary punishment',[32] although our observations suggested this was rare and both context- and role-specific. Early observational studies of the police suggested the criminal law was *invoked* to justify the actions an officer wished to take, particularly in keeping the peace on the officer's beat, rather than acting as a set of rules that guided their actions. In other words, officers fitted legal powers around their decisions rather than vice versa.[33] The criminal law thus becomes vague, uncertain and manipulated.[34] In this way, 'police decisions not to invoke the criminal process largely deter- mine the outer limits of law enforcement';[35] the outcome is that rather than the police officers apprehending criminals, the police play a direct role in *constructing*

---

[28] Though we would not go so far as to describe it as 'an almost infinite range of lawful possibilities' (L Lustgarten, *The Governance of the Police* (London, Sweet and Maxwell, 1986) 10).

[29] J Goldstein, 'Police Discretion Not to Invoke the Criminal Process: Low-Visibility Decisions in the Administration of Justice' (Yale, Faculty Scholarship Series 2426, 1960).

[30] Ericson, *Reproducing Order.*

[31] E Bittner, 'The Police on Skid Row: A Study of Peacekeeping' (1967) 32 *American Sociological Review* 699; S Holdaway, *Inside the British Police: A Force at Work* (Oxford, Basil Blackwell, 1983).

[32] S Choongh 'Policing the Dross: A Social Disciplinary Model of Policing' (1998) 38(4) *British Journal of Criminology* 623, 625–26.

[33] M Banton, *The Policeman in the Community* (London, Tavistock, 1964); Bittner, 'The Police on Skid Row'; JQ Wilson, *Varieties of Police Behaviour: The Management of Law and Order in Eight Communities* (Cambridge, MA, Harvard University Press, 1968).

[34] J Reiman, 'Is Police Discretion Justified in a Free Society?' in J Kleinig (ed), *Handled With Discretion: Ethical Issues in Police Decision Making* (London, Rowman & Littlefield. 1996) 71.

[35] J Goldstein, 'Police Discretion' (1960) 69 *Yale Law Journal* 543.

the criminal population.[36] The constructivist argument remains a powerful one, but we need to take care in assuming that many of the early accounts – particularly of the police in the United States – are still applicable to contemporary policing in England and Wales.

One of our key arguments in this book is that the police service is in constant flux and is subject to varying differing degrees of transformation in response to force policy, organisational readjustment, supervisory change, and techno- logical development. Even potentially short-term changes, such as cutbacks to Neighbourhood policing and an increased focus on Response policing, have the potential to change how the police utilise the law. As an example, let us take Bittner's finding that, 'in discretionary law enforcement involving minor offences, police- men use existing law largely as a pretext for making arrests ... the real reasons for invoking the law are wholly independent of the law that is being invoked'.[37] Our observations indicated that this was reflected in the behaviour of Territorial Support units (particularly early on in our research) but not for other policing roles (see Chapter 7). Further, as our fieldwork progressed and arrest was made less attractive for all officers, even the Territorial Support units preferred to avoid a visit to custody for minor offences unless absolutely necessary. Police discretion in law enforcement remains both omnipresent and essential[38] but it operates in a very different way for twenty-first century Response officers with body-worn cameras, location trackers, and handheld devices with check-boxes, than it did for beat officers in the United States in the 1960s.

## II.  The Common Law Regulation of the Police

Unfortunately, the continued importance of police discretion in both law enforce- ment and the wider duties and working lives of officers all too often combines with criticism about police failings in their duty of care, treatment of suspects, and ability to apply their powers in a way that is proportionate to minority or under- privileged populations. The regulation of police powers, and how this relates to the accountability and legitimacy of the police, is the central theme of this book and the remainder of this chapter will consider the steps that have been taken to manage, regulate, and control the power and discretion that individual frontline officers possess. We will consider the common law and legislative position before considering the impact of human rights and, finally, policy and guidance.

It is a long-standing principle of English law that there should be some restric- tions on the use of executive power against the citizen, probably most famously

---

[36] M McConville et al, *The Case for the Prosecution: Police Suspects and the Construction of Criminality* (London, Routledge, 1993).

[37] E Bittner, *The Functions of the Police in Modern Society* (University of Minnesota, National Institute of Mental Health, Center for Studies of Crime and Delinquency, 1970) 109.

[38] K Davis, *Police Discretion* (St Paul, MN, West Publishing Co, 1975) 140.

set out in the eighteenth century case of *Entick v Carrington*.[39] However, rather than providing citizens with any rights against the use of power by the police (in John Entick's case a warrant to search his property which lacked authority either in statute or common law), *Entick v Carrington* merely established that in order to commit acts that would otherwise be unlawful (in this case trespass to property), the agents of the state simply needed legal authority. Civil *liberties* rather than *rights* are therefore talked about with regard to the relationship between British citizens and the state. Furthermore, as cases started to come before English courts in the twentieth century, rather than providing further protections for citizens from the power of the executive, instead we witnessed a common law extension of police powers. Ewing draws our attention to Sir Robert Megarry V-C's statement with respect to executive power (in this case phone-tapping) in *Malone v Metropolitan Police Commissioner (No 2)* that, 'England, it may be said, is not a country where everything is forbidden except what is expressly permitted: it is a country where everything is permitted except what is expressly forbidden'.[40] Dixon also notes that twentieth-century cases were more likely to extend than restrain police powers, providing the example of *Moss v MacLachlan*,[41] which extended the definition of 'imminence' in the context of the power to make arrests to prevent a breach of the peace. Controversially, the extension of this power in this case also enabled the police to assist the Government's attempt to break the Miners' Strike in 1984–1985. Other cases, such as *Dallison v Caffery*[42] and *Holgate-Mohammed v Duke*,[43] supported the power of the police to make arrests in order to carry out reasonable investigations and obtain evidence to justify a potential future charge.

The historical creep in the number of criminal offences also had the effect of increasing police powers over the population.[44] Obviously the more potential crimes there are available for the police to respond to, the more opportunity there is for use of coercive powers (though whether a growth in the number of offences leads to more police activity is another matter). Some offences have also had a disproportionate impact on the use of police powers, by providing special powers of enforcement or investigation, most famously section 4 of the Vagrancy Act 1824 which provided police officers with the power to stop, search, and arrest any person suspected of an intent to commit an arrestable offence in a public place. The 'sus laws', as they became known, were implicated in the use of arbitrary stop and searches which disproportionately affected ethnic minority populations. The Scarman Report found that the mass use of 'sus law' searches as part of the

---

[39] *Entick v Carrington* [1762] 275 95 ER 807.
[40] *Malone v Metropolitan Police Commissioner (No 2)* [1979] Ch 344 at 357.
[41] *Moss v MacLachlan* [1985] IRLR 76; Dixon, *Law in Policing* 74.
[42] *Dallison v Caffery* [1964] 2 All ER 610.
[43] *Holgate-Mohammed v Duke* [1983] 3 All ER 526.
[44] For example, in 2010–11, 1,760 new offences were created. Whether this increase is accelerating or not is disputed (J Chalmers and A Shaw, 'Is Formal Criminalisation Really on the Rise? Evidence from the 1950s' (2015) 3 *Criminal Law Review* 177).

Metropolitan Police's 'Operation Swamp' played a significant role in increasing tensions that led to the 1981 Brixton riots.[45]

At the same time as common law and statute were increasing police powers in England and Wales, there was little in the way of regulation of police use or misuse of power by the courts. As judges have the ultimate control over whether or not evidence is adduced in court, they can also influence police behaviour by exclusion of prosecution evidence obtained improperly (eg through an unlawful search or detention, a forced confession, or entrapment). Prior to PACE, the power of judges to exclude evidence was set out in the 'Judge's Rules,' which included the requirement to caution suspects, and also requirements for the form of written statements.[46] However, a failure by officers to follow the rules would not lead to automatic exclusion of the evidence; a decision here remained at the trial judge's discretion and was sparingly used.[47] Common law decisions also provided trial judges with the discretion or direction to exclude certain other types of evidence, for example forced confessions,[48] or more generally evidence that had a prejudicial effect outweighing its probative value.[49] However, none of these powers purported to give judges control or supervision over how the police conducted their enquiries: 'The judges control the conduct of trials and the admission of evidence against persons on trial before them: they do not control or in any way initiate or supervise police activities or conduct'.[50] Ultimately, as McConville et al conclude, 'due process has never been the dominant principle of English criminal justice'.[51]

# III.   Legislation and the Police and Criminal Evidence Act 1984

Arguably the most significant change to the regulation of policing in England and Wales came from the introduction of PACE, which followed decades of 'official dissatisfaction' with the previous rules.[52] It created for the first time a

---

[45] Lord Scarman, *The Brixton Disorders 10–12 April 1981: Report of an Inquiry* (London, HMSO, 1981). See also B Bowling et al, 'Policing minority ethnic communities' in T Newburn (ed), *Handbook of Policing*, 2nd edn (London, Willan Publishing, 2008) 611; and K Reid, 'Race Issues and Stop and Search: Looking Behind the Statistics' (2009) *Criminal Law Review* 165. See S Hall et al, *Policing the Crisis: Mugging, the State and Law and Order* (London, Macmillan, 1978) for a wider discussion on policing of race in this period. The 'sus laws' were repealed by the Criminal Attempts Act 1981 and the general stop and search power is now governed by PACE 1984.

[46] *Practice Note (Judge's Rules)* [1964] 1 WLR 152.

[47] D Ormerod and D Birch, 'The Evolution of the Discretionary Exclusion of Evidence' (2004) *Criminal Law Review* 767, 776.

[48] *R v Ibrahim* [1914] AC 599.

[49] *R v Sang* [1980] AC 402.

[50] Lord Parker CJ in *Practice Note (Judge's Rules)* [1964] 1 WLR 152, 152.

[51] McConville et al, *Case for the Prosecution* 185.

[52] M Zander, *Zander on PACE: The Police and Criminal Evidence Act*, 6th edn (London, Sweet and Maxwell, 2013) xi.

comprehensive legislative framework setting out the limits of police powers and suspect rights in relation to areas of interest key to our research, including stop and search, arrest, and detention. It also created the Crown Prosecution Service (CPS) and set on a statutory footing many of the judicial powers to exclude prosecution evidence. However, as Lord Judge noted, PACE was not 'greeted with universal acclaim' and drew criticism from the outset that on the one hand it failed to properly protect the rights of suspects against police abuse, and that on the other it still placed restrictive and bureaucratic restrictions that made it harder for police officers to do their job.[53] Around a decade after its introduction, a number of reports, articles, and monographs were published, many based upon ethnographic fieldwork, which looked to assess its impact and debate how (if at all) police powers and discretion had been affected by its enactment. These included Maguire and Norris (1992), McConville, Sanders and Leng (1993), Rose (1996), Brown (1997), and Dixon (1997),[54] and there was considerable disagreement on the extent to which the new legislation, and the comprehensive and detailed Codes of Practice attached to it, changed policing.

For McConville et al, PACE (and other legislation) did not provide a strong constraint on police behaviour. For example, the requirement for 'reasonable suspicion' to conduct a stop and search or summary arrest remained 'sufficiently vague and flexible to allow the police very extensive discretion'.[55] Similarly, McKenzie questioned the role of the Custody Sergeant in assessing the necessity of detention, identifying no post-PACE decline in arrests and no case in 1,800 custody records examined of detention not being authorised.[56] For many scholars, the failure of PACE simply demonstrated once again that legality was not a strong constraint on police behaviour. The police would always, McConville et al argued, find ways to work around the rules. This police practice is well documented, and the police themselves refer to the 'Ways and Means Act'.[57] This is a metaphorical piece of legislation which officers claim to use to find ways around any laws or rules which place bureaucratic barriers in the way of their work, and some officers express bravado about using it to find a way around restrictions on their behaviour.[58] Another way of explaining this gap is through the 'law of inevitable increment – whatever powers the police have, they will exceed by a given margin'.[59] It is clear,

---

[53] Lord Judge, in *Zander on PACE* v.

[54] M Maguire and C Norris, *The Conduct of Criminal Investigations Royal Commission on Criminal Justice Research Study #5* (London, HMSO, 1991); McConville et al, *Case for the Prosecution*; D Rose, *In the Name of the Law* (London, Jonathan Cape, 1996); D Brown, *PACE Ten Years On: A Review of the Research: Home Office Research Study 155* (London, HMSO, 1997); Dixon, *Law in Policing*.

[55] McConville et al, *Case for the Prosecution* 182–84.

[56] I McKenzie et al, 'Helping the Police with their Inquiries: The Necessity Principle and Voluntary Attendance at the Police Station' (1990) *Criminal Law Review* 22.

[57] Holdaway, *Inside the British Police*; Waddington, *Policing Citizens*. The 'Ways and Means Act' was still referred to by officers during our fieldwork.

[58] Dixon, *Law in Policing* 304.

[59] Reiner, *Politics of the Police* 173.

therefore, that there is a significant difference between what the law requires of the police, and the actual use of powers by frontline police:

> The law appears to exert less moral force on the police than is often believed, for there is a gap between many legal rules and the working rules of the police. This means that much of the law is presentational in nature, providing a misleading appearance of a system subject to numerous inhibitory due process safeguards. In reality law breaking by the police and lesser failures of due process are tolerated.[60]

For many commentators, therefore, PACE has become merely a list of 'presentational rules' that do not guide police conduct.[61] As Ericson so eloquently notes, new laws rarely change police decision-making because '… rules are literally dead letters, dying as the ink on them dries on the paper on which they are published'.[62] Attempts to impose legislative change often run the risk of failure without an attempt to understand the 'working social context' in which the real 'rules of the game' are created and maintained.[63] External legal rules can often fail to compete with existing internal rules and established practices, and those imposing them often presume their deterrent effect upon behaviour with scant evidence.[64]

Moreover, even where some change is effective, this frequently carries with it 'unplanned and unexpected consequences',[65] and with regard to PACE and other apparently restrictive legislation, it has been argued that this not only fails to prevent abusive practice, but also enables officers to cover procedurally-suspect behaviour with a 'legal canopy'[66] of protection from scrutiny. Rather than following the rules it can be argued that the police are using the law for their own crime control agenda.[67] The effect is therefore not neutral but instead that, 'most of the presentational rules (…) are part of a (successful) attempt by the wider society to deceive itself about the realities of policing'.[68] Further, it can be argued that these consequences are not unintended or unexpected; PACE and other legal regulation of the criminal justice system may follow a rights-based rhetoric, but tend to expressly permit deviation from this through statutory exception and executive and judicial discretion. McBarnet claims (pre-PACE) that, '[i]f the practice of criminal justice does not live up to its rhetoric one should not look only to interactions and negotiations of those who put the law into practice but to the law itself'.[69]

---

[60] A Sanders and R Young, 'Police Powers' in T Newburn (ed), *Handbook of Policing*, 2nd edn (Cullompton, Willan, 2008) 305.

[61] D Smith and J Gray, *Police and People in London: the PSI Report* (Aldershot, Gower, 1985).

[62] R Ericson, 'Rules in Policing: Five Perspectives' (2007) 11 *Theoretical Criminology* 367, 379.

[63] S Falk-Moore, 'Law and Social Change: The Semi-autonomous Social Field as an Appropriate Subject of Study' (1973) 7 *Law and Society Review* 719.

[64] A Goldsmith, 'Taking Police Culture Seriously: Police Discretion and the Limits of Law' (1990) 1 *Policing and Society* 91.

[65] Falk-Moore, 'Law and Social Change' 723.

[66] McConville et al, *Case for the Prosecution* 174–75.

[67] Ericson, 'Rules in Policing'.

[68] Smith and Gray, *Police and People* 441–42.

[69] D McBarnet, *Conviction: The Law, the State and the Construction of Justice* (London, Palgrave MacMillan, 1981) 155–56.

The gap between rhetoric and reality is not just one between formal equality and situational equality, between the law in the books and the law in action, but a gap between
the rhetoric of justice and the reality of criminal procedure: it is a gap within the law in
the books, which has to be traced not to the petty administrators of the law but to the
people with the power to make it – the judicial and political elite of the state.[70]

In other words, the rhetoric of the law (with regard to curtailing executive power
and the rights of the individual) is subverted *within* the law, not by 'policemen
bending the rules'.[71] The 'law in books' realistically sets out police powers,[72] including the wide discretion granted to officers, and is closer to the law in action than
many believe.[73]

However, not all commentators are so pessimistic about the limits of legal
regulation and the failures and ambiguous effects of PACE upon the use of police
powers. Although acknowledging that officers would sometimes completely
ignore, or work around, legal restrictions, Herbert argues that this does not mean
such restrictions are 'unimportant in shaping police behaviour'.[74] While Long
was also critical of the lack of scrutiny given to necessary detention by custody
officers, he found 'a more grounded evidential basis' for arrests than had existed
before.[75] Similarly, Skinns' more recent study in Custody Suites found that officers
worked *within* the rules, although probably because the forms of communication
and bureaucracy forced them to do so.[76] Nevertheless, she identified a 'profound
regard' for the legal rules relating to custody by Custody Sergeants.[77] Rose also
identified post-PACE attitudinal and behavioural shifts,[78] and Maguire and
Norris's study found that PACE rules were inhibitory upon officers, altering police
behaviour not because officers believed it was the right thing to do, but because
it was forced on them. Over time, these inhibitory rules then became normalised
by officers.[79] Overall, Brown found that the research on PACE's impact identified
progress with regard to improving suspects' rights, but that the legislation had not
achieved the balance it had aimed for.[80] When we assess criminal justice outcomes,

---

[70] D McBarnet, 'Pre-trial Procedures and the Construction of Conviction' (1983) 23 *Sociological
Review Monograph on the Sociology of Law* 172, 199.

[71] McBarnet, *Conviction* 156.

[72] D McBarnet, 'Arrest: The Legal Context of Policing' in S Holdaway (ed), *The British Police* (London,
Edward Arnold, 1979) 24.

[73] D McBarnet, 'False Dichotomies in Criminal Justice Research' in J Baldwin and A Bottomley (eds),
*Criminal Justice* (London, Martin Robertson, 1978) 23, 31.

[74] S Herbert, 'Police Culture Reconsidered' (1998) 36 *Criminology* 343, 353.

[75] J Long, 'Keeping PACE? Some Front Line Policing Perspectives' in E Cape and R Young (eds),
*Regulating Policing* (Oxford, Hart Publishing, 2008) 91, 95.

[76] L Skinns, *Police Powers and Citizen Rights: Discretionary Decision Making in Police Detention*
(London, Routledge, 2019) 26.

[77] Skinns, *Police Powers and Citizen Rights* 112.

[78] D Rose, *In the Name of the Law* (London, Jonathan Cape, 1996) 216–17.

[79] M Maguire and C Norris, *The Conduct of Criminal Investigations Royal Commission on Criminal
Justice Research Study #5* (London, HMSO, 1991); M Maguire and C Norris, 'Police Investigations:
Practice and Malpractice' (1994) 21 *Journal of Law and Society* 72.

[80] Brown, *PACE Ten Years On* 254. Similar progress in terms of controlling the abuse of police
discretion by legal means in the United States was identified by Walker following the introduction of

we find a significant reduction in appeals against unsafe convictions referred by the Criminal Cases Review Commission on the grounds of police misconduct post-PACE,[81] leading Quirk to conclude that, 'the safeguards offered by PACE in particular have made an enormous difference'.[82]

Dixon agrees that policing changed post-PACE, but that 'its impact cannot be adequately grasped at the level of generalities', with wide variation across the police and even between different stations in the same force.[83] There was not, however, a 'mass conversion to due process'[84] and some provisions remained largely of presentational effect.[85] In particular the failure of the regulation of stop and search provided an excellent example of the 'limits of legalism'.[86] Bringing together the wealth of previous research, including our own, we would conclude that there appears, therefore, to be a difference in terms of how successfully PACE operates in regulating police behaviour pre- and post-arrest, with the impact on the latter appearing to be more significant.

It may be that PACE's more modest progress in adequately protecting suspects pre-arrest has been the result of failures of the appeal courts to rein in judicial discretion to allow evidence to be adduced that was gained by police impropriety or in contravention of PACE Codes of Practice.[87] In a series of cases, the courts have made it clear that a breach of the Codes of Practice with regard to investigation, detention, interviewing, and suspect treatment will not lead to automatic exclusion of evidence, and the Court of Appeal has stated that, as a more general principle, it will not readily second guess a trial judge's decision to admit evidence.[88] This includes inculpatory or mixed statements gained from interviews where legal advice has been denied, although significant, repeated, or deliberate breaches of the Codes are more likely to see such evidence excluded under PACE, section 78,[89] which provides the trial judge with the discretion (but not the direction) to exclude prosecution evidence which may lead to 'an adverse effect on the fairness of proceedings'. Through section 78 (and other exclusionary powers),[90] the

---

rules preventing the adduction of illegally obtained evidence following the *Mapp* and *Miranda* cases (S Walker, *Taming the System: The Control of Discretion in Criminal Justice 1950–1990* (Oxford, Oxford University Press, 1993)).

[81] D Kyle, 'Correcting Miscarriages of Justice: The Role of the Criminal Cases Review Commission' (2004) 52 *Drake Law Review* 657.

[82] H Quirk, 'Identifying Miscarriages of Justice: Why Innocence in the UK Is Not the Answer' (2007) 70 *The Modern Law Review* 759, 773.

[83] Dixon, *Law in Policing* 87–88.

[84] Dixon, *Law in Policing* 163.

[85] Dixon, *Law in Policing* 283.

[86] Dixon, *Law in Policing* 303.

[87] D Ormerod and D Birch, 'The Evolution of the Discretionary Exclusion of Evidence'.

[88] *R v Z* [2009] 1 Cr App R 34.

[89] *R v Walsh* (1990) 91 Cr App R 161; *R v Alladice* [1988] Crim LR 608; *R v Devani* [2008] 1 Cr App R 4; *R v Keenon* [1990] 2 QB 54.

[90] For example PACE, s 76 and s 77 (confessions). Additionally, s 82(3) preserves a trial judge's common law exclusionary discretion.

protections of PACE should facilitate judicial control on police behaviour,[91] but the policing of these in the appeal courts has provided no such certainty.[92] This can be summarised by the comments of Lord Lane in *R v Delaney*, that '[i]t is no part of the duty of the court to rule a statement inadmissible simply in order to punish the police for failure to observe the Codes of Practice'.[93]

Nevertheless, despite the relatively free hand given to trial judges by the appeal courts to allow evidence gained in contravention of the Codes, frontline officers in our research remained concerned about breaching the Codes in a way that might make evidence unusable. However, this was largely not directly due to fears about what might happen at trial, but as a result of more immediate concerns that the Custody Sergeant may be critical of their practice, or determine there should be no further action. Additionally, they expressed concern about the possibility of a decision by the CPS that the evidence was too risky, which would lead to the case collapsing and subsequent further criticism, this time from the officer's Sergeant or Inspector. A case collapsing could be personally embarrassing and lead to severe censure, and these fears appeared to outweigh concerns about the legality or otherwise of evidence gathering. PACE and the Codes of Practice have clearly changed how the police operate, but this change is, in part, the result of work rules, practices, and fears of career damage, rather than simply deference to PACE or an awareness, for example, of the potential exclusionary operation of PACE ss 76–78 in the courts.

When we revisit PACE and the arguments about its effectiveness as a tool for changing police behaviour, there is one striking difference between our work and the studies carried out in the 1990s that dominated debate in this area. In contrast to the officers that were the subject of fieldwork back in the 1990s, most of our research participants simply had no experience of policing prior to PACE. Participants typically referred to working their '30 years' service', though they were very aware that the length of service before reaching retirement was increasing. We encountered very few frontline officers who had worked for the full 30 years. The upshot of this is that we came across little evidence of pre-PACE working practices that had survived attempted reform, or officers who still used these practices. In this sense the laws and procedures of PACE and its Codes, mediated through experience and working realities, was ingrained in much police practice for our participants.[94] When it came to interviewing and evidence gathering in the context of custody, the fear of evidence exclusion did act as a

---

[91] D Dixon et al, 'Consent and the Legal Regulation of Policing' (1990) 17 *Journal of Law and Society* 245, 345.

[92] Decisions in relation to prosecution evidence gained as a result of entrapment have also indicated a wide margin of discretion on the part of trial judges to include evidence (eg *R v Christou* [1992] 1 QB 979; *Nottingham City Council v Amin* [2000] 1 WLR 1071; *R v Jones* [2007] 3 WLR 907).

[93] *R v Delaney* (1989) 88 Cr App R 338.

[94] Skinns similarly found that PACE was taken for granted in her study of police custody (L Skinns, *Police Custody: Governance, Legitimacy and Reform in the Criminal Justice Process* (London, Routledge, 2011) 9–10).

guide to police behaviour (although we could not determine to what extent that had changed from the pre-PACE situation). In contrast, when it came to stop searches and arrests, the situation was considerably different and seemed to be less settled. As we will see in Chapters 6 and 7, it was certainly not the case here that PACE was acting as the main driver of police decision-making practice.

## IV. The Human Rights Act 1998

In 1998, the HRA 1998 was enacted, coming into operation at the turn of the century. Although the UK had ratified the ECHR in 1953, and the UK government could be sued in the European Court of Human Rights (ECtHR) in Strasbourg for police breaches of Convention rights,[95] in reality this was an unsatisfactory way of protecting the individual from state (and police) abuses. In contrast, the HRA 1998 provides a domestic remedy, with section 6(1) establishing that, 'It is unlawful for a public authority to act in a way which is incompatible with a Convention right'. An infringement of the ECHR rights can now lead to police forces being subject to litigation in the domestic courts, meaning that in practice, and for the first time, the police were given an obligation to directly consider Convention rights when using their powers. As such, some commentators have argued that the HRA 1998 is the most important development in policing in modern times.[96]

Officers considering using coercive street powers would, it was claimed at the launch of the HRA 1998, now be required to consider not only the domestic legality of the power, but also the proportionality and necessity of its utilisation where it engaged ECHR rights.[97] Decisions to use force needed to be weighed against the risk to Article 2 (right to life), searches to property and persons needed to be weighed against the Article 8 right to privacy, and arrests needed to be proportionate and necessary to avoid being an unlawful breach of Article 5 (right to liberty). Treatment of suspects on the street and in custody had to satisfy the absolute prohibition on 'inhuman or degrading treatment' in Article 3. Further, when deciding whether or not to respond to a job, officers needed to be aware that a failure to prevent a foreseeable breach of the rights or freedoms on the part of the victim could bring the force into breach of their positive obligations under the HRA 1998.[98] This would require significant changes not only in high-level strategic

---

[95] For example, turning to the phone-tapping case of *Malone* above, the claimant then took the case to the ECtHR and successfully claimed a breach of Art 8 (the right to privacy) (*Malone v United Kingdom* (1985) 7 EHRR 14).

[96] Dixon, 'Changing Law' 32.

[97] Starmer, *European Human Rights Law*.

[98] Other positive obligations relevant to police forces include Art 9 (freedom of religion), Art 10 (freedom of Expression), and Art 11 (freedom of association and assembly). While particularly important in the policing of protest (H Fenwick, 'Marginalising human rights, breach of the peace, "kettling", the Human Rights Act and public protest' (2009) 4 *Public Law* 737) and other crowd events

decision-making, but also at the tactical and operational levels that would affect frontline officers on a day-to-day basis. It was not simply the case that human rights compliance would be a 'tick box' bureaucratic exercise, but that, 'at an operational level, police need to move from a philosophy of justification by results (ie ends justify the means) to justification by a balance of compliance and appropriate outcome'.[99] Like legality, claim Neyroud and Beckley, necessity in the use of police powers should provide 'a substantial discipline on discretion'.[100]

Given what we have already seen with regard to the effectiveness of legal regulations on the utilisation of police discretion, it is probably not surprising that the extent to which human rights pose an additional restraint on the discretion of police officers has been contested. It has been suggested that human rights are reduced to 'minimal safety nets', with crime control goals continuing to dominate in the minds of officers.[101] It has also been argued (with respect to Northern Ireland), that there may be police resistance to human rights, which is seen by officers as impinging on their ability to fight crime,[102] and that the HRA 1998 has not embedded a 'culture of human rights awareness' into police decision-making.[103] Instead, change (albeit significant change) has been experienced by frontline officers largely at a bureaucratic level.[104] Echoing some of the arguments we have seen about the inconsistent substantive impact of the PACE reforms, human rights can take the form of merely presentational rules, used to support courses of action or decisions that have already been taken with an enhanced form of justification. This can provide 'a mechanism to structure and facilitate both advanced and post-hoc rationalization of a wide range of decision making',[105] and in reality enables, rather than constrains, police discretion.[106] In this form, human rights become '... a procedure to be followed rather than a paradigm to be cultivated, adopted and practised, underpinning all aspects of policing and forming part of its very rationale'.[107]

However, we should not assume that the arguably underwhelming impact of the HRA 1998 on frontline policing is a result of 'cultural' police resistance to

---

(M James and G Pearson, 'Public Order and the Rebalancing of Football Fans' Rights: Legal Problems with Pre-emptive Policing Strategies and Banning Orders' (2015) 3 *Public Law* 458), these did not raise issues during the current fieldwork.

[99] P Neyroud and A Beckley, *Policing, Ethics and Human Rights* (Cullompton, Willan Publishing, 2001) 217.

[100] Neyroud and Beckley, *Policing, Ethics and Human Rights* 66.

[101] A Sanders, 'Reconciling the Apparently Different Goals of Criminal Justice and Regulation: the "freedom perspective"' in H Quirk et al (eds), *Regulation and Criminal Justice: Innovations in Policy and Research* (Cambridge, Cambridge University Press, 2010) 42, 68.

[102] M Lamb, 'A Culture of Human Rights: Transforming Policing in Northern Ireland' (2008) 2 *Policing* 386, 391.

[103] K Bullock and P Johnson, 'The Impact of the Human Rights Act 1998 on Policing in England and Wales' (2012) 52 *British Journal of Criminology* 630, 646.

[104] Bullock and Johnson, 'Impact of the Human Rights Act' 631–35.

[105] Bullock and Johnson, 'Impact of the Human Rights Act' 643.

[106] Bullock and Johnson, 'Impact of the Human Rights Act' 642.

[107] C Harfield, 'Paradigm not Procedure: Current Challenges to Police Cultural Incorporation of Human Rights in England and Wales' (2009) 4 *The Journal of Law and Social Justice* 91, 104.

either human rights ideology or the effect that human rights compliance should have in practice on police work. What, post-2000, has been required by officers is a fairly complex process of decision-making, which is a fundamental change to what came before. These demands were made on top of the existing requirements of the law, the PACE Codes, and force policy, posing a significant challenge to frontline officers often making split-second decisions:

> Human rights policing demands that police officers become adept at balancing compet-
> ing rights, demonstrating clear and justified decision-making and keeping this under
> constant review. A rigid, rule-bound bureaucracy would simply be unable to create
> and sustain an operating culture flexible enough to cope with this challenge. Increased
> professional autonomy and a more reflective practitioner are essential for the develop-
> ment of public policing.[108]

While, as we have noted above, few of our participants were in post prior to the introduction of PACE, many remembered policing prior to the HRA 1998. Further, the proportion of officers au fait with the pre-HRA 1998 approach to policing increased when it came to supervisors, mentors, and trainers (who tended to be officers longer in post), meaning that new recruits schooled in a human rights-based approach to policing could find their understanding subsequently challenged. This may have reduced the 'vital' role that training needed to play in ensuring that officers were able to apply human rights considerations appropriately.[109] Albeit with a modest sample, Bullock and Johnston identified considerable confusion amongst officers about how to apply human rights, particularly when applying the test of proportionality. They found that, '[o]fficers consistently conflated necessity with legitimacy', considering the test of necessity satisfied if the use of the power prevented or detected crime.[110] As we will see when we consider arrest in Chapter 7, we also observed confusion about the meaning of 'necessity' in this study, alongside inconsistent use and understanding of other human rights principles. We are maybe not as pessimistic about the impact of human rights on policing over the medium- to long-term as some of the commentators we have cited here. Nevertheless, ensuring that the HRA 1998 operates in a way that was anticipated when it was introduced remains a major challenge.

## V.  Policy, Procedure, and Guidance

Finally, we need to consider the impact of policy, procedure, and guidance. The rather catch-all nature of this section aims to address the fact that 'the law' as

---

[108] Neyroud and Beckley, *Policing, Ethics and Human Rights* 86.
[109] Neyroud and Beckley, *Policing, Ethics and Human Rights* 177. We could also speculate that 'recruitment freezes' that affected both forces under observation may have diluted the impact of training upon the wider personnel.
[110] Bullock and Johnson, 'Impact of the Human Rights Act' 637.

it affects frontline officers does not merely exist in an abstract and black-letter form that is accessed directly by officers through training or their own research. As we have seen, culturalist approaches to understanding policing suggest that it is the police's occupational 'culture' that mediates law as it appears in statute and case judgment and how it is applied on the street; in Holdaway's view, for example, law is not 'obliterated within the occupational culture but reworked'.[111] As we will see in more detail over the following chapters, our research suggested that there was not a guiding 'culture' or set of 'sub-cultures' that altered, mutated, or manipulated laws into working rules for frontline officers. However, the law that was applied on the street was frequently different from that which is found in the black-letter case reports and statutes. The view that we will be setting out is that this is a result of the interpretation of individual officers, which is governed by many factors. While there are regular overlaps in this understanding, the differences in application of the law between officers was a striking feature of our fieldwork.

An officer's understanding of the law is mediated through her interpretation, or 'sensemaking',[112] of a number of messages which may be consistent or inconsistent in nature. These include: (a) the officer's individual understanding of the law and interpretation of how it should be applied in different situations; (b) instruction, guidance or censure from divisional, station, shift, or Custody Suite supervision (usually from a Sergeant or Inspector); (c) advice from colleagues and mentors; (d) the mode of delivery of training (be it courses for new recruits or personal development or legal update packages) combined with the trainer's own interpretation of the law; (e) instruction or guidance through force policy; (f) guidance from official Codes of Practice and the College of Policing's Authorised Professional Practice (APP); (g) a host of other unofficial prompts or reminders coming in forms as varied as desktop screen-saver messages to posters stuck above urinals or sinks in police station toilets; and (h) broader social influences, including from the news and from popular representations of policing and the criminal justice system.

We have already considered the status and influence of the PACE Codes above, but it is important here to briefly address the status and potential value of force-wide policies and APP, because one of our foci will be the extent to which policies and guidance such as these can significantly affect police behaviour and effect police change. National guidance and force-wide policy can gain quasi-legal status when it comes to police discretion, in particular the utilisation of coercive powers against suspects. Jefferson and Grimshaw's account of the operation of the police considered the extent to which force-wide policies were effective. For this they used a narrow definition of policy as, 'an authoritative statement signifying a

---

[111] S Holdaway, 'Discovering Structure: Studies of the British Police Occupational Culture' in M Weatheritt (ed), *Police Research: Some Future Prospects* (Avebury, Police Foundation, 1989) 55, 65.

[112] R Worden and S McLean, *Mirage of Police Reform: Procedural Justice and Police Legitimacy* (Oakland, CA, University of California Press, 2017) 14.

settled practice on any matter relevant to the duties of the Chief Constable'[113] and identified a difference between administrative and operational policies (the latter would pertain to the use of street powers). Their conclusion was that as a result of an officer's discretionary freedom, 'effective *operational* policy cannot exist. The universality of constabulary independence makes operational policy effectively redundant' (emphasis added).[114] Jefferson and Grimshaw's data and analysis was based on the regulation of the police under the now repealed Police Act 1964. It was also primarily pre-PACE (on which, as we have seen, there is a broad consensus that it had a not-insignificant impact on frontline police behaviour) and considerably before other key structural changes such as the launch of the College of Policing and the introduction of Police and Crime Commissioners. From a 'bottom-up' approach, we did not find their narrow definition of policy helpful in identifying the supervisory drivers behind the operational decision-making of frontline police, and their understanding of the laws they were enforcing or that were regulating them. These, we have observed, come from multiple sources. Further, as we will see, our observations suggested that force-led policy (according to the Jefferson and Grimshaw definition) on operational matters *was* used to change the activities of frontline officers and *did* have an effect in this respect.

As a result, our use of 'policy' in this book will refer not only to force-wide policies cascading down from the Chief Constable, but also the College of Police's APP and other guidance and directives from senior officers or supervisors. The latter may come in many forms, from orders or reminders in regular or extraordinary briefings, to divisional or station-specific circulars, to individual censure. The key features of our use of policy in this book are that: (a) these directions came from an officer (almost always of a more senior rank) with the power of censure (ie that there was some way the direction would be supervised); and (b) they were understood by officers in this manner. In other words, it was the interpretation of the officer rather than the source of the power (or the intention of the original policy from senior command) that is central to our analysis. The only way in which our view of what falls under policy will be narrowed is that we are only considering instructions or guidance that is not understood by frontline officers to be transient in nature (eg in relation to a particular job or shift). However, we stray from Jefferson and Grimshaw's 'settled in practice' because it makes sense to include instructions which were intended to be long term but were quickly changed or re-interpreted, or which were operating differently in different divisions or stations. As officers indicated, 'settled practice' was not something they associated with policy, and for the fieldworkers, learning new policies was often a thankless task, as they were sometimes changed or interpreted differently by the next observation.

---

[113] Grimshaw and Jefferson, *Interpreting Police Work* 204.
[114] Grimshaw and Jefferson, *Interpreting Police Work* 291.

There is evidence from both the United States and the UK that policies understood in this way have the potential to fundamentally change police behaviour.[115] In contrast, others have been sceptical about the effectiveness of policy, particularly where the proposed changes clash with institutional barriers and police views of their role in terms of fighting crime.[116] It may be that policies and practices seen as unfair by officers encourage resistance and opposition, rather than changing behaviour in the way intended.[117] However, as we will argue in the coming chapters, policy – be it national, force-wide, divisional, or station-specific – was usually at the forefront of a frontline officer's mind when they utilised their street powers, providing both an opportunity for change, but also a barrier to the application of national guidance or legal principles.

[115] For example, Worden and McLean, *Mirage of Police Reform* 191 (with respect to procedural justice in the United States).
[116] A Myhill and B Bradford, 'Can Police Enhance Public Confidence by Improving Quality of Service? Results from Two Surveys in England and Wales' (2012) 22 *Policing & Society* 397, 419.
[117] B Bradford and P Quinton, 'Self-Legitimacy, Police Culture and Support for Democratic Policing in an English Constabulary' (2014) 54 *British Journal of Criminology* 1023.

# 4

# Power, 'Culture' and Discretion

We have begun to draw attention to the problems that are inherent in the consistent imposition of national or force policies on frontline officers. Many commentators on the subject of police regulation have suggested that this can be explained by the fundamental feature of police discretion. As public servants, operating out of sight of immediate supervision, frontline police officers have significant scope to exercise discretion. What influences this apparent freedom will be the central concern of this chapter. While this is in part about decision-making at the individual level,[1] in this chapter we are also interested in the role of supervision, procedures, policies, briefings, structures and so forth, in shaping and directing officer interest and decisions.[2] In particular, we will draw upon the idea of street-level bureaucracy[3] as a framework with which to understand the dilemmas officers encounter and resolve on a daily basis. Michael Lipsky argues that street-level workers are 'public service workers who interact with citizens in the course of their jobs, and who have substantial discretion in the execution of their work'.[4] Indeed, 'decisions of street-level bureaucrats, the routines they establish, and the devices they invent to cope with uncertainties and work pressures, effectively *become* the public policies they carry out'.[5]

---

[1] H Simon, *Administrative Behavior: a Study of Decision-Making Processes in Administrative Organizations* (New York, Free Press, 1957); H Drummond, *The Art of Decision-Making: Mirrors of Imagination, Masks of Fate* (Chichester, John Wiley & Sons, 2001); WK Muir, *Police: Streetcorner Politicians* (Chicago, University of Chicago Press, 1977).

[2] H Pepinsky, 'Better Living Through Police Discretion'(1984) 47 *Law and Contemporary Problems* 249; FA Shull et al, *Organizational Decision Making* (New York, McGraw-Hill, 1970); E Campbell, 'Towards a Sociological Theory of Discretion' (1999) 27 *International Journal of the Sociology of Law* 79; GP Fletcher, 'Some Unwise Reflections about Discretion' (1984) 47 *Law and Contemporary Problems* 269; J McGregor, 'From the State of Nature to Mayberry: The Nature of Police Discretion' in J Kleinig (ed), *Handled with Discretion: Ethical Issues in Police Decision Making* (Lanham, MD, Rowman & Littlefield, 1996).

[3] M Lipsky, *Street-Level Bureaucracy: Dilemmas of the Individual in Public Services* (New York, Russell Sage, 1980); S Maynard-Moody and M Musheno, 'State Agent or Citizen Agent: Two Narratives of Discretion' (2000) 10 *Journal of Public Administration Research and Theory* 329; MK Brown, *Working the Street: Police Discretion and the Dilemmas of Reform* (New York, Russell Sage Foundation, 1988).

[4] Lipsky, *Street-level Bureaucracy* 3.

[5] Lipsky, *Street-level Bureaucracy* xii.

# I. Understandings of Discretion

At the heart of concerns about policing, and of the state more generally, are questions of the meaning and limits of discretion.[6] At street level, the utilisation of discretion is the point at which 'the legal system touches the people', and 'where the tensions, dilemmas, and sometimes contradictions embodied in the law are worked out in practice'.[7] Yet we know surprisingly little about the topic. One reason for this is the lack of focus on the concept of 'discretion' in the law regulating policing in England and Wales. There is nothing in common law and legislation that defines police discretion or which directly informs an officer how it should be used. Before gaining their powers as Constables, all would-be officers must perform an attestation, where they declare to,

> well and truly serve the Queen in the office of constable, with fairness, integrity, diligence and impartiality, upholding fundamental human rights and according equal respect to all people; and that I will, to the best of my power, cause the peace to be kept and preserved and prevent all offences against people and property; and that while I continue to hold the said office I will, to the best of my skill and knowledge, discharge all the duties thereof faithfully according to law.[8]

On an earlier iteration of the oath, McArdie J in *Fisher v Oldham Corporation* noted that it was to serve the state rather than the borough.[9] In this way, the discretion of Constables to preserve and enforce law was enshrined in common law, albeit without mentioning the word discretion once. Therefore, discretion should not, Jefferson and Grimshaw argue, be seen as officers ignoring the law but as them using powers of discretion granted to them by law.[10] This can be seen as *formal* discretion,[11] powers that are positively conferred by law rather than a deviation from law.[12] Since the Police and Criminal Evidence Act 1984 (PACE), the police should no longer be seen as 'citizens in uniform';[13] the law grants them powers and privileges[14] not enjoyed by ordinary citizens. This situation is mediated somewhat by the Police Reform and Social Responsibility Act 2011 which refers to the 'direction and control' that a Chief Constable has

---

[6] Maynard-Moody and Musheno, 'State Agent or Citizen Agent'.

[7] K Hawkins, 'The Use of Legal Discretion: Perspectives from Law and Social Sciences' in K Hawkins (ed), *The Uses of Discretion* (Oxford, Oxford University Press, 1992) 11.

[8] Police Act 1996, sch 4 (as amended by the Police Reform Act 2002, s 83).

[9] *Fisher v Oldham Corporation* [1930] 2 KB 364, 370.

[10] R Grimshaw and T Jefferson, *Interpreting Police Work: Policy and Practice in Forms of Beat Policing* (London, Allen & Unwin, 1987). See also D McBarnet, *Conviction, Law, the State and the Construction of Justice* (London, Palgrave MacMillan, 1981).

[11] Hawkins, 'The Use of Legal Discretion' 14–15.

[12] D Galligan, *Discretionary Powers: A Legal Study of Official Discretion* (Oxford, Clarendon, 1986) 1.

[13] R Reiner, *The Politics of the Police*, 4th edn (Oxford, Oxford University Press, 2014).

[14] Police Act 1996, s 30.

over her force and its officers,[15] to enforce the Police and Crime Commissioner's police and crime plan.[16] This covers crime, disorder, anti-social behaviour and other behaviour 'adversely affecting the environment' (misuse of drugs, alcohol and other substances, and re-offending).[17] However, once again, the new legislation does not tackle the meaning of discretion, or its best use, on the part of Constables. Instead the legislative framework, supported by the PACE Codes of Practice, gives officers powers (for example to stop and search or arrest) which in turn are limited by human rights principles of necessity and proportionality, an absence of discrimination against those with characteristics protected by the Equality Act 2010, and the broad principle of reasonable suspicion which underpins PACE.[18]

While we know that officers 'have' discretion or 'use' discretion, that we can apply the word in these two ways illustrates some of the problems. Is it a quality that officers possess or a tool that they can choose to use?[19] For some, an officer 'has discretion whenever the effective limits on his [sic] power leave him [sic] free to make a choice among possible courses of action or inaction'.[20] Such a definition suggests a good deal of latitude and freedom to choose among different courses of action, and suggests there is no right or wrong answer.[21] Indeed, it might embrace unauthorised actions, even illegal ones, and Davis appears to accept that.[22] A tighter definition is offered by Dworkin, who has famously likened discretion to the 'hole in the doughnut', an 'area left open by a surrounding belt of restriction'.[23] This image, of a 'sphere of autonomy within which one's decisions are in some degree a matter of personal judgment and assessment',[24] has the benefit of identifying some limits to the freedom to choose. For Dworkin, discretion could be viewed as either strong (indicating that the official could use their own standards to apply in the decision), or weak (where the standards by which decisions were made were determined elsewhere and had to be applied).[25] Socio-legal scholars see discretion as central and inevitable[26] in the legal system precisely because law is a 'fundamentally interpretative enterprise'.[27] As Cotterrell contends, 'the dichotomy

---

[15] Section 2(3).

[16] Police Reform and Social Responsibility Act 2011, s 8.

[17] Police Reform and Social Responsibility Act 2011, s 101.

[18] R Munday, 'The Royal Commission on Criminal Procedure' (1981) 40 *The Cambridge Law Journal* 193.

[19] EL Nickels, 'A Note on the Status of Discretion in Police Research' (2007) 35 *Journal of Criminal Justice* 570.

[20] K Davis, *Police Discretion* (St Paul, MN, West Publishing Co, 1975) 4.

[21] Galligan, *Discretionary Powers* 16.

[22] K Davis, *Discretionary Justice: A Preliminary Inquiry* (New Orleans, Louisiana State University Press, 1969) 4.

[23] R Dworkin, *Taking Rights Seriously* (Boston, Harvard University Press, 1977) 1.

[24] Galligan, *Discretionary Powers* 8.

[25] Dworkin, *Taking Rights Seriously*; Galligan, *Discretionary Powers* 20.

[26] Galligan, *Discretionary Powers* 1; Hawkins, 'The Use of Legal Discretion' 11.

[27] Hawkins, 'The Use of Legal Discretion' 11.

of rule and discretion seems an unsatisfactory way to refer to a *continuum*: an immense array of standards, prescriptions, and modes of interpretation and decisions in modern regulatory systems'.[28] These discussions tell us of the importance of discretion in looking at the application of police powers, and they tell us where we might find their source, but they don't tell us what discretion *is*. It embraces decisions both to act and not to act, or to see and not to see.

Ethnographic work has instead sought to describe discretion as it is observed. And in taking this approach, these works have tended to downplay the importance of the law as a consideration.[29] It has been noted that, while legal scholars tend to think of discretion, other social scientists are more likely to view the same concept as an issue of decision-making.[30] They are more likely to focus on the officers' *perception* of their authorised capacity to make choices about different courses of action or inaction.[31] They pay attention to other influences and constraints on the decisions officers make, including training, supervision, resources, and guidance,[32] and note that discretion in policing increases the lower down the hierarchy the officer.[33] Lipsky's work on street-level bureaucracy explores the dilemmas and competing pressures and demands as they affect public service workers.[34] Resolving these dilemmas is, in effect, the exercise of a bounded discretion,[35] whether that discretion is exercised consciously or unconsciously.[36] However, such work can suggest that everything is discretion and every officer has a different take on it.[37] All decisions, whether to turn left or right when on patrol, can be considered discretion. And the focus is on the decisions made by officers at the front line and not on those decisions taken by senior officers, about policies and resources for example, that form some of the dilemmas themselves.[38]

## A.  Officers' Understandings

While academics may debate definitions and models, in keeping with our commitment to understand policies as officers see them, officers have their own sense of the word that we must consider. Once again, however, from our observations, it

[28] R Cotterrell, *Law's Community: Legal Theory in Sociological Perspective* (Oxford, Clarendon Press, 1996) 284.
[29] E Bittner, 'The Police on Skid Row: A Study of Peacekeeping' (1967) 32 *American Sociological Review* 699.
[30] Hawkins, 'The Use of Legal Discretion' 14.
[31] L Skinns, *Police Powers and Citizen Rights: Discretionary Decision Making in Police Detention* (London, Routledge, 2019) 21–22.
[32] JQ Wilson, *Varieties of Police Behaviour: The Management of Law and Order in Eight Communities* (Cambridge, MA, Harvard University Press, 1968); Brown, *Working the Street*.
[33] Wilson, *Varieties of Police Behaviour*.
[34] Lipsky, *Street-level Bureaucracy*.
[35] Shull et al, *Organizational Decision Making*.
[36] Maynard-Moody and Musheno, 'State Agent or Citizen Agent'.
[37] Muir, *Police: Streetcorner Politicians*.
[38] NJ Sekhon, 'Redistributive Policing' (2011) 101 *Journal of Criminal Law and Criminology* 1171.

quickly became apparent that it could mean different things at different times and from one officer to the next. We do not here offer an exhaustive list of these, but illustrate the range.

First, discretion can mean good judgement or common sense. It is evident in the ways Neighbourhood officers handle long-running disputes that might otherwise develop into conflict.[39] It can be observed in the ways officers approach people in distress and at risk.[40] And officers recognise these instances as requiring good judgement as they weigh up the choices available to them. Second, discretion is also closely associated with questions of risk. In making difficult choices, and particularly ones that officers believe contradict policy or common practice, they place themselves at risk of criticism, or worse, if at some future date something goes 'wrong'. Discretion will, then, be accompanied by paperwork to document a decision and to cover officers against those unknown future risks, a discussion to which we will return later in this chapter.

The anticipation of future events leads to a third understanding of discretion: making decisions in anticipation of decisions others will make. While an offence may have been committed, officers will act in the belief that pursuing a case will be pointless. Either investigations will lead to no further action (NFA), or the CPS will not charge the offender. Or even that it will go nowhere at the magistrates' court.[41]

But discretion can also mean 'cuffing' jobs: not seeing offences, issuing words of advice and a whole range of other options that entail less effort than setting the wheels of the formal criminal justice process in motion. Officers will joke about only looking straight ahead as they return to the police station with hot food.

> We leave custody after 90 minutes, which isn't bad. Thomas's partner on this shift suggests it is time for a break. A 45-minute break? They discuss the hours and the rules. Thomas doesn't normally bother to take a full break and certainly doesn't time it, but his partner checks the rules. A 10-hour shift gets one hour, a 9 hour shift gets 50 minutes and 8 hours gets 45 minutes. They should have 50 minutes. But he will delay signing off with the Control Room to squeeze out some more time. As he drives to Brandham, he speeds up to drive alongside cars that are obviously speeding. But he just warns them by glancing over and slowing down. He isn't going to stop them on the way to dinner.[42]

They will stop a vehicle for a traffic offence but not issue a ticket if the driver passes 'the attitude test' (that is they admit the offence and are polite and respectful in their manner and tone). Those that fail this test will generally get slow and punctilious treatment.

> Late at night, a car comes the other way at some speed and with fog lights on. It is an SUV. Toby pulls it over to have a word but asks the driver into the back seat of his police

---

[39] Neighbourhood, Abbey, June 2016.
[40] Territorial Support, Brandham, December 2014.
[41] Response, Abbey, April 2016.
[42] Territorial Support, Brandham, December 2013.

car to issue a ticket. I am slightly puzzled that this should be necessary, but then the driver gets into the back. He is rude and abrasive. 'Can you hurry it up?' He is going to the train station to pick up his son and the train was due in five minutes ago. 'Well, you are late already'. 'Seriously, have you got nothing better to do? No crime? Nothing?' 'Seems not'. He proceeds to slowly write out a ticket, pausing to check the details with the driver even though he has the information already. When he is finished, Toby would normally wind the electronic window down and suggest the male lean out and open the door from the outside. But, just to take things a little more slowly, he gets out and goes round to open the rear door. All very polite, but deliberate. And the man does say 'thank you' as he walks back to his car.[43]

But officers then have a multitude of ways of avoiding work they do not want to do, and creating space for the type of policing jobs they prefer. What we might call 'airwaves discretion' was used by officers to avoid unattractive jobs (such as domestic abuse or missing persons). Officers would sometimes ignore the radio, or claim they were 'just finishing up a job' that had already been completed.

> There is an hour and a half left of the shift and the radio crackles into life. Grade One. A kid is kicking off at a school for 'troubled and naughty children'. No one is respond-ing and the call is from the other side of the division. Aidan says 'Ooooh … no fucking chance!' He continues to patrol his 'beat' until the end of the shift. [A little later there is another Grade One call radioed through, again at the other end of the division]. Again Aidan doesn't want to go. He can see that [with the likely arrest] it will take five hours … Nobody wants to go to this. There is silence on the radio. The call handler on the radio then starts saying, 'I can see that some of you aren't tasked, so unless somebody volun-teers I'm going to start calling you up individually'. Still silence, no-one wants to go (…) At least four officers on this shift tried to ignore the request. They are pretending they are 'wrapping up' jobs that they have already finished to avoid this call.[44]

As another officer noted, 'around handover time no-one wants to be picking a proper job up'.[45]

However, even *after* an officer had agreed to respond to a particular job, there was often plenty of opportunity to be distracted by a preferable job. It was not uncommon in a 10-hour shift for an officer tasked with an unattractive Grade Two job to still have that job outstanding at the end of the shift, having diverted to Grade One jobs along the way, performed stop checks on vehicles, or simply 'gone the long way round' in the hope of seeing something more interesting.

> We are in the station having coffee at the start of a Night shift. Over the radio, a call comes through about hate crime in a shop. A car with two officers responds. On the way, they report seeing a woman running down the hard shoulder of the motorway without any shoes. They are stopping to deal with this and so they won't be able to make the hate crime. In the station, several officers laugh and groan. 'That'll

[43] Traffic, Knapford, July 2014.
[44] Response, Wilderland, October 2016.
[45] Kenny, Response, Esgaroth, December 2016.

be [the female officer] running down the road, then!' They know the officers involved. They believe they are doing anything to avoid the hate crime case with all the paperwork and with their shift due to end soon.[46]

That these examples are understood not just as cuffing jobs but as a form of discretion was made evident at a briefing where our work was introduced. An officer declared, 'You won't see any discretion with Thomas. He takes the job too seriously.'[47]

These multiple and conflicting understandings of discretion reflect some of the lack of clarity to be found in the academic literature. But it also presents a practical problem for the supervision of frontline officers. Indeed, senior officers will often refer to discretion as both the solution to the problems they face (that is, it is a way of reconciling demand with diminishing resources) and a cause of problems (that is that officers make poor decisions which cause subsequent problems and give rise to litigation etc). The College of Policing offers little by way of clarity when it sets out one of its core purposes:

> Authorised Professional Practice is the body of consolidated guidance for policing. It has significantly reduced the volume of national guidance in circulation, bringing consistency and encouraging the use of professional discretion.[48]

Elsewhere, there is a little more detail on what they mean by discretion:

> Police discretion is necessary, but must be used wisely. When making decisions about using your discretion you must:
>
> - use your training, skills and knowledge about policing
> - consider what you are trying to achieve and the potential effects of your decisions
> - take any relevant policing codes, guidance, policies and procedures into consideration
> - ensure you are acting consistently with the principles and standards in this Code.[49]

However, to encourage the use of discretion (or police discretion, or professional discretion) without being clear what is meant by the term does offer the prospect of confusion and misunderstanding. Research has shown the ways in which ideas of well-being[50] or of bullying[51] can be interpreted and misinterpreted at different levels in the police organisation. We will argue, and illustrate, that the same can be said of discretion.

---

[46] Response, Hackerbeck, June 2015.

[47] Neighbourhood, Brandham, December 2013.

[48] College of Policing, *Standards and Guidance* (2017) www.college.police.uk/What-we-do/Standards/Pages/standards-guidance.aspx.

[49] College of Policing, *Code of Ethics* (Ryton, College of Policing, 2014).

[50] J Ferrill, *Buzzwords, Bureaucracy and Badges: an Ethnographic Exploration of how Versions of Wellbeing are Constructed Through Social Ideology Projects in a UK Police Organisation* (Loughborough, unpublished PhD thesis, Loughborough University, 2018).

[51] D Callaghan, *Seeing Through a Bourdieusian Lens: a Field-level Perspective of Anti-bullying Interventions in a UK Police Force* (Liverpool, unpublished PhD thesis, University of Liverpool, 2019).

Despite the obvious challenges in reaching a clear and precise definition of discretion, it is important to set out our own understanding. This in turn will underpin our later arguments about regulating the use of police street powers. The more fieldwork we conducted, the more it became clear to us that, irrespective of the view of many officers that their discretion in responding to reported criminality was being curtailed by bureaucracy, procedure, and monitoring, officer discretion needed to be understood more broadly. In fact, officers possessed a wider range of discretion than that associated with formal action (or inaction) when confronted with a suspect. This form of 'invocation discretion'[52] was indeed being subjected to ever-more intrusive monitoring and direction through force policies of 'positive action', NCRS categorisation, and the presence of body-worn cameras (BWCs). However, discretion must be understood more widely than this to include other aspects, such as decisions about priorities (which jobs to respond to and in which order), patrolling (when and where to patrol), and engagement (who to follow or speak to). Excluding these uses of professional judgement from the definition of discretion would lead us to take invocation discretion completely out of context. Further, as we will see, it is impossible to address issues of disproportionality and community legitimacy without considering the decisions officers make that lead them to be in a particular place at a particular time where a decision to utilise a street power is made or not.

## II. Training

Much has been written about the training, and socialisation into the 'police culture', of new recruits at the Academy,[53] although relatively little in recent years.[54] Clearly, it is a key process for instilling an understanding of what is expected of officers and of what is to be understood by discretion. That message is then reinforced by a probationary period, during which new recruits are tutored and required to demonstrate their competence through a learning portfolio that covers all the basics they can be expected to have learned and experienced before passing.[55] Of the two processes, we observed three training sessions, some of the material used at the Academy, and were present with tutors mentoring probationary officers. These were largely concerned with our initial research interest in stop and search

[52] J Goldstein, 'Police Discretion Not to Invoke the Criminal Process: Low-Visibility Decisions in the Administration of Justice' (Yale, Faculty Scholarship Series 2426, 1960).

[53] N Fielding, *Joining Forces: Police Training, Socialization and Occupational Competence* (London, Routledge, 1988); J van Maanen, 'Observations on the Making of Policemen' in P Manning and J van Maanen (eds), *Policing: a View from the Street* (Santa Monica, CA, Goodyear, 1978).

[54] D Cassan, 'Police Socialisation in France and in England: How Do They Stand Towards the Community Policing Model?' (2010) 16 *Cahiers Politiestudies* 243.

[55] S Charman, *Police Socialisation, Identity and Culture: Becoming Blue* (London, Palgrave Macmillan, 2017).

and, while we would not make great claims on the basis of these observations, we can note two points.

Training at the Academy consists largely of preparatory reading and class-room input reinforced by role-playing. Observing one classroom session, we left confused as to the law concerning stop and search, and less clear on the circum-stances in which a lawful search under PACE could take place than we had been when we entered the classroom. From our observations of the role-playing part of the training, the environment seemed too relaxed to reflect the situations offic-ers would find themselves in during a shift, failing to test the officers on the finer points of what are reasonable grounds on which to conduct a search. Instead, training focused upon the performance, the use of the mnemonic GO WISELY[56] and the conduct of the search itself. What such training does not do is prepare an officer for the street.[57] The mnemonic is a clumsy one and, from our observations, no officer experienced in the use of stop and search on a regular basis used it in the way taught at the Academy. That is not to say that they forgot elements of the expected script but that they developed an approach to encounters that turned a formulaic approach into a more conversational one, often done at speed and with-out thinking. These officers know that they also need to have an eye on the person detained. What is their manner and demeanour? What are they doing with their hands? What about any friends or bystanders? Are there any threats to the officer's safety while this search is underway? This is typically not learned in the Academy but is passed on by the tutor and developed with experience. And this is a simple illustration of the point made frequently by officers and academics: you learn in the field – and not in the Academy – how the job is really done.[58]

Given the importance of the process of tutoring, it is surprising how little atten-tion has been given to it, either in research or within the police. The process through which tutors are selected appears haphazard.[59] Officers put themselves forward. At times of high recruitment levels, when demands for tutors are high, there may be no choice but to take these volunteers. Talking to officers performing the role, it is clear that the motives of tutors can be very varied. During a shift observing a tutor and tutee, Spencer spoke at length about the role. There is little training for the tutor and so they bring their own experience of learning and coaching to the role. But it is also clear that, in many ways, there is less stress in the role. Tutor officers have a different radio call sign and so will be sent to unusual jobs, to ensure the tutee can complete their portfolio, or they might request particular kinds of job

[56] GO WISELY stands for: Grounds; Object searched for; Warrant card; Identification of the officer; Station they are based at; Entitlement to a copy of the record; Legislation under which the search is conducted; and You are being detained.

[57] M Rowe et al, 'Learning and Practicing Police Craft' (2016) 5 *Journal of Organizational Ethnography* 276.

[58] Fielding, *Joining Forces*; van Maanen, 'Observations on the Making of Policemen'; Charman, *Police Socialisation, Identity and Culture.*

[59] Charman, *Police Socialisation, Identity and Culture.*

on a specific shift. The pressures of time are less, allowing space for learning, but this lack of pressure is an incentive for some to undertake the role, another form of discretion as 'shirking'.[60] What is being learned from tutors is, then, not always clear. A good Sergeant will be involved in the process but, as we will discuss in the next section, the quality of supervision is just as varied.

What we have also been able to observe more rigorously during our time in the field is the process of ongoing training and professional development that officers go through. In particular, we observed the materials used to communicate changes in the powers to stop and search that were introduced in 2014.[61] For many officers, particularly those on Response duties, the use of stop and search is a very marginal part of their duties. Changes to the process or to the records required could be the cause for some confusion.

> Having just stopped a young male and then searched him, Bertie talks of stop and search. He is aware of the recent changes but not the details. I mention changes to Section 60 and that more details are now required on stop forms. Bertie looks a little blank. 'Stop forms? I thought they were no longer filled in'. He says he hadn't filled one in for years. 'I asked the lad if he wanted one and would have filled it out if he had said yes. But I thought it was no longer required?' I explain that he may be confusing the change to stop and account. There is no need to fill a form in then. But stop and search still requires a form. He looks slightly taken aback. I laugh and try to put him at ease. This is exactly what we should be seeing in this research. We know the statistics are a bit of a joke. So this just proves it.[62]

Bertie confused changes to stop and search with those, some years earlier, to stop and account (see Chapter 6 for further details). But he was also largely unfamiliar with the details of the changes, made only months before, to stop and search. While he was an experienced officer, trained some years before at a time when recording of all involuntary encounters with the public was required, he had not kept up-to-date because it was a power he rarely used in his current role.

Even those officers who used the power regularly were unclear on some aspects. After the numbers of recorded stop and search incidents dropped dramatically, in both forces and across the country, in a matter of months, efforts were made to clarify the purpose of the powers and how officers should be using them. But this was communicated by online learning materials that simply added to the confusion.

> As I join the shift at the start, the Inspector suggests I watch the most recent computer-based training materials they have had. An officer logs in and sets it running. A video starts by mentioning the disciplinary consequences of failing to use the powers to

---

[60] Response, Arlesdale Green, February 2018.
[61] Home Office/College of Policing, *Best Use of Stop and Search Scheme* (2014) assets.publishing. service.gov.uk/government/uploads/system/uploads/attachment_data/file/346922/Best_Use_ of_Stop_and_Search_Scheme_v3.0_v2.pdf.
[62] Neighbourhood, [Redacted] 2014.

stop and search appropriately! A great start. There is then some history leading to the introduction of PACE. There is then a simple statement that a search requires the same evidential basis as an arrest. As I am watching this, there is an audience of other officers behind commenting. 'So why don't we arrest then?' The video moves straight on to protected characteristics. [Equality Act 2010] Stop and think, it exhorts. Mentions the 2011 riots and the 2013 Home Office review of stop and search. There is then a clip of Theresa May speaking at the Police Federation conference, which attracts derogatory comments from my audience. It then goes on to specify the criteria for stop search. It must be fair and effective, justified and lawful, stand up to scrutiny and be based on a 'genuine belief' and 'reasonable grounds'. Intelligence is not enough, nor is OCG status. There is a two-tier test. First, there must be genuine suspicion in your own mind – the suspicion that the object will be found must be reasonable. And it must be based on facts and/or intelligence (I am confused at this point) and must be such that 'a reasonable person would reach the same conclusion'. To understand this, the video suggests that an innocent bystander must be able to see they are treated with dignity and understand why they are being searched. It then declares 'you cannot question to gain suspicion' but officers are expected to 'remove their suspicion by questioning and thereby removing the need to search'. This is all very confused. And it ends with Theresa May again.[63]

These are notes from watching this 'training' material. It left us and officers confused and uncertain. Far from being clear about the use of the powers, officers were less likely to search after watching this video and, indeed, the numbers recorded remained very low in comparison to the past. A subsequent briefing by senior officers only aggravated the situation. In seeking to correct misunderstandings, they merely reinforced scepticism.[64] Only when the force invested in a one-day training session, involving detailed discussion and scenarios, did officers begin to both clearly understand the powers as revised and the attitude of senior officers to their use. This underlines a point we have made elsewhere.[65] Online learning packages are poor substitutes for proper training. Officers tended to value and look forward to their regular refresher courses, such as Personal Safety Training or Advanced Driving. The day away was seen as an investment in them. An online package was more associated with the appearance of learning, and communicating changes through supervision and briefings was unreliable.

# III.  Supervision

What research there is on Sergeants, and there is surprisingly little, is largely descriptive.[66] More analytical work has explored the influence of Sergeants on

---

[63] Territorial Support, Knapford, October 2015.

[64] Brandham, October 2016.

[65] Rowe et al, 'Learning and Practicing Police Craft'.

[66] J van Maanen, 'The Boss: First-line Supervision in an American Police Agency' in M Punch (ed), *Control in the Police Organization* (Boston, MA, MIT Press, 1983); J van Maanen, 'Making Rank: Becoming an American Police Sergeant' (1984) 13 *Urban Life* 155; M Chatterton, 'Frontline Supervision

patrol officer behaviours[67] but this does not extend to their influence on the use of street powers and on interactions with the public. Allen[68] sought to examine the connection between supervisory contact and officers' actions. He examined the frequency of contacts, assuming that this would have an influence on key indicators of officer activity – the time spent on interactions with the public and on officer-initiated encounters. However, no relationship was established, suggesting that the role of Sergeants in this respect was a weak one. Contemporary work has looked at the impact of supervisory styles (traditional, innovative, supportive or active) on officer conduct,[69] inferring a connection between identified styles and subsequent patterns of arrest or use of force, for example. But these studies only infer that effect through reported arrests and use of force rather than through any direct observation.

This surprising gap in our understanding of the role and impact of Sergeants is not one that this work is able to fill. However, as our research progressed, we noted the importance attached to the role by Constables and the way in which Sergeants could influence the application of policy and the law on the frontline. Our focus remained on frontline officers and, except in particular teams, such as the Organised Crime Disruption teams, or particular duties, such as Football duties or the night-time economy, supervision was largely invisible on the streets. Where Sergeants, and sometimes Inspectors, did make an appearance in the field, it was normally associated with a particular incident (reports of a series of attempted break-ins in a neighbourhood[70] or at the end of a brief pursuit,[71] for example). Otherwise, their presence was at a distance. Seeking authorisation from a Sergeant or Inspector was mandatory in some situations (eg leaving a house unsecured instead of waiting for it to be boarded-up).[72] Otherwise, officers sought advice from Sergeants only where they respected their judgement. They were as likely to confer with each other or with another colleague over the radio as with a Sergeant. Where the Sergeant's influence could not be so easily avoided was in

---

in the British Police Service' in G Gaskell and R Benewick (eds), *The Crowd in Contemporary Britain* (London, Sage, 1987).

[67] AP Brief et al, 'Correlates of Supervisory Style among Policemen' (1976) 3 *Journal of Criminal Justice and Behaviour* 263; MA Wycoff and WG Skogan, 'The Effects of a Community Policing Management Style on Officers' Attitudes' (1994) 40 *Crime and Delinquency* 371.

[68] DA Allen, 'Police Supervision on the Street: an Analysis of Supervisor/Officer Interaction during the Shift' (1982) 10 *Journal of Criminal Justice* 91.

[69] RS Engel, 'The Supervisory Styles of Patrol Sergeants and Lieutenants' (2001) 29 *Journal of Criminal Justice* 341; RS Engel, 'Patrol Officer Supervision in the Community Policing Era' (2002) 30 *Journal of Criminal Justice* 51; RS Engel, *How Police Supervisory Styles Influence Patrol Officer Behavior* (Washington, Office of Justice Programs, 2001); RS Engel and S Patterson, 'Leading by Example: the Untapped Resource of Frontline Police Supervisors' in JM Brown (ed), *The Future of Policing* (London, Routledge, 2014); J Maskaly and W Jennings, 'A Question of Style: Replicating and Extending Engel's Supervisory Styles with New Agencies and New Measures' (2016) 39 *Policing* 620.

[70] Response, Hackerbeck, March 2015.

[71] Response, Kirk Machan, July 2015.

[72] Response, Hackerbeck, May 2015. We should note that it was this officer's interpretation of policy that he needed authorisation from an Inspector.

the completion of paperwork (a term that is policing shorthand for report writing and record-keeping that is, increasingly, performed online and without paper). They were expected to sign-off on cases and incidents, to quality check stop and search records and to review and sign an officer's pocket notebook. We will return to this aspect of the work in our next section.

A more obvious source of supervision, particularly for Response officers, was the Radio Control Room.[73] The interpretation of a call for assistance, the prioritisation of one call over another, and decisions to deploy officers are taken by police staff under the supervision of Sergeants and Inspectors. They will make judgements about each situation, assigning domestic violence jobs to officers patrolling in pairs, where possible, or providing background history on an alleged offender so that officers are forewarned. Through these decisions, they influence the understanding an officer has of the offence and of the offender as they approach an address or other location. And they then expect an officer to inform them of the outcome in line with this understanding.

> Two proactive officers, Arthur and Stepney, assigned to the proactive patrol of a community in response to recent incidents of burglary, hear the Control Room report a vehicle driving without insurance. Static Automatic Number Plate Recognition (ANPR) cameras nearby have picked up a white van and the operator passes this out to the police officers on proactive duties. The officers both interpret this as a potential burglar and I assume this is what the operator is thinking as well. Vans are good vehicles for carrying off stolen goods. And criminals don't pay attention to the niceties of driving with insurance etc. The officers set to working out where the camera is and where the van might be going. No more than a couple of minutes later, they see the van ahead. It is pulling off the main road into a residential area. Everything is confirming their beliefs about this van. As they approach, the van is pulling over to the side and the driver gets out. He is wearing working clothes. A moment of doubt, but the officers get out and speak to him. He has pulled up outside his grandmother's address and is there to do some work for her. He is a general builder and handyman and the van is full of the tools of his trade. When asked about his insurance, he is confused. He has insurance. Some checks are made and it appears he has insurance, but it is on his old van and not this one. He has sold that but didn't change the records. He is embarrassed. Arthur considers the situation and decides to take no action. The man is on the phone to his insurance company to resolve the issue and transfer the insurance. He is not going anywhere at the moment. So Arthur decides to leave it be. He is not in the business of harassing 'decent working folk'. Both officers agree and as we leave, they turn their attention back to their proactive duties. However, the control room operator calls back some two hours later. 'Shall I order a tow truck for that van?' 'Do you need the tow truck yet?' Arthur reluctantly responds and has to justify his decision not to seize the van.[74]

[73] A Black and K Lumsden, 'Precautionary Policing and Dispositives of Risk in a Police Force Control Room in Domestic Abuse Incidents: an Ethnography of Call Handlers, Dispatchers and Response Officers' (2020) 30(1) *Policing and Society* 65.
[74] Neighbourhood, Maron, February 2016.

Standard procedure would be to tow the van and issue tickets to the driver. For Arthur, this would hamper a man about his legitimate business who had made a simple mistake. The control room had no such sense of the specifics and expected an explanation that could be entered on the record of this incident.

Over the course of our observations, changes to the National Crime Recording Standards (NCRS)[75] altered this process.[76] Operators are now recording as crime any offences reported to them, however tenuous or open to doubt those reports might be (see Chapter 9 for more discussion). This was a source of frustration and of work for officers. They are no longer able to determine whether an offence has been committed on arrival at a scene. And should they find that the reported (and recorded) offence is not what it appeared, they have to work hard to change the original record.

> Barry is sent to a report of a sexual offence. As a Specially Trained Officer (STO), trained to deal with cases of rape or sexual assault, he is assigned to jobs like this. They can take a lot of time and patience. But this one is several days old by now and it is not clear why it needs to be dealt with on Response. The report is of an exchange student who has moved out of her host family's house. It seems she has been filmed with her boyfriend by the father of the host family. And the reports also suggest that the son has made unwanted advances. This is not going to be a simple case. When Barry gets to the new address where the student is staying, a few doors down the same street, she is embarrassed. She has not reported anything and doesn't want any action taken. Her new host family made the reports when she arrived a few days ago and appeared upset. It is a misunderstanding. She was filmed, but by the security camera and the footage has been deleted. She didn't know the camera was there and the family threw her out. She is desperate that Barry doesn't interview the first host family. They are friends of her family through church. Barry reassures her he will take no further action. But he spends much of the rest of the shift changing the status of the job from a crime to nothing more than a welfare check. He can't do this. It has to be done by a central team and he has to explain to them what has gone on.[77]

In this context, the presence of the control room operators directing, determining, and recording was more pervasive than any sense of supervision by Sergeants or Inspectors. Barry was not available for Response duties for a period of hours, dealing with a case that was not urgent and that, it turns out, was not a case at all. He was directed by the control room and then had to row back on the original 'criming' of the case. Before NCRS, this would have been resolved in a fraction of the time by the officer sent to deal with the call. If the Radio Control Room is a more evident form of supervision when it comes to decisions on criming, it is one that is characterised by policies, procedures, and record keeping.

---

[75] M Maguire, 'Criminal Statistics and the Recording of Crime' in M Maguire et al (eds), *The Oxford Handbook of Criminology*, 5th edn (Oxford, Oxford University Press, 2012).

[76] We will discuss the attempts officers make to 'cuff' crimes despite NCRS in Chapter 7.

[77] Response, Westmarch, February 2018.

# IV. Bureaucracy

Police work has often been described as bureaucratic in character.[78] By bureau-cratic, commentators do not refer to Max Weber's ideal typical rational-legal authority[79] but to a looser sense of a job dominated by record-keeping and paper-work. In this sense, the term is often much more a pejorative statement than an analytical one.[80] But the bureaucratic nature of much of the work is evident to observers as well. Long hours typing reports and statements, recording evidence, preparing warrants, and logging intelligence are a significant part of many shifts and, at times, the office can resemble some kind of typing pool.[81] These examples of written work have a clear purpose. Statements might be used in a subsequent prosecution. Evidence must be recorded to show a chain of custody. Warrants have to be presented to a magistrate for authority. What is less clear to officers is the value of the many other documents and reports they prepare, often as a follow-up to some of the jobs they least enjoy.

We have already noted the association between discretion and risk. This is in practice mitigated by the very paperwork officers object to. In cases involving domestic disputes, the importance of this paperwork comes to the fore. Indeed, the handling of domestic disputes well illustrates our arguments about officers' understandings of policy, of discretion, and of risk. What officers understand to be policy varies. The policy to take positive action in the case of a domestic violence allegation has morphed, over time, to be understood by many officers as a policy to arrest (see Chapter 7). Others understand that there are alternatives but, if anything were to go wrong, questions might later be asked about why someone was not arrested. Paperwork forms a record of the decision, of the risks considered and assessed, of the other vulnerable people involved, such as children, and so on.

> On a Night shift dominated by domestic calls, Spencer and a tutee complete one job and go straight to the next. It is another domestic call. A woman with two daughters reports a man threatening to stab her with a knife. They have been arguing all day. The woman has the knife, so there is no immediate threat. The man has left and she will call the police if he returns. She has locked the door and he doesn't have keys. On arrival at the address, they are both there. The man opens the door and the officers separate the two. Spencer goes through to the kitchen with the man, but everything said in each room can be heard. Two young girls are seated on a couch watching television but also listening to everything.
>
> The woman tells the story as being much ado about nothing that got out of hand. He grabbed her arm, but that is not an assault in her eyes. But she can hear the conversa-tion in the kitchen has turned to the knife. And it becomes clear she picked up the

---

[78] Wilson, *Varieties of Police Behaviour.*

[79] D Beetham, *Bureaucracy* (Buckingham, Open University Press, 1996).

[80] M Herzfeld, *The Social Production of Indifference: Exploring the Symbolic Roots of Western Bureaucracy* (Chicago, University of Chicago Press, 1993).

[81] Neighbourhood, Maron, February 2016. Some officers also had 'desk days' set aside predominantly for this type of work.

knife and threatened him. She called the police when he said something to the effect of 'if you stab me, I'll stab you!' She is furious he has mentioned the knife and comes across as controlling.

Spencer and the tutee go outside, leaving the door ajar in case they need to intervene. Who is the victim? The man lives elsewhere but has no money to get home. He has nothing until his wages are paid in tomorrow. He can't get home. Should they arrest him? For what? Leave him there? What if it kicks off again? Where could he go to cool off? He is a young lad. It is cold and wet, but he will survive until his money comes through. They settle on this solution, but they are not sure about it. It is a risk. If it does kick off again, how do you explain that you didn't arrest?

They go back in and the man understands the proposal. However, the woman is being unhelpful. His coat is on the radiator drying after being washed. So he has no coat, but she won't lend him one. He offers to leave his bankcard as guarantee. But she is the problem now. She turns to the television while the officers try to help the man work out how to see through the hours until his money comes through. Eventually, the man leaves with a coat to walk around until midnight at least. We leave with a sense that this is a risk but no other solution made sense either.[82]

Forms completed back at the station require responses to questions about the 'victim' and 'perpetrator'. It asks 'why did you not arrest?' 'Does the victim deny the assault?' And for whom should he complete the vulnerable person referrals for? The mother and her daughters? Or the man? Spencer finds it hard to respond. He wants to record no offences, but the case has already been crimed. Everything suggests it would have been easier to arrest and proceed as the case first appeared to the call handlers. But Spencer's judgement is that this would be wrong and unfair on the man. He is also trying to tutor a young officer. He uses discretion, but he becomes bound up in paperwork long after the end of the shift.

The connection between risk and bureaucracy is most clearly expressed in the Custody Suite. Sergeants receive detained persons and ask a series of questions about injuries, health, mental health, medication, and many other personal details. Some do it almost robotically. The list only ever gets longer, each new question being included because of some oversight that resulted in injury to, or an investigation over the treatment of, someone detained. They describe their role as classically bureaucratic. They believe they exercise no discretion in the role anymore. In Chapter 7, we will see that they do retain an important role in the detention process, but we also want to indicate another aspect of discretion. On a Night shift in the period just before Christmas, a succession of homeless men were brought in as part of a joint operation between the local authority and the police. Each was a familiar guest (the Sergeants tried to guess who would come in next) and each also knew the Sergeants. They knew which of the Sergeants they would prefer to be handled by. While much of what those Sergeants did appeared to them to be bureaucratic, to the homeless men they were very different. The favoured one

[82] Response, Arlesdale, February 2018.

would ensure they had a hot drink and had some hot food coming as a priority. The paperwork could wait.[83]

While apparently a small difference, and one that fits under the very widest interpretation of the sense of discretion, it is significant. Officers affect the lives of others. In the words of Lipsky quoted earlier, they make policy in the way they treat those they encounter.[84] They are gatekeepers who can open doors or bar the way.[85] But they do it very often without deliberate thought. By our presence, we found that we would frequently cause officers to reflect on the decisions they were making, not least because we would ask them about those decisions at a later point. This revealed something of the underlying assumptions about the laws, codes, rules, procedures, policies, and risks associated with the courses of action. But it also revealed that officers frequently made decisions without thinking about them. Similarly, we encountered many officers who were not comfortable with the decisions they felt constrained to take.

## V. 'Culture' and Discretion

Part of the discomfort some officers felt could be explained by the idea of 'police culture'. We have noted in Chapter 2 the way in which the concept of 'police culture', the artefacts, values, and assumptions[86] shared by officers, can *appear* to shape and explain behaviours. Indeed, research into 'police culture' has largely been driven by efforts to understand why it is they don't simply follow the rules and enforce the law.[87] And in observing officers, it is easy to identify many of the characteristics that have been distilled into a simple and widely-used list of those values: sense of mission, suspicion, isolation and solidarity, conservative, macho, racist, and pragmatic.[88] In the rest room (talk of the 'canteen culture' needs to acknowledge the absence of canteens in recent years), officers do share stories of incidents. Either they were funny,[89] or action-packed, or entailed danger.[90] Macho attributes appeared to be prized. Physical fitness and exercise regimes were regularly the topic of conversation. And officers moaned about change, especially about any changes that affected either their powers as officers or their shift patterns. In this sense, they were conservative.

[83] Custody, Tidmouth, November 2013.
[84] Lipsky, *Street-level Bureaucracy* xii.
[85] Maynard-Moody and Musheno, 'State Agent or Citizen Agent'.
[86] E Schein, *Organizational Culture and Leadership*, 3rd edn (San Francisco, Jossey-Bass, 2004).
[87] C Shearing and R Ericson, 'Culture as Figurative Action' (1991) 42 *British Journal of Sociology* 481.
[88] Reiner, *The Politics of the Police* 119–32.
[89] SM Gayadeen and SW Phillips, 'Donut Time: the Use of Humour Across the Police Work Environment' (2016) 5 *Journal of Organizational Ethnography* 44.
[90] M van Hulst, 'Storytelling at the Police Station: the Canteen Culture Revisited' (2013) 53 *British Journal of Criminology* 624; PAJ Waddington, 'Police (Canteen) Sub-culture: an Appreciation' (1999) 29 *British Journal of Criminology* 287.

Souhami discerned that the police service was 'pervaded by an undercurrent of racism, sexism, and homophobia', with LGBTQ and BAME officers reporting 'a climate of intangible yet pervasive discrimination'.[91] We encountered 'banter' between officers that was regularly sexist and occasionally homophobic,[92] and officers would sometimes complain in a humorous manner about the 'politically correct' nature of contemporary policing: 'You can't say that any more, Dave'. Or officers might joke that they had been insulted: 'I have a disability and I am offended by that'.[93] However, none of the openly LGBTQ participants made any reference to us of feeling uncomfortable due to their sexuality. Although this may not denote more than a presentation of inclusivity, LGBTQ awareness and support posters, rainbow lanyards and Pride mugs were dotted around the police stations.

When it came to race and religion, our observations mirrored those of Loftus. In terms of *overt* racism, 'racist language was virtually non-existent' and some officers challenged members of the public over their own racist language.[94] This was despite the fact that the officers we observed were predominantly white (although in both forces we saw a handful of black officers and a greater number of Asian officers and Police Community Support Officers (PCSOs)).[95] We did not encounter overtly racist comments or jokes, although occasionally an officer might make stereotypical and generalised remarks about how religious 'cultures' operated. However, mirroring Waddington's findings, regardless of such comments, we did not see evidence of overt discrimination in the use of street powers and discretion.[96] Nevertheless, statistics for stop search and for arrest in both force areas still demonstrated that ethnic minorities were much more likely to be subjected to coercive police powers. That we saw no overt discrimination might be a result of our presence, but it might also reflect other aspects of the use of these powers. We will return to the issue of discrimination in Chapter 6 when we consider stop and search.

Returning to our more general discussion about 'police culture', as studies focusing on 'police culture' have noted, not all officers think and act the same. Research has recognised that there are variations between ranks,[97] between roles and functions, and between police forces.[98] Nevertheless, these studies assume some connection between this 'culture', varied as it may be, and behaviour. While Traffic officers may be different in some respects to Response officers, they share

[91] A Shouhami, 'Constructing Tales of the Field: Uncovering the Culture of Fieldwork in Police Ethnography' (forthcoming) *Policing and Society* 6.

[92] There were many openly gay officers and we saw no evidence of 'banter' directed 'at' them. Nevertheless, we saw several instances of officers claiming others were gay as part of 'banter' in the office or canteen and other officers acting out stereotypically camp behaviour in response.

[93] Neighbourhood, Brandham, January 2014.

[94] B Loftus, *Police Culture in a Changing World* (Oxford, Oxford University Press, 2009) 155.

[95] PCSO teams were noticeably more diverse.

[96] P Waddington, *Policing Citizens: Authority and Rights* (London, UCL Press, 1999) 108.

[97] E Reuss-Ianni, *Two Cultures of Policing: Street Cops and Management Cops* (London, Transaction Books, 1983).

[98] Wilson, *Varieties of Police Behavior*.

some fundamentals as police officers. And these studies tend then to suggest that, while there may be differences between different specialisms, there is something in common within a specialism. Traffic officers, for example, can be grouped together as sharing a 'sub-culture'. Some further studies have sought to look at individual styles, classifying officer attitudes and conduct into types,[99] but again these can be seen almost as drivers of the conduct of those officers. Because officer A is type Y, she will behave in this manner in this situation. Finally, those studies that have focused upon conversations in the canteen and elsewhere do recognise that there is a distinct difference between what is said in the police station, in front of an audience, and what occurs in the field.[100] Despite these caveats and reservations, and despite warnings about 'cognitive burn-in,'[101] the concept of 'police culture' appears to still hold some attraction to both academics[102] and practitioners.[103] Indeed, senior officers, with whom we first had discussions about this research, used the idea of 'culture' and the need to change it frequently and casually. As we noted in Chapter 2, what they understood by 'culture', and how they proposed to change it, was less clear.

To illustrate the point, during our research many officers, both frontline and in a supervisory role, took the view that Constables would look for the easiest or quickest way to solve a problem. This can be expressed by the view that 'Bobbies take the path of least resistance'.[104] Is this a shared cultural meaning that, in turn, can help us explain, or even predict, common practice in policing? Is this approach to decision-making part of the 'police culture'? Actually, when we dig a little deeper into how 'the path of least resistance' was played out in practice, what strikes us is not homogeneity but completely differing understandings and subsequent approaches. For some officers, the path of least resistance could be found by cutting corners. They might achieve this by avoiding paperwork, filling in the bulk of a DASH[105] form themselves rather than going through each question individually with the victim, ignoring difficult or time-consuming jobs, or patrolling quiet areas towards the end of a shift. However, for other officers, the path of least resistance meant almost the opposite. It meant doing police work 'by-the-book' to avoid 'in the job' trouble.[106] For these officers it was less important what the job

---

[99] Muir, *Police: Streetcorner Politicians*; P Ramshaw, 'On the Beat: Variations in the Patrolling Styles of the Police Officer' (2012) 1 *Journal of Organizational Ethnography* 213.

[100] Waddington, *Policing Citizens*.

[101] DA Sklansky, 'Seeing Blue: Police Reform, Occupational Culture, and Cognitive Burn-in' in M O'Neill et al (eds), *Police Occupational Culture: New Debates and Directions* (London, Elsevier, 2007).

[102] Loftus, *Police Culture*; and even Sklansky, 'Seeing Blue'.

[103] Much of the College of Policing's efforts to develop Leadership, Fast Track and Direct Entry schemes is in order to 'impact on and positively influence the management and culture of policing', see recruit.college.police.uk/Officer/leadership-programmes/Pages/Fast-Track.aspx.

[104] Interview, Neighbourhood, Shiloh, September 2015.

[105] DASH stands for Domestic Abuse, Stalking and Honour-based Violence.

[106] M Chatterton, 'The Supervision of Patrol Work Under the Fixed Points System' in S Holdaway (ed), *The British Police* (London, Edward Arnold, 1979); P Waddington, *Liberty and Order: Policing Public Order in a Capital City* (London, UCL Press, 1994).

was, it would fill up the allotted time until the end of the shift regardless. Finally, for other officers, the path of least resistance was simply to adhere to whatever they believed their Sergeant wanted. Therefore, rather than revealing a shared meaning and practice that might fall into the traditional view of 'culture' (see Chapter 2),[107] a brief investigation of 'the path of least resistance' instead merely demonstrates, once again, an *absence* of homogeneity of approach by frontline officers to their job and the use of their street powers.

What we observed over time was a much more problematic picture of 'police culture' such that, for us, the term has little real meaning or interpretive value. It obscures more than it reveals. We observed officers performing similar roles at different police stations. We observed different shifts at the same police stations. We observed the same officers in different roles and in different police stations. But fundamentally we observed a large number of officers, directly and indirectly, over a period of time. From these observations, we found that different officers deal with similar cases in different ways. These differences are not simply down to roles, to styles, or to personality, though these were factors. They also reflect different understandings of the purpose of policing. For some, keeping people safe and being there in times of need were as important as crime fighting, and indeed these gave them their sense of mission. It was not clear to us that any simple set of shared values or assumptions underpinned the decision-making of the officers we observed, and that was one of our early puzzles. We could not readily make sense of the variety of attitudes and behaviours we observed using the simple framing device of 'police culture'.

Despite training and supervision, despite policies and procedures, rules and forms, and despite apparently enforcing the same criminal law, officers still responded to similar situations in a variety of different ways. By way of illustration, during the six years of our observations, BWCs were rolled out in both of the police forces. Reactions from officers varied greatly, and we shall explore this a little further in Chapter 9. If they were equipped with a camera, officers responding to a domestic incident were required to activate the camera. They were also expected to use them in cases where they conducted a stop and search. Beyond that, their use was voluntary. We observed officers using BWCs extensively to record road traffic accidents, seized property and the condition of a house before and after executing a search warrant. We observed teams playing back an incident, discussing and seeking to learn from what occurred. But we have also observed officers, suspicious of their real purpose, in effect refusing to use the cameras. And in between, there were many others who either forgot to switch on their BWC or turned it on half-way through an encounter. And these variations were in the same teams.[108] Frontline officers were not simply conservative and resistant to change.

---

[107] M Agar, 'Culture: Can You Take it Anywhere?' (2006) 5 *International Journal of Qualitative Methods* 1.
[108] Rowe et al, 'Learning and Practicing Police Craft'.

They each adopted or adapted to the change, more or less consciously, in a way that suited them.

Brought together, the policies that are open to interpretation, the variable training, the varying degrees of supervision, and the form filling do shape the way officers' work. We do not contest that. For some officers, it was a cause of frustration and of humour.

> In the middle of a shift, while waiting for a briefing to commence, officers played an elaborate prank that had been days in the planning. An officer who was a keen cyclist, riding to work every day, has been eager to use a police bike for some time, but he needs to go on a course. The chief prankster in the team has a plan to wind him up. He radios through and asks the officer if he is free to speak on the phone? A moment later he rings back and tells him that the Training Academy has been in contact. There is a course available next week if he can make it. It is his rest day, but he is keen and will be there, he responds immediately. The prankster then reels him in and details the online training packages he will need to do first. The cycling awareness package. The Proper Use of Police Issue Bicycle Clips package. The officer is noting these down quite seriously on the other end of the phone. It is only when the prankster asks if he can give the Inspector a lift to the Academy on his bike that the officer begins to smell a rat. And at that moment the Inspector arrives to berate the officers for being so childish in front of a guest.[109]

The story is not a profound one, but it is as illustrative of the conversations that went on around the station as any of the more macho or action-filled stories. And it illustrates both the absence of supervision and the contempt in which much of the training they receive is held by officers. The humour is a bit schoolboyish, but the prankster practises on all his colleagues, and they all enjoy it. The victim officer in this case returned to the station to mock himself. He showed everyone the notes he had taken of the phone call, right down to the Inspector needing a lift: 'You had me there!' It is important to be made fun of in this team, and to take it and to laugh at yourself. It is what makes this team distinct from others we have observed. But did this particular 'culture' or 'sub-culture' in this particular team affect the ways in which those officers responded to situations? No, not in ways that we could determine.

# VI. The Police Career

The range of roles was one of the attractive features of policing as a career. Even if an officer had no ambition for senior ranks, there was plenty of opportunity to learn new skills, to specialise and to progress. Over our six years, many of those we observed moved on to new roles, often having talked it through with us as

---

[109] Neighbourhood, Arlesdale, October 2014.

impartial and independent sources of advice. Each, in their own way, was trying to find either where they fitted best, or to develop a portfolio of experience that would fit them for promotion. For one, this meant training as an STO, becoming a tutor constable and other similar roles. He was happy in Response but was aiming for promotion. At time of writing, he was Acting Sergeant. Another had moved from Response to Neighbourhood, and enjoyed the proactive work. During the time of the research, he moved on to the Organised Crime Disruption team and then made Sergeant. Another went from Traffic to a specialist Vehicle Crime team before resurrecting his military training to become an Authorised Firearms Officer (AFO). Another was trying to be accepted into the dog handling unit. A further officer went from Traffic to the Specialist Search Team, a role that might take him all over the country. What senior officers struggled with was recruitment to CID. One participant had left CID to return to uniform. He explained that there was no 'let-up' in CID. You carried your cases with you, taking them home literally and metaphorically, until they were completed, 'working silly hours' at times. It was too much.[110]

Our point here is that officers aren't simply shaped by 'police culture'. Rather, they develop as individuals within the role. Are Traffic officers different because they choose the path, or does moving to Traffic change you so that you become different through some process of socialisation? Of the two, we would say it is more likely to be the former than the latter. And this is the case in most of the roles. Perhaps the one exception is Neighbourhood. While some officers chose the role as a distinct one, it was apparent that some chose it for the easier shift patterns. There were no Nights.[111] And unlike other specialist roles, Neighbourhood officers received no training in the new role. Yet an understanding of the role is key because Neighbourhood officers are expected to work alongside PCSOs to establish deep roots in a community. They are expected to engage with that community very differently to Response or Territorial Support. And they are expected to work in very different ways, developing intelligence and knowing their patch. Much like tutor officers, the selection and development of Neighbourhood officers is one of those little-remarked-upon weaknesses in current policing. However, it is against this background that recent efforts to professionalise, or re-professionalise, the police might be understood. This is a topic to which we will return in Chapter 10. But before we do so, we will turn in more detail to the ways in which officers work and use their powers and the temporal and geographical context that influences their use of discretion.

---

[110] Territorial Support, Maron, January 2015.

[111] We should also note that a good number of career decisions were made to accommodate family commitments.

# 5

# On the Beat: Temporal
# and Geographical Influences
# on Police Discretion

Surprisingly little is written about the shift as it affects discretion and decision-making. What commentary there is tends to be in passing rather than the focus of sustained attention. In our observations, the shift, in all its aspects, affected the ways officers saw the world around them, responded to calls, utilised their discretion, and, most significantly for the purposes of this book, used their powers. We also reached the conclusion that it was not possible to understand the true nature or extent of police discretion without considering the temporal and geographical context of the shift. We will seek to give these features of the shift some attention in this chapter.

## I. The Archetypal Shift

It would be too easy both to assert that no two shifts are the same and also to ignore the regularities that are evident across the range of shifts. The purpose of this chapter is to explore the effects of an apparently simple and necessary management system for deploying resources upon the way officers work and the way they use their powers. That it will affect the use of powers is familiar to anyone reading the work of Brogden[1] about inter-war policing, or ethnographies of policing in the 1970s[2] and contrasting these with modern approaches to deployment, including the use of intelligence and 'hot spots' policing,[3] to target officer time and attention. To explore this, we will develop a model of an archetypal shift, noting as we do so the significant points with respect to time, place, and interactions with others as they impinge upon the ways in which officers think and act.

---

[1] M Brogden, *On the Mersey Beat: Policing Liverpool Between the Wars* (Oxford, Oxford University Press, 1991).
[2] S Holdaway, *Inside the British Police* (Oxford, Basil Blackwell, 1983); J McClure, *Spike Island: Portrait of a Police Division* (London, Macmillan, 1980).
[3] JH Ratcliffe, *Intelligence-led Policing*, 2nd edn (London, Routledge, 2016); DM Kennedy, 'Pulling Levers: Chronic Offenders, High-crime Settings, and a Theory of Prevention' (1997) 31 *Valparaiso University Law Review* 449.

Before proceeding, a word about the shifts themselves. They vary according to role, but, as a general rule, officers work a ten-hour shift. There are Early, Late and Night shifts, and we shall refer to them as such hereafter. Earlies will normally start at 07:00, Lates at 14:00 and Nights at 21:00. In each case, there is an overlap at the start of each shift as a new team comes on duty, except at a handover between Nights and Earlies. Many police forces will now have variations to allow for peaks of demand, splitting shifts and varying start times to ensure there is cover. Officers will also on occasion work different hours, for example when tasked with the policing of a time-limited event such as a sporting event. There are also variations in the patterns of shifts over time. For example, a unit might have a shift pattern that starts with two Earlies, then two Lates followed by two Nights and four days off before starting again. There are then also variations according to the function an officer performs. Neighbourhood teams will commonly work Earlies and Lates, but not Nights. But these variations do not represent significant deviations from the standard shift for our purposes at this stage.

## II. Time

### A. 'You should have been Out with Me Last Night'

The assumption is that, if you are observing police officers, you want to see them in action, making decisions. Thus, particular shifts are considered more or less likely to be productive ones. In Response, the Late shift will generally be busiest, in terms of calls for service. This is peak time for drunk and disorderly behaviour and for domestic violence. The Night shift can be much quieter, though one never says the word 'quiet' (often known as 'the Q word') for fear of jinxing the shift, and will often present opportunities for officers to be a little more proactive in the work they do. Earlies can be slow, but they will be the best time for officers to catch up on outstanding paperwork, to follow-up on cases and to arrange inter-views with witnesses or suspects. These patterns are then affected by the day of the week. Friday and Saturday Lates and Nights will be dominated by the night-time economy and associated drink and violence problems, particularly those just after a payday at the start of a month. 'Even criminals enjoy their Friday and Saturday nights out' as one officer remarked.[4] Saturday and Sunday Earlies will then be much quieter, but Sunday Lates and Nights are considered the start of the working week for criminals.

Beyond these regular patterns, there are levels of *folk wisdom* and superstition in policing. The weather is believed to affect behaviours. On one shift, an Early on what promised to be a very warm summer day, officers predicted the offences they would deal with. Accompanying one officer as she drove around the terraced

---

[4] Traffic, Midgewater, August 2018.

streets, we observed people bringing out their furniture, their beer and even a television at 10:00, settling down for as long as the sun was on the street. Sure enough, later in the shift, she was called to deal with disturbances and neighbour disputes in just such streets as drink took effect.[5] On other shifts, the rain apparently played a key role in keeping the streets safe. Most often referred to as 'PC Rain', she was sometimes promoted to 'Inspector Rain'. Whatever the rank, rain ensured that crime remained indoors and would tend towards domestic violence. We have already used the 'Q word' too often in the previous paragraph, but officer superstitions go much further. In particular, they note the full moon and will tell stories of the crazy things they have seen or that people have done on such nights. Custody Sergeants, in particular, regaled us with tales of their cells brimming with the strangest cases.[6] Whether these variations in anticipated activity play out in practice is, in our experience, hard to tell. It was evident that they did not in all cases we observed. What is interesting is the ways in which officers then deal with the variations in shifts as they evolve, the ways they manage time, and how that affects their approach to their encounters with the public and the use of their street powers.

## B.  Start of the Shift

On arrival to conduct an observation, we will be let in by the officer (sometimes after a lengthy wait outside), there being few public reception areas remaining open in many forces. Officers are almost always already kitted up. They have arrived early. Some will have been to the gym, whether a commercial gym or a small facility in the station. Others will have showered after a cycle ride to work, often some considerable distance. Concern with fitness is evident among many officers, although healthy packed lunches are regularly put to one side if a colleague offers to do a 'run' to the chip or kebab shop for 'dirty scoff'. The workspace they occupy will generally be open-plan, often shared with other teams and other functions. As observers, then, it is not always clear who is who, where to sit, and who knows or does not know about our work. It is a moment of tension, of uncertainty for all. Only with time does a degree of familiarity emerge, and with it confidence in the use of the space. Once briefing or parade is called, the key personnel on the shift for this observation become clearer.

Briefing for Response officers will take place more or less at the start of any shift, though officers on a slight variation may not receive a briefing at all. Accompanied by a presentation pack, sometimes put together by the intelligence analysts and sometimes just a review of the recent notices pertinent to a Division, much of the information communicated is the same from one shift to the next. It will consist

---

[5] Response, Kirk Machan, July 2015.
[6] Custody, Lakeside, June 2014.

of *information* about recent incidents of note, of suspects wanted and of the vulnerable to be attended to. Most of the faces are well known to officers and, very often, they will have more up-to-date intelligence than is provided in the briefing. A man listed as wanted might have been locked up that afternoon, for example. Or a vulnerable young woman, potentially a victim of child sexual exploitation, may have been found, apparently safe and well. Only rarely do officers pay close attention. Only very rarely are they tasked to follow-up on specific individuals. They almost never take notes unless tasked to a particular job, and those notes will often be scrawled onto the back of the hand with a pen. The briefing might also list 'hot spots' to be attended to. These will be typically associated with a spate of burglaries,[7] but there might also be ongoing attention given to particularly vulnerable or threatened communities.[8] In our observations, it was rare for an emergency Response team briefing to significantly alter an officer's conduct and attention during a shift. The briefing sometimes finishes with an update on the terrorist threat-level, and any direction on personal protective equipment, and duties and call signs are issued, but the duties only rarely relate to any specific intelligence given out during a briefing.

Where briefings do affect the work officers undertake is in those teams with a focus on proactive policing. In particular those targeting gangs and organised crime will be deployed to specific areas based either on recent occurrences or intelligence about potential incidents. They might be tasked to conduct a search warrant or to back up colleagues in doing so. These differences in briefings reflect the different tasks of the teams. But they also reflect a very different relationship with supervision. Targeted and proactive officers will, as we have noted in Chapter 4, often operate in small teams under relatively close supervision from a Sergeant, and be briefed by an Inspector. In contrast, Response officers will infrequently see their Inspector and, after a briefing by their Sergeant, operate largely without hands-on supervision throughout a shift. They may seek advice and may need to gain permission for some decisions, but in many observations, the Sergeant might appear only at the start and the end of a shift.

## C. Managing Time

For the most part, officers will want to finish their shift on time. To achieve this more often than not, officers adopt a number of different approaches to jobs. The key point we are making here is that officers have the time remaining on their shift at the forefront of their minds when making decisions about the jobs they take, as far as they are able. Therefore, we can only understand how officers use their powers if we understand the context of the shift on which they are working.

---

[7] Response, Westmarch, August 2017.
[8] Response, Trollshaws, September 2016.

First, to enable the previous shift to finish on time, emergency response officers will begin to take calls as they leave the briefing. This will depend on the availability of a car, but any Grade One call, that is those requiring an immediate response which can (and almost always does) involve using blue lights and sirens ('blues and twos'), will be taken by the new shift. As we saw in the previous chapter, no officer would want to take a complex domestic violence case or a job involving an arrest in the last hour of their shift, so an unwritten rule demands that the new shift takes the call (see text in Chapter 4, section I.A and accompanying notes).

Aside from such emergencies, the start of a shift will involve tea and coffee, often with cakes, whether because of someone's birthday or as a penalty applied because of some gaff on a previous shift. Any cakes or biscuits that have been left unattended are fair game. Emails, force briefings, announcements and adverts, booking leave or training courses, and completing paperwork from a previous shift all occupy the first few minutes, delaying the time for an officer to go to her car. If finishing on time is important, being on top of paperwork is a second prime consideration. Carrying paperwork over into the next shift is fraught with potential problems. Should the officer get landed with a case requiring an arrest, witness statements, interview, reports and so forth, she will find herself struggling to catch up. This rule of practice, that paperwork should not be carried over, will define other aspects of the way time is managed over a shift. After a job, many officers will look to complete all the associated paperwork before making themselves available for a further job. As we have seen in Chapter 4, this is also a way of 'shirking' (see text in Chapter 4, section I.A and accompanying notes). Only rarely will an officer go from job, to job, to job without a break to tidy up loose ends. While sometimes this is unavoidable, creating a backlog of paperwork will increase the likelihood of the officer having to stay on after the end of the shift.[9]

If excitement and action dominate impressions of policing in television dramas or fly-on-the-wall documentaries, quiet time is valued on any shift. For Response officers, quiet time might allow for them to park the car for a few minutes, watching passing traffic, sometimes with a purpose, often more idly.[10] But such quiet time needs to be balanced out by more substantial work. On a Night shift, an officer will struggle to stay awake and time will drag painfully unless there is a call, one that consumes two or three hours.

> At 23:12, Barry is called to back up an ambulance crew called to a threatened suicide. It is from a man well known to the officers and, indeed, he was Tasered only recently by another officer on the shift who also responds. The man has rigged the door so that, when opened, he believes it will pull a rope tight and he will be hanged. But the door opens inwards and not out, so it has no effect. But he is clearly in distress. They arrest for a Breach of the Peace, because he has disturbed his neighbours who are all on the landing of the block of flats. Once out of his flat, they detain him under s 136 of the

---

[9] Response, Arlesdale Green, February 2018.
[10] M Cain, *Society and the Policeman's Role* (London, Routledge and Kegan Paul, 1973).

Mental Health Act and take him to a local hospital. With constant observation duties and report writing, Barry doesn't leave the hospital until 03:06. That is the back broken on this shift. Time to eat and it will be near time to finish, though on this evening food is interrupted by reports of a burglary in progress at a warehouse.[11]

Other tasks will consume time with even less effort.

A Specially Trained Officer, one trained to deal with offences such as sexual assaults, assigned to deal with an attempted rape at the start of the shift knows how the next ten hours will play themselves out. Aside from the sensitive handling of the complainant, the work itself can be routine and boring. While the complainant is undergoing forensic examination, the officer will wait for more than three hours in a hospital waiting room with little to do. Before smartphones, a book was an essential piece of kit. Now, officers will while away hours engrossed in their phone or, perhaps, completing work-related tasks on a tablet. On this occasion, the officer was calm and unconcerned about his apparent inactivity. He would finish on time and would get home safe at the end of the shift. What more could he ask for?[12]

For most, these hours would be dull and pointless, the inactivity only emphasised by the radio conversations about ongoing incidents. Finding themselves in the Holding Cell waiting to go into Custody for more than three hours, two officers became more and more frustrated, overhearing reports of two burglaries on 'their patch' that they were unable to do anything about.[13] Officers assigned to the constant observation of a prisoner due to concerns for their mental health and safety, or to the guarding of a crime scene, will experience similar frustrations. Staying alert is a real challenge, particularly on a Night shift.

Those in Neighbourhood teams, when nothing is happening, might be inclined to drive around housing estates they would not normally visit. Sometimes this is labelled a 'high visibility patrol', but it represents little more than keeping out of the office while appearing to be active. One officer drove 97 miles in a single routine shift, hardly getting out of the car. There were numerous traffic infringements (tail-lights not working, driving too fast in a residential area), but all were handled merely with words of advice.[14] Officers on proactive and Traffic teams will more often drive to and around areas of interest, whether known for drug dealing or for speeding and other offences. They might call it 'mooching', a commonly-used term that implies some form of intelligence gathering or crime-fighting work, but consists merely of driving around. And these hours will drag the more because it contrasts so much with their own image of their purpose, to be proactive.[15]

Consuming time, or what Margaret Cain refers to as easing,[16] is important, but consuming it in a purposeful manner is key. And one of the more important ways

[11] Response, Bree, August 2016.
[12] Response, Ravenhill, May 2018.
[13] Territorial Support, Brandham, March 2014.
[14] Neighbourhood, Shiloh, September 2015.
[15] Territorial Support, Knapford, October 2015.
[16] Cain, *Society and the Policeman's Role*.

of consuming time is to take a break for a meal, referred to variously as 'refs' or 'scoff'. While breaks should be staggered within a shift, it is common for officers to engineer it, emergency calls permitting, so that they take refs together. In some teams, the Sergeant and Inspector might also be part of this same arrangement,[17] while in others, officers would meet at a location away from the station.[18] On a quiet shift, these breaks could become extended,[19] but the timing of them was also important. Too early and the end of the shift would drag on. Too late and you risk not getting a break at all if a significant incident occurs. Just over half-way through a shift appeared to be the most widely preferred choice. Attempts to timetable and monitor staggered break times have proven both unpopular and impossible to enforce.[20] As our research progressed and officer numbers declined, or officers were moved to new stations, the regularity with which officers gathered together socially for refs appeared to diminish. At some stations and on some shifts, it was hard to discern whether a 'canteen culture' had ever existed.

Although refs played a key role in making even the dullest shift bearable, on occasion an opportunity might arise that promised sufficient excitement that meant meals could be overlooked or even abandoned half-way through. The following vignette reflects the experience of one of the authors shadowing a Territorial Support team on a Late shift, although we should emphasise just how unusual this incident was. The team had just sat down with 'dirty scoff', midway through a Late shift, a refs break they had been planning and looking forward to for hours:

> The officers break off from their food almost as one and bend their heads down or pick up their radios to listen. I can't hear the details, but it is clear that something unusual is occurring as they start conferring about how long it would take to get to the location of the incident. Then they are suddenly rushing as one out of the kitchen area and towards the exit where their vans are parked, struggling to put on stab vests, some still carrying or eating their food as they go (...) We head down the motorway at high speed in a convoy of two vans, blue lights on. A group of [men] have apparently barricaded themselves in a pub and are refusing to leave. Response officers think they have identified weapons, and requested assistance. I have never seen these officers so excited, I think they are positively giddy at the prospect of getting to use some of the riot gear stashed in the back of the van.
>
> Then one shouts up. 'Sarge!' He nods at me. 'We've got ...' He tails off and I suddenly feel guilty I may be about to spoil the fun. But Sarge just shrugs and says, 'He can get stuck in

---

[17] One team of Response officers in Kirk Machan would gather around a table that comfortably seated six. There would be eight or more officers, the Sergeant and the Inspector at almost every break time.

[18] This seemed to apply particularly to Traffic officers, who would meet for coffee at motorway service stations as a way of remaining available while taking a break.

[19] On one occasion, and trying to be subtle in front of an observer, an Inspector ordered officers out of the station and back on patrol after one much extended break (Territorial Support, Knapford, October 2015).

[20] J Ferrill, *Buzzwords, Bureaucracy and Badges: An Ethnographic Exploration of how Versions of Wellbeing are Constructed Through Social Ideology Projects in a UK Police Organisation* (Loughborough, unpublished PhD thesis, Loughborough University, 2018).

if he wants'. I think he is being serious. But the fun is spoilt anyway. The Response officers have talked the men in the pub down and they have agreed to leave. No assistance is now required. The blue lights go off, the van slows down and the driver indicates to leave at the next junction to head back to the station. The sense of disappointment is palpable.[21]

This example is indicative of a couple of things we need to take note of. First, as has been noted in a number of previous studies,[22] excitement is prized by many police officers, particularly on otherwise mundane shifts. However, we would fall short of describing this as a culturally-shared meaning. We cannot say it is necessarily different from other forms of shift-work, nor do we argue that all police officers share this desire. This was a specialised proactive and public order Level Two trained unit. Other officers we observed would prefer to avoid the opportunity for physical confrontation if they could. The risk of injury and complaints meant it was by no means the 'path of least resistance'. Clearly, the Response officers handling the incident preferred to talk than to fight. Second, it demonstrates that, while ref breaks and the end of the shift dominated officer thoughts, where jobs arose offering the opportunity for excitement or kudos, or where there was an immediate physical risk to other officers or 'decent people', most officers were willing to put in the extra time and effort.

## D. Custody

A further key component in determining the pattern of a shift will be a decision to arrest. We will discuss the legal considerations in more detail in Chapter 7, but some practical ones also arise. Principal among these is the fact that an arrest takes time and, second, it might lead to either more or less paperwork, depending on the offence and the way prisoners are handled.

Arrest was handled differently in the two forces we observed. In one, it was common for officers to simply bundle the person detained into the rear seat of a patrol car and take them to Custody without any further fuss. Officers realised it was official policy[23] to await a van with a cage, but that just wasted time and was only followed if there was any threat of violence. The arresting officer was then always the one to present the prisoner to the Custody Sergeant, to explain the grounds etc (see Chapter 7 for a fuller discussion). In the other force, officers would wait for a van. This was usually driven by two further officers who could spend a good deal of their shift escorting prisoners to Custody. Because the van could be tied up at another job, officers might spend some time waiting for it to

---

[21] Territorial Support [Redacted] 2014.

[22] Most famously R Reiner, *The Politics of the Police*, 4th edn (Oxford, Oxford University Press, 2014).

[23] While many policies might be followed rigidly for fear of any consequences, this was one policy routinely ignored by all.

arrive to take a prisoner.[24] The arresting officer would hand the prisoner over and pass details to the van crew of the time of arrest, the offence and, on occasion, the reason and/or necessity criteria. The van crew were the ones to then present the prisoner to the Custody Sergeant, rather than the arresting officer who could continue with their duties.

At Custody, officers wait in a Holding Cell, a bare room with a few posters on the wall reminding officers of key procedures, until there is a Custody Sergeant ready to deal with the prisoner. This can be a swift process, a pause of a matter of a few minutes, or it can take a long time. Officers, in the force where they were responsible for taking their own prisoners, were very aware of who was on duty in the Custody Suite on any particular shift. On one notable occasion, the researchers were observing different teams on a similar shift pattern. One team of officers arrested two brothers for breach of the peace (BOP) at a hospital and took them in to Custody. However, they had to wait for more than three hours in the Holding Cell, for reasons that were not clear to anyone.[25] Meanwhile, the second unit had stopped a man who was acting suspiciously on the street. The man had a history of convictions and in his possession was a halogen oven. His attempts to explain why he was carrying the oven around at this time in the evening were unconvincing but as the officers were aware of the delays at Custody, rather than simply arresting the suspect as they would have normally done, they decided to make further enquiries in the hope they would not need to make the arrest. Only when these merely confirmed their suspicion of burglary did they make the decision to arrest.[26] Such considerations appear nowhere in PACE, in the Academy training, or in any formal policies, but they were very real considerations for officers when determining whether or not to make an arrest, and some senior officers were well aware of it. Closing down Custody Suites increased these delays in the Holding Cell and meant that officers started to give more serious consideration to the alternatives for arrest, such as asking the suspect to voluntarily attend (VA) for interview – consideration they should have been giving in any case.[27]

Once a suspect is arrested, their case then has to be processed to some form of resolution. The arresting officer would have to write up a report of the arrest which, for minor offences, could potentially take longer than the suspect's period of detention lasted. In the two cases above, a BOP entailed a cooling off and no more. That the cooling off took place in the Holding Cell was unplanned but, once into Custody, they were there for no more than 20 minutes. In the second case, officers had a number of potential lines of enquiry, including possible credit card fraud. The detainee was tested positive for cocaine and there was no solicitor available

---

[24] Response, Bree, August 2016.

[25] Territorial Support, Brandham and at Tidmouth Custody, March 2014. See also n 13 above.

[26] Territorial Support, Knapford and at Cronk Custody, March 2014.

[27] G Pearson et al, 'Policy, Practicalities, and PACE s 24: Police Understanding and Subsuming of Necessity in Decision-Making on Arrest' (2018) 45 *Journal of Law and Society* 282, 288; see also Chapter 7 for a fuller discussion.

until the morning, so the case would be handled by an Investigating Officer the next day. But the arresting officers spent some time writing their reports and detailing the lines of enquiry that might be followed.[28] Other cases required follow-up, including interviews and witness statements, to be conducted by the arresting officers. If a shift was short-staffed, a Sergeant might not be too pleased that officers were off the street and involved in casework of this sort. Indeed, on night-time economy duties, the rule was that officers avoided arrest unless unavoidable. It was more important to have officers on the street than to arrest for a BOP, for example. Instead officers were encouraged to issue a 'Section 27 to leave' a defined area and not return that same night.[29]

An exception to this rule applied in one force at the start of our observations. Once arrested, all prisoners were handed on to a Prisoner Processing Unit. The arresting officer wrote up their statement, but all other actions were passed on to this team. For officers, the incentive was clear. It was often easier to arrest and hand the case on than it was to deal with it by way of a VA or other process. Some months in to our fieldwork, this was changed and officers would now have to handle the investigation of minor offences. This often meant that enquiries might have to wait until an officer was next on an Early shift and might then cause delays, but it did reduce demand for the Custody Suites.

## E. End of the Shift

An arrest early in a shift might meet the need for what officers perceive to be all necessary purposeful activity. But an arrest towards the end of a shift was not something to be contemplated unless it was unavoidable.

> At 04:25, Winston hears a burglar alarm going off. His partner winds down the passenger side window and listens closely. It is coming from behind them and, looking in the rear-view mirror, they can see a man running across the road with a bag over his shoulder. It might as well say 'SWAG' on it! Winston turns the car around and they follow the man into a side road. He runs into bushes but they pursue on foot and quickly catch him. Bringing him to the side of the car, they are joined by a Traffic officer who heard the radio calls. As the man starts to have a fit, the Traffic officer leans over. 'That won't work. Open your eyes. Remember me? I remember you. I know you are putting it on. I've seen it before.' The guy calms down a bit, but he has spat out his teeth in the process of faking a fit. He complains about use of force and then starts protesting that this is his first commercial job. Winston is jubilant – it is his first as well! While other officers are checking out the pharmacy where the alarm is going off, he is inspecting the bag. Full of pills.

[28] Territorial Support, Knapford, June 2014.
[29] Night-time Economy Team, Brandham, August 2014. This referred to the now-repealed alcohol dispersal orders under the Violent Crime Reduction Act 2006.

05:00 they head off to Custody. The rest of the shift and long into overtime is spent writing reports, bagging up property and logging it as evidence. This is boring stuff. But the two officers are excited. Many officers never catch someone in the act. And I feel the excitement too. Normally, going into overtime on a Night shift would drain the energy levels. But this is the last of a set of Nights, so they have some rest days coming. And it is worth it for this. They count the cash. £305.17. And they count each and every pill. Some of them are out of date and they pause to wonder about the pharmacist. But that is not their concern now. A screwdriver found in the bag means he was going equipped. As the end of the shift approaches, Winston turns to me and thumps the desk several times with both fists. 'Have I told you how much I love this fucking job?!' I leave them at 07:00, still bagging up exhibits.[30]

As we saw in the previous section when discussing meal breaks, for some jobs, time is no consideration. More normally, officers manage the approach of the end of their ten hours of duty very carefully. We have noted in Chapter 4 that officers will avoid jobs they believe might run on past the end of a shift. Those officers coming on to the new shift, they believe, should be tasked to take them, and there is generally a common understanding about this. But, much as with meal breaks, there is a delicate balancing act to be played. Taking two or three calls back-to-back will usually occupy most of a shift with purposeful activity and leave plenty of paperwork to run down the clock at the end of the shift. On a Night shift, this might also fit the pattern of demand as well. At the start of the shift, calls to domestic disputes or reports of burglary will be more frequent than at 04:00. But there is an art to selecting the jobs you respond to.

## F. Choosing Jobs

The researchers got a sense of pushing water uphill at times. Response officers got to know the regulars on their patch. These were street-drinkers and beggars, drug users and dealers, domestic abuse calls and some of the persistent prolific offenders (PPOs). They also knew key addresses. A call over the radio for officers to respond was, frequently, greeted by exclamations of fake surprise or by groans. For some officers, these calls were easy because they tended to follow a familiar pattern. For others, they were frustrating and to be avoided, precisely because they had attended that address too many times already. But their predictability meant that an officer will have a better idea of how to manage the rest of the shift.

Other duties also provided a good deal of certainty. The Specially Trained Officer (STO), trained to handle sexual assault and rape cases, sent to hospital with a woman to gather forensics evidence following an attempted rape, knew how his ten-hour shift would pan out (see n 12 above). While standing guard at a crime scene or on constant observation over someone detained deemed at risk

---

[30] Response, Kirk Machan, July 2015.

of self-harm might be boring work, they too provided a deal of certainty. Officers assigned to deal with missing persons for that shift often complained about the work. Much of the work was concerned with people reported missing from care, whether that be a children's home or adult care. The names were often familiar, some being reported two or three times a week. Responding to missing persons entailed checks on likely addresses, taking statements from relatives or carers and recording all these efforts, usually to find that the person returned of their own accord sometime after their official curfew. It was frustrating and thankless work, and definitely not deemed 'proper police work'. However, for some, and much like the STO, the work 'has to be done by someone, so why not me?'[31]

These choices make some sense and follow from our points about the management of time. But officers then expressed other preferences that were more personal. One officer said he 'doesn't do sudden deaths'. He hated dealing with dead bodies (not an unreasonable phobia) and so he was never sent to them.[32] Others openly declared that they 'don't do traffic'. In one team, the Sergeant set a challenge to get some traffic tickets. It wasn't so much performance management as an effort to get officers to use their time productively between emergency calls. He called it his 'OSCO Challenge'.[33] Spencer refused to engage with the challenge. Spotting a taxi one night, he noted that it was doing 40mph in a 30mph zone, had taken an illegal right turn and had a broken brake light. Pulling it over, he spoke to the driver, who wasn't particularly polite or respectful. Returning to the patrol car, Spencer commented, 'I was in danger of giving an OSCO there!'[34] For others, traffic was a specialty that they enjoyed, and it was in these ways that officers began to think about where they might want to go after they became bored with Response.

## III. Place

As the geographical area of beats and divisions[35] has grown during austerity, we noted the importance of local knowledge to the work of police officers. This sounds like an obvious statement but it does need some discussion, as it affects decision-making. If discretion is about the use of good judgement and policing with the consent of the community, knowing the people and places you are policing must be a part of that. What we have observed is a change in an understanding of local knowledge. Technology has been a part of this change. Each force developed and

---

[31] Response, Farquhar Road, November 2016.
[32] Response, Arlesdale Green, February 2018.
[33] OSCO standing for Officer Seen Conditional Offer and also known as a TOR, Traffic Offence Report.
[34] Response, [Redacted] September 2016.
[35] We use the label 'division' to refer to the sub-areas into which the geographical area of the Constabulary is divided for administrative purposes. However, different forces use different labels for these sub-areas.

rolled out new systems during the course of our research, all intended to allow officers access to information and intelligence on mobile and handheld devices. We will discuss these further in Chapter 9, but they promised more than they delivered. One Sergeant, involved in the user-testing of these new systems, was very enthusiastic about their potential. He described a world in which Response officers would drive through an area and be able to see that it is a burglary hotspot, or that the address they have been despatched to was connected to drugs or firearms. It would reduce radio traffic, which would help because the number of channels has been cut back.[36] But for all the promise, to use the technology while responding required a second officer in the car, and that was a rare sight. We provided company for officers who spent most shifts alone because, as a rule, only tutors and their tutee would be double-crewed.

When we started the fieldwork, Radio Control Room staff were dedicated to working with one geographical area. They knew the patch and they also knew the officers. They would meet new officers as they joined a unit and, where it worked, the Control Room staff became almost part of the team. As time went by, this changed. Operators were expected to cover wider areas, just as Response officers were. Officers began to joke about the mistakes made by Control Room staff, sending officers to the wrong London Road, for example. But they began to notice that they were attending incidents with less information. One Neighbourhood officer complained that a Response officer had undone all his efforts to resolve a long-running neighbour dispute. Unaware of the history, the Response officer had reached a quick conclusion based on limited and largely superficial information. He assumed the frail old woman was the innocent party rather than the noisy family with vehicle parts and unwashed children in the front garden. This was not an unreasonable assumption, drawing on most officers' experience, and Response officers are under pressure to clear jobs quickly.[37] However, had the Response officer known the area better, or had the Control Room had the time to pass on information, the Neighbourhood officer might not have had to subsequently apologise to the family concerned.

Having said that, we were often struck by just how well officers knew parts of the city. In quiet moments, we would be taken on a tour, highlighting features of the towns and cities that are familiar to the officers but go largely unremarked upon by others. It is a very particular view of the city.

> On one Late shift, a Response officer pointed out some key landmarks. A water tower that was lit up acted as a beacon for people who don't know the area who come looking for drugs or prostitutes. It is always worth watching out for people navigating towards it. Then, shortly after midnight, he points out a strange nocturnal migration, one that will be familiar to many officers. As money is paid into a bank account at midnight, queues form at cashpoints to withdraw the money before any direct debits are taken out.

---

[36] Response, Kirk Machan, September 2015.
[37] Neighbourhood, Abbey, June 2016.

They then go to the 24-hour off-licence for booze and cigarettes. As the officer commentates on this pattern, he stops to speak to two young girls, maybe sixteen years' old. They have been sent out by their parents to do the cashpoint run and to buy the booze. 'What a life! What a world!'[38]

This officer couldn't understand this life, in many respects, but he kept an eye on those midnight migrations. These were vulnerable people, carrying cash. There was always the potential for trouble. The importance of a knowledge of place became more apparent when things began to happen at speed. However, the growing size of Neighbourhood beats and the stretching of Response officer resources that resulted from austerity undermined this local knowledge.

# IV. Austerity

In a written statement to Parliament, reporting the funding grant for the police in 2016/17, the then Minister of Policing announced a better than expected settlement.[39] Security concerns, following – among others – the terrorist attacks in Paris, had made it politically inexpedient to continue to cut the budget. However, in the same announcement, he referred to the previous years of austerity. He declared that forces were reducing 'costs and duplication', working with other emergency services through 'co-location and collaboration' and moving officers from the 'back office' to the 'front line'. At the same time, the Inspectorate of Constabulary had identified scope for further efficiencies through better use of IT, smarter procurement, and improvements in productivity.[40] Our observations have been of street-level officers, performing routine patrols and responding to emergency calls for service on a daily basis. Our perspective is, therefore, that of the subaltern. However, in engaging with senior officers as we present our research material and with a steering group, we have also been aware of the discussions and debates developing at a senior level. These debates have then filtered down to officers, partly as rumours and then as finished, polished, strategies for change. While we have not been insiders in the debates, we have nevertheless discerned distinct tiers of decision-making in response to austerity. There was a strategic level, one in which senior officers discussed rational models of change. At a middle management level, that is those Chief Inspectors, Inspectors and Sergeants concerned with the oversight of the day-to-day, there were coping strategies developed to make

---

[38] Response, Ffarquhar Road, June 2015.

[39] House of Commons, *Police Grant Report England and Wales 2016/17*, HCWS426, *Written Questions and Answers and Written Statements* HCWS426, 17 December 2015 www.parliament.uk/business/publications/written-questions-answers-statements/written-statement/Commons/2015-12-17/HCWS426/.

[40] Her Majesty's Inspectorate of Constabulary, *Increasing Efficiency in the Police Service: the Role of Collaboration* (London, HMIC, 2012); Her Majesty's Inspectorate of Constabulary, *PEEL: Police Efficiency 2015* (London, HMIC, 2015).

ends meet in the short term. At the street-level, officers recognised these choices and adopted their own ways of making sense of the competing demands and the expectations placed upon them. We will briefly consider the first two before turning in more detail to the third tier.

## A.  Strategic Choices

At the outset of our research, Force A operated using a model that separated out key functions, noticeably Response teams from Neighbourhood teams, but they were aligned in geographical divisions. Since then, strategic decisions have been taken to change the way business is carried out. First, key functions have been centralised. While Neighbourhood teams remain decentralised across the force, the number of officers has fallen and they each cover a bigger beat. At one point, there were serious discussions about the future for the role of Police Community Support Officers (PCSOs). Response was 'brigaded' together and placed on a much more fragmented shift rota to better manage peaks and troughs in demand. These larger teams covered wider patches and, in theory, might be deployed across 'fuzzy boundaries' to cover the whole force area. Technology, in the form of mobile devices, would facilitate such flexibility. Training became an entirely central role and not something done (at least officially) within local units. Communications (that is the Radio Control Room) formed discrete teams working with the same police officers and covering the same geographical beats. They were now also centralised and operated to achieve economies of scale.

Second, the number of police stations open to the public was drastically cut back and the hours of opening also reduced. Plans for the closure and selling off of some stations and other estate assets were announced, but progress proved slow. Nevertheless, a number of stations were mothballed. Some new facilities were built to accommodate specialist teams and to enable the wider reorganisation. As we have already alluded to, the number of Custody Suites has been significantly reduced.

At face value, these measures represented economies, simply trying to continue to deliver the same service with fewer resources. The 'fuzzy' boundaries recognised that the demand for services was not evenly distributed across the force. However, they also recognised, if belatedly, that demands have changed. Foot traffic through police stations was not very heavy, so the closure of some receptions for public visitors recognised that most people use the phone to contact the police, either in an emergency or for more routine interactions. And on paper, there were economies of scale to be realised in centralising certain functions. These choices also maintained the force's activities across the array of duties it had carried out in the past. Talk of merging Armed Response Vehicles with Traffic, or of cutting Neighbourhood personnel would have represented a significant shift in the way the force went about its business. The changes, as they were set out, avoided any such hard choices. The investment in new technologies, in part funded by central government innovation funding, did represent an effort to develop efficiencies and new ways of working. Despite this, the changes represented more retrenchment and reorganisation than repositioning and were a very rational and top-down response to the challenges of austerity.[41]

## B.  Local Expediencies

While such strategies were developed, it was the responsibility of supervisory ranks (by which we mean Inspectors and Sergeants) to cope with diminishing resources and undiminished demand. Again, these ranks have not been the focus of our research. However, we have noted the ways in which resources were stretched more thinly. At the very basic level, officers were increasingly deployed in singly-crewed cars rather than in pairs. Sergeants recognised there were safety concerns in doing this, but this was often a less pressing issue than the need to have cars on the road. Neighbourhood officers were frequently deployed (or 'abstracted') to cover gaps in Response teams, or on operations that took them to other areas of the force. The fleet of vehicles was worked harder and replaced less frequently. At the outset of the research, cars were taken off the road after 120,000 miles. Three years later, this had risen to 140,000 miles. Other resources that officers might previously have drawn upon were similarly stretched, whether that was the Dog Team or a helicopter. This last was shared with other neighbouring forces and became a rare sight in parts of the force. This stretching of resources meant that, on a busy shift, a Sergeant might find her team thin on the ground, if officers were tied up in Custody with prisoners, or waiting for Traffic or the Dog Team to assist.

## C.  Austerity at Street Level

These rational strategic responses and more pragmatic coping mechanisms fed through to affect the context in which officers were making decisions during the six years of our research. On the surface, some of this was cosmetic, not fundamentally affecting the way officers worked. However, over a period of months, observing one Neighbourhood officer, Bertie, in Arlesdale police station, the team slowly reduced in size, losing officers to transfers who were not replaced. The Response team in the station was moved to be 'brigaded' elsewhere, leaving much of the station empty. Shortages of vehicles meant that Bertie and colleagues would often have to act as a taxi service for the PCSOs who were attending surgeries or walking beats at some distance from the station. At break times, they no longer sat with Response officers, sharing information and stories about their patch.

---

[41] G Boyne and R Walker, 'Strategy Content and Public Service Organizations' (2004) 14 *Journal of Public Administration Research and Theory* 231.

For information and intelligence, they spent the first part of every shift browsing the records of recent incidents on the police database.[42] This loss of connection and camaraderie seemed very real to Bertie and his fellow officers. And around them, Arlesdale police station had no future and was being cannibalised to meet the needs of those stations that were part of the longer-term plans. Similar neglect at another station meant that officers had to drive 23 miles to clean their car. The pressure hose, air pump and other equipment no longer functioned at Maron, so they had to go to Kildane instead and when they arrived there one afternoon, they found a queue of officers' vehicles waiting to use the valeting facilities.[43]

At about the same time, in Ffarquhar Road police station, a Response team had grown in numbers and in the area it was responsible for. Officers from another station were relocated to join the team and, while the new colleagues integrated well, officers struggled to get to know the streets in the expanded district.

> An officer, despatched to a Grade One call, gets lost. He radios for advice, but the Radio Control Room operator doesn't know the area either. He used to cover another area altogether and is covering this patch today for the first time. With the increasing distances to cover and the confusion over directions, the officers arrive to find the incident largely resolved, an ambulance having long since attended the scene.[44]

For officers only peripherally affected by changes, the smallest things still disrupted their work patterns. When the Radio Control Room worked well, the operator would send officers they knew to jobs they were suited to. They would avoid sending a singly-crewed car to a domestic dispute. And they would always pass on the details of previous calls from an address or a telephone number so the officer was better prepared for what was to come. But as the Radio Control Rooms became more stretched, there was less time to handle each incident and less local knowledge to call on. Officers were required to call a service desk for further details rather than clog up the air on the radio with further queries about an address or a vehicle registration. As mobile devices, including laptops and handheld tablets, were introduced, officers might search for the information themselves, but this depended on finding a good spot to park up and get a signal and, again, took time.[45]

Stretching Response in this way brought apparent efficiencies, distributing work more evenly and ensuring coverage without having to draw on Neighbourhood officers to fill in during times of high demand. But lots of things were lost. Sergeants deployed officers in singly-crewed cars more frequently, unless there were not enough cars available. Changes to technology and the working patterns of the Radio Control Room made that simple stretching of resources amplify the problems those officers encountered as they tried to perform even relatively routine duties.

---

[42] Neighbourhood, Arlesdale Green, September and October 2014.
[43] Territorial Support, Maron, January 2015.
[44] Response, Ffarquhar Road, June 2015.
[45] Response, Hackerbeck, March 2016.

Similarly, for a Neighbourhood officer in Abbey police station, a small town on the edge of the force area, the accumulated changes meant he thought about jobs differently. He tried to avoid arresting anyone at all costs. It could take hours to process someone through Custody and, because there were fewer cells available, an officer might have to go 30 miles to lock up a shoplifter. Once you were there, you were in the hands of the Custody Sergeant and so lost control of time which, as we have discussed, is something officers avoid where possible. It was no longer worth pursuing shoplifters.

> Simon is called to deal with a shoplifter who has been detained by store detectives. Response are all busy. Simon arrives to find a drunk woman. She has arrived in town on holiday with her family. They are all booked into the hotel and expecting her to join them. Simon turns a blind eye to the fact that her breath smells of alcohol. She sounds sober in the manner of her speaking and she is contrite. He has a poor sense of smell, he tells us, and couldn't detect alcohol on her breath. In theory, he should have arrested her and taken her in to Custody to sober up before she was interviewed. Instead, he seeks the consent of his Sergeant and interviews her there and then. He takes an image of her on his BWC for the records. All she will be getting is a Fixed Penalty Notice in any case, so why make more of it than needed?[46]

In this way, Simon's use of discretion was significantly affected by resource considerations, principally that of time. He was on his way to another job, a neighbourhood dispute that he had been involved in resolving for some time. Because Response were busy, he was called away. He needed to get back, not least because there were two PCSOs out on foot to pick up at appointed times and places later on. Everything reinforced his natural inclination to avoid Custody and we might argue that there were good grounds for this (see Chapter 7 for a discussion of the alternatives to arrest). But the decisions were not taken in the interests of justice or, we might argue, with the best interests of the shoplifter in mind. Fully sober, might she have been better advised to act differently? The overriding factors behind the decisions were ones of time and resource.

## D. Other Agencies

An aspect of austerity that was largely omitted from the rational plans developed in police forces was the simple fact that austerity did not occur in one organisation in isolation. This was most apparent to Response officers as they picked up the pieces of broken lives. Much of a Response officer's time was spent dealing with domestic disputes, mental ill-health, or with missing persons. All other services were being withdrawn and cut to the bone. For example, on one occasion two officers spent hours with a woman who represented a danger to herself. They did not want to take her into Custody or to hospital because she had a young daughter and they

---

[46] Neighbourhood, Abbey, April 2016.

did not know what would happen to her. So they waited for a GP or a social worker to become available.[47] A growing awareness of vulnerability and, in particular, of child sexual exploitation meant that people missing from care were more regularly reported to the police, even if they had only missed their curfew by a few minutes. One agency's risk management procedure becomes a high-risk missing person for the police. On one shift in one Response team, Spencer dealt with one missing person report while another colleague took three reports and a further officer took two more.[48] Each demanded the completion of paperwork, the identification of family, known friends and associates, places to look and actions to take. Police risk management procedures then ensured that action was taken to find someone or to ensure their safety. The attention to the paperwork and record-keeping, evidencing the actions taken and the assessments made, was much greater given the growing concerns for vulnerability. This work consumes resources and could not be passed off, deferred, or refused. Other work could become merely an optional extra.

## V. The System

In Chapter 2 (see the text at fn 63 of that chapter), receiving a nod from an officer signified more than thanks. It indicated that we had understood the situation and the choices and decisions the officers were making as events unfolded. On a very different occasion, another form of understanding coalesced during a Night shift with Spencer, a Response officer.

> At 02:25, we hear radio traffic. There is a scramble (that is a pursuit) going on further north. Way too far off for Spencer to think about joining in. He has finished checking a van parked in an odd location and is at a junction watching traffic while listening to the scramble on the radio. Cars have joined the pursuit, but the car giving directions is a Traffic officer I have met while observing one of his colleagues. He is giving clear details of the pursuit, the direction of travel and the traffic offences committed. The helicopter is up as well. Four lads then run from the car and scatter. Officers pursue, again others I recognise from the Territorial Support team. They are making arrests, but it is unclear if they have got all four.
>
> As we listen, a car passes us at speed. Spencer responds and pursues down narrow residential streets with cars parked on both sides. It is very tight, but there is nobody on the streets. He tries to shout up for help on the radio, but the airways are still full with the other pursuit. He gets a brief call out, but his radio is old and the button is awkward. He couldn't give a commentary anyway with all the other radio traffic. And the pursuit is a short one. The car is abandoned in a cul-de-sac. Traffic and other officers begin to arrive, but it is a job for a dog now. Spencer is partly exhilarated, but partly embarrassed. He is an Advanced Driver, but this is not something he does very often on Response. He fluffed it a bit.

---

[47] Territorial Support, Brandham, December 2013.
[48] Response, Hackerbeck, October 2016.

For Spencer, the accumulation of small changes and efficiencies mean he cannot easily radio for assistance. He feels isolated, following a car without knowing who is on board and what he might be dealing with. Should he just back off for his own safety? Is it worth the possibility of injury to a passer-by or of damage to parked cars? He does find the car, a couple of streets over. There might be some forensics, but that is doubtful and so may not be worth the cost. The car will probably just be returned to the owner who, at this time, is probably still unaware it has been stolen. The sense is of frustration. Radio kit that is getting a bit old, with a button falling off. A car not really up to pursuing a newer, faster car. No air time on the radio.[49]

Much like catching a thief red-handed, a pursuit, even a short one, is a bit of a rush for officer and observer alike. For an officer, trained in this form of short pursuit, practice is an important part of retaining the skills learnt on a course.[50] But the episode reveals something of the way the different functions interact and come together at key points in time. Officers, who were, moments ago, mooching or taking a break at a motorway services, quickly coordinate and, knowing the roads and likely routes, look for opportunities to stop or to box in the fleeing car. No police dogs arrived before the foot pursuit was over, but from other observations such an incident is what they have trained for and relish.[51] Having also observed some of the other officers, during the course of this research, allowed for some insight into the actions of those other participants. And as Spencer engaged in his short pursuit, struggling to drive at speed in narrow streets while also trying to communicate over the radio, we learned something of the skill it entails. Finally, we also got some insight into the pace with which an officer is expected to switch from being tired in the middle of a quiet Night shift to being alert and automatically switching to a high-speed, adrenaline-fuelled pursuit. For all the shift can be about managing time and jobs, there remains always the possibility of excitement and of danger. And, in important ways, these too affect the decisions officers make.

## VI. Concluding Remarks and Recap

An awareness of all the factors noted in this chapter is absolutely key to understanding how and when officers will use their street powers. We have tried to explain here the fundamental role that the shift plays in the mind-set of an officer when she is placed in positions where she has discretion over whether, and how, to utilise her street powers. We need to understand practicalities such as the time

---

[49] Response, Hackerbeck, March 2016.
[50] M Rowe et al, 'Learning and Practicing Police Craft' (2016) 5 *Journal of Organizational Ethnography* 276.
[51] A Dog Handler, being observed on another occasion, expressed disappointment when a short vehicle pursuit came to an end when the car ahead stopped. The officer remarked, 'I lost interest at that point. I wanted him to run to give the dog a good stretch of his legs!' (Dog Team, Midgewater, September 2018).

remaining on the shift or until refs, and the local knowledge an officer may or may not possess. These largely under-explored factors can all influence whether a vehicle is stopped, a search carried out, or an arrest made. But we also need to understand better how the often-dramatic changes in pace of police work affect decision-making. How, for example, does the sudden change from boring desk-work or waiting for hours in a car to high-speed chase influence how an officer uses their powers? Finally, as we noted towards the end of Chapter 4, we also need to consider the fluidity of the police service – the fact that the officer tasked to respond to a particular job may have previously been in a different role, or with a different team. Policing careers and the realities of frontline police work, which we believe can often only be uncovered by long-term ethnographic work with officers, play an under-reported role in the utilisation of street powers.

Before we move on to consider the specific use of certain powers, we should pause to reflect on the discussion so far. The last two chapters in particular have sought to draw attention to the way in which the working practicalities of the police Constable tend to dominate their decision-making process. However, these practical realities and constraints have largely been under-estimated in the debates about the regulation of police powers. Our argument is that focus on an overarching 'police culture' is fundamentally misplaced. 'Police culture' does not explain the use of discretion, nor the outcomes in terms of any disproportionate use of powers. There are undoubtedly many shared working understandings, practices, and priorities across units, shifts, stations, and even forces, but the police forces we observed were fragmented along all these lines. To understand how police street powers are utilised in practice we must take into account police careers and roles, supervisory relationships, the shift, and available resources. We must also acknowledge that police 'discretion' is far wider than merely the invocation discretion available to an officer when confronting a suspect. Discretion, in terms of choosing jobs and managing when and where to patrol, also plays a fundamental role in how powers may be used later on.

# 6

## Stop and Account! Proactive Interactions with the Public

Regardless of the role of an individual officer, or the shift they are working, a fundamental feature of frontline police is proactive interaction with members of the public. This chapter focuses on police-initiated public encounters that occur prior to any arrest, request for voluntary attendance at a police station, other disposal, or words of advice. It focuses on the legal powers that officers possess to stop vehicles (a 'stop check'), or to stop and search an individual. It also focuses on situations where an officer approaches a member of the public to ask their identity or their business (usually referred to as a 'stop and account'). These interactions with members of the public are usually undertaken when the officer possesses some suspicion about the individual. Depending on their outcome, the stop can escalate to a search which, should anything be found, can be the start of a formal criminal justice process. The initial stop, which is not usually recorded, provides officers with significant discretion in terms of who is approached and who is left alone, and an officer has little supervision or accountability. These encounters can be inconvenient, embarrassing, even traumatising for members of the public, and can contribute to individuals or groups believing they are being harassed by the police. As with all elements of police work where discretion is at its most unfettered, police stops can result in discriminatory effects, and over-policed groups.[1] However, officers see these powers as essential to investigating or preventing crime and, for some officers in certain roles, the stopping of members of the public can become the dominant tactic to uncover or disrupt crime.

## I. Stop and Account

Stop and account should be a strange focus for a book on police street powers. This is because, while the state grants British police statutory powers to stop vehicles, stop and search suspects, and arrest those suspected of committing offences, they are not – in contrast to many other jurisdictions – granted any power to

---

[1] P Waddington, *Policing Citizens: Authority and Rights* (London, UCL Press, 1999) 38–39.

force members of the public to stop and account.[2] However, stop and account was seen by officers to be an essential tool in frontline policing, and on occasion briefings would recommend that officers stopped named individuals in order to update the force intelligence system.[3] That said, the manner and extent to which stop and account was used varied widely between roles and individual officers,[4] and in some areas appeared to be diminishing in use. In 2008/09, the last year in which records were kept, there were 2,211,598 recorded stop and accounts (in contrast to 142,763 recorded stop and searches) in England and Wales.[5] As it does not exist as a statutory power, or even one enshrined in guidance in the Codes of Practice supporting the Police and Criminal Evidence Act 1984 (PACE), defining stop and account can be problematic. In 2011, then Police Minister Nick Herbert described it as the situation '… where individuals are merely asked to account for their presence, actions and so on. It is not a statutory power. It is one step on from the general conversations that officers have with members of the public every day'.[6] Previous guidance from PACE Code A noted that it *did not* include:

> general conversations, such as when giving directions to a place, or when seeking witnesses. It also does not include occasions on which an officer is seeking general information or questioning people to establish background to incidents which have required officers to intervene to keep the peace or resolve a dispute'.[7]

The stereotypical "Ello 'ello 'ello, what's going on' ere then?', is the classic example of a stop and account, but there are no particular words or standard phrases that need to be used. A typical stop and account would occur when an officer slowed down or stopped their patrol car, wound down the window and started a conversation with a member of the public such as 'Hi, are you alright?' Usually the short conversation would see the member of the public volunteer information about what they were doing or where they were going, but occasionally an officer would be more direct in asking questions such as, 'Where have you come from?', 'Where are you going now?', and 'Are you known to the police?' Repeat offenders would usually be chatted to and addressed by name: 'Everything alright, Michael? How long have you been out [of prison] for now …? I hear you're hanging around with Chrissie these days …' Conversations with previous offenders were usually

---

[2] Although under the Police Reform Act 2002, s 50, an officer may request the name and address of an individual who is acting in an anti-social manner and it is an offence for them not to comply.

[3] Response, Trollshaws, September 2016.

[4] Norris suggests that Constables are wary of the risk in interactions with the public, believe they can easily go wrong and result in a disciplinary process. While this was true, we found that only a few participants seemed to avoid interactions unless absolutely necessary (C Norris, 'Avoiding Trouble: The Patrol Officer's Perception of Encounters with the Public' in M Weatheritt (ed), *Police Research: Some Future Prospects* (Avebury, Police Foundation, 1989).

[5] *The Guardian* (22 January 2011).

[6] Hansard HC First Delegated Legislation Committee, 2 February 2011, Col 4.

[7] Now repealed PACE, Code A, paras 4.12 (2003) and 4.13 (2009).

good humoured from both sides and, ironically, officers often adopted a more cheerful demeanour with them than with members of the public not known to them.

Following the McPherson Report, officers were required to make a brief official record of each encounter, along with the ethnicity of the individual, but in 2009 the mandatory requirement to record these encounters was abolished,[8] principally to reduce pressure on police time.[9] In neither of the forces observed was a record of stop and accounts made. There is also no legal requirement that a member of the public acquiesces to the request of the officer to either stop or engage in conversation: 'Police officers have no power to require a person to Stop and Account. Officers are not obliged to inform a person that he need not stop.'[10] Consent on behalf of the member of the public to stop and provide information is therefore essential to the utility of stop and account. The extent to which this consent is genuine is, however, highly questionable.[11] In other areas of law, consent is an agreement made through choice by someone with the freedom and capacity to make that choice.[12] Applying that here, the member of the public should be in a position where they both understand that they do not have to comply with the request and have the power to refuse. However, when a police officer faces a member of the public, there is not an 'equality of power', and 'full consent is therefore, in practice unattainable'.[13] Put another way, the definition of consent in the context of stop and account covers a sliding scale from genuine agreement, to agreement resulting from ignorance of alternative courses of action, through to reluctant submission.[14] Regardless of how polite and cheerful a request to stop and account (and most requests were both), there was still likely to be – in the minds of the member of the public at least – the underlying and unspoken threat of force, either of a stop search or an arrest, that so characterises the police.[15]

---

[8] Police and Criminal Evidence Act 1984 (Codes of Practice) (Revisions to Code A) (No 2) Order 2008, SI 2008/3146. Code A, para 4.12 now states, 'There is no national requirement for an officer who requests a person in a public place to account for themselves, i.e. their actions, behaviour, presence in an area or possession of anything, to make any record of the encounter or to give the person a receipt'. See K Reid, 'Race Issues and Stop and Search: Looking Behind the Statistics' (2009) 73 *Journal of Criminal Law* 183 for more on the brief life of the stop and account form.

[9] The Independent Review of Policing Report 2008 (the Flanagan Report) noted that it took an officer an average of seven minutes to record a stop and account. It was subsequently claimed that abolishing reporting requirements would save 450,000 police hours each year (Hansard HC First Delegated Legislation Committee, 2 February 2011, Col 5).

[10] *R (on the application of Diedrick) v Chief Constable of Hampshire* [2012] EWHC 2144 (Admin) para 9.

[11] Waddington, *Policing Citizens* 140.

[12] Sexual Offences Act 2003, s 74.

[13] D Dixon et al, 'Consent and the Legal Regulation of Policing' (1990) 17 *Journal of Law and Society* 245, 346. See also A Sanders and R Young, 'Police Powers' in T Newburn (ed), *Handbook of Policing*, 2nd edn (Cullompton, Willan Publishing, 2008).

[14] D Dixon, *Law in Policing: Legal Regulation and Police Practices* (Oxford, Clarendon, 1997) 91.

[15] E Bittner, *The Functions of the Police in Modern Society* (University of Minnesota, National Institute of Mental Health, Center for Studies of Crime and Delinquency, 1970).

As Ewing argues, 'it is far from clear that stop and account is an entirely non-coercive process'.[16]

> [We are l]ooking for a suspect who allegedly tried to groom some children. We see a man in a hoodie walking along a path through a park. 'Can I have a word, please?' says Kenny as the man passes. [The man] doesn't look up and starts to walk past. 'If you don't stop I will have to hold you to stop and account' [says Kenny]. The man continues walking, his back now to us and he is about six-yards away. Kenny holds up his hand even though the man can't see him. 'Stop and Account!' he calls. The man stops in his tracks and Kenny walks [up to the man] to ask where he is going. The man grudgingly responds and explains who he is and where he is going.[17]

This is an extreme example of an officer utilising the lack of knowledge of the member of the public to essentially coerce information from them. It should be noted that in six years of research this was the only example of this practice we observed. However, it was also a rare occasion when a member of the public, asked to stop and account, did not do so:

> A young lad walks up ahead and just casually ducks into a side street that is bollarded off. Spencer is sure he knew that and did it to dodge us. He drives around to see him coming out of another little close. Spencer follows and calls to the man. He doesn't even stop, just turns around to say he is off to the cafe. He has no intention of passing the time of day. Does he know he doesn't have to? This raises Spencer's interest. As he is puzzling, a car with two lads on board pulls out ahead. I note them for discussion later. He is trying to work out where the original lad is going, where the cafe might be and then drives around. The lad is then to be seen walking across open land towards some shops. Spencer drives around to park the car and discreetly watch him. He does go to the shops next to a cafe. Spencer is satisfied, but still has a sense that the lad was not right.[18]

It is impossible to assess from our research in how many of these encounters the individual realised they did not have to respond. But we would conclude from our observations that, while a police officer may have no statutory *authority* to 'stop and account' members of the public, in effect it remains one of the most significant police *powers*.

There is currently no formal statutory or common law guidance as to when and under what circumstances officers should utilise stop and account.[19] As we will see, this is in contrast with the power of stop and search (although not vehicle stop checks). Without formal guidance, officers draw upon training, the guidance

---

[16] K Ewing, *Bonfire of the Liberties: New Labour, Human Rights, and the Rule of Law* (Oxford University Press, 2010) 20.

[17] Response, Bree, September 2016.

[18] Response, Hackerbeck, March 2016.

[19] Although as employees of a public authority, officers should use all their powers in a manner which is compliant with the European Convention on Human Rights' provisions on discrimination (Art 14) and not use them in a way which discriminates against any of the Equality Act 2010's 'protected characteristics'.

of more experienced officers, their own experience and their freedom and desire to be proactive, when determining whether to stop a member of the public. Certain roles were more conducive to conducting stop and account. Officers involved in Territorial Support, for example, were more likely to stop individuals than Response officers – the former role being a more proactive one. Additionally, Night shifts saw a higher proportion of stops than Early shifts. Finally, on an individual level, some officers would stop more individuals than their colleagues, usually explaining this as being a result of their penchant for 'proactive' policing. Identifying why officers chose to stop some members of the public and not others was, therefore, difficult and, while officers were usually able to explain why they had stopped a specific individual, they often struggled to explain in more general terms what factors would make a stop likely.[20]

In line with Sacks' description of the police's use of 'incongruity procedure',[21] officers targeted individuals who looked 'out of place' or not 'seeming to fit',[22] or someone 'out of the ordinary'.[23] This was also the case for vehicle checks (below). However, this by itself is not particularly helpful without further investigation of what it was that made an individual 'seem out of place'. Looking different in terms of dress style could also arouse suspicion, although as we will see, looking 'the type' to be involved in criminal activity was also a factor in attracting police attention even in areas where this was commonplace. Avoiding eye contact, or acting 'shifty',[24] or 'shying away' from or avoiding the police[25] (for example choosing to use side alleys rather than a main road when officers were present)[26] would arouse suspicion and make a stop and account more likely.

Contextual factors also affected the likelihood of an individual being stopped. Presence in areas associated with previous or regular criminality (usually burglary or drug dealing),[27] or where a crime or suspect was reported,[28] increased the chance of a stop and account. A direction to attend such hot-spots sometimes took officers away from their usual area (the term 'beat' was rarely used), which could also lead to more stops, as one Territorial Support officer explained:

> It depends on how well we know the area. If we don't know the area we have to stop and question everyone to find out what's going on … anyone that's walking around we will tend to just stop and speak to and just see who they are and if they are of any interest to us.[29]

---

[20] See also B Loftus, *Police Culture in a Changing World* (Oxford, Oxford University Press, 2009) 123.

[21] H Sacks, 'Notes on Police Assessment of Moral Character' in D Sudnow (ed), *Studies in Social Interaction* (New York, The Free Press, 1972) 280; also Loftus, *Police Culture* 124.

[22] Response, Bree, September 2016.

[23] Night-time Economy Team, Knapford, October 2015.

[24] Territorial Support, Knapford, June 2014.

[25] Territorial Support, Knapford, September 2015.

[26] Territorial Support, Knapford, May 2015; Territorial Support, Knapford, September 2015.

[27] Specials, Maron, July 2015; Neighbourhood, Brandam, January 2014.

[28] Response, Bree, September 2016.

[29] Territorial Support, Knapford, March 2015.

The time of day was also an important factor. A member of the public on the street late at night was far more likely to be stopped. This was because, first, many officers felt that presence on the street after the pubs had closed demanded an explanation: 'This time of night (2am) we stop anybody because what are people doing out now?'[30] Second, officers were more likely to have the time to embark on proactive policing. Although Night shifts could be busy, they often entailed 'dead' hours where even Response officers could effectively go on patrol. For certain roles, especially Territorial Support ('We are more nosey'),[31] at night almost everyone would be stopped apart from the elderly: 'This time of night your sense of suspicion is heightened'.[32]

At other times, officers would stop and account after seeing (and indeed looking out for) certain 'trigger' behaviour from members of the public, particularly when the individual became aware of the police:

Annie: 'How they react to us …'

Alf: 'Yeah'.

Annie: '… you'll probably have noticed it as well, but when we drive past someone they will automatically go to their pockets, and you'll feel them checking … you know what's going through their heads – have they got drugs on them? Have they got something on them, have they left it at home, have they brought it out …? And you're looking for how they react to you … and you're trying to pick up on things, like people who won't even look at you, or even engage … Is it because they are wanted, is it because they don't want to speak to you, do they just not like the police … there could be a whole host of reasons'.

Alf: 'Certain officers will get onto body language a lot more than others and that's just based on your skills as a police officer'.[33]

However, as we will see when we consider stop and search, sometimes officers interpreted bodily behaviour in a different way or considered behaviour at either end of the spectrum to be suspicious. Acting nervously could lead to a stop – maybe the individual had something to hide? But so could acting too confidently – clearly they had a lot of experience of dealing with the police. Ultimately the police were trained and encouraged to be suspicious, and their experiences of occasionally being duped by someone who later committed an offence (sometimes combined with a loss of face in front of more experienced colleagues) made them more likely to take action. For some officers this was more pronounced than others:

Alf: 'It also depends on whether you have a proactive officer looking for crimes … rather than someone just reacting to them. … [our] predominant role is to go out there and disrupt and arrest and target criminals'.

Researcher: 'So the crime is always out there …?'

---

[30] Territorial Support, Lakeside, January 2015.
[31] Territorial Support, Knapford, February 2014.
[32] Territorial Support, Knapford, February 2014.
[33] Territorial Support, Knapford, March 2015.

Annie: 'We just have to go and find it, yep!'

Alf: 'It's all around you, you just have to find it' [laughs].[34]

The officers who considered themselves more proactive were often disparaging of officers they perceived to be purely reactive: 'If you're not smelling criminals everywhere, you're not doing your job'.[35] Inevitably, this led to officers admitting to stopping individuals based purely on a hunch, or 'a sense that something is not quite right'.[36] The lack of guidance from the law, and the lack of clarity expressed by officers as to the circumstances in which they decided to stop and account, raises serious questions as to how this de facto power is used. Individuals who were stopped regularly complained to officers about their treatment, often alleging harassment,[37] highlighting that a stop and account cannot be considered a merely harmless and two-way conversation between individuals, even though officers often interpreted it in this way. Further, as we will see later, a stop and account frequently led to a search, where individuals were faced with more overt coercion, inconvenience, and sometimes embarrassment or humiliation. While there were genuine concerns from the Government and the police about the effect of recording all stops, not least the additional inconvenience for the member of the public, our research indicated that the current situation of unfettered discretion, combined with a lack of regulation or structured guidance, can adversely affect the relationship between officers and members of the public. Indeed, it can potentially undermine the legitimacy of the police amongst communities, particularly in heavily-policed areas, an issue we will return to in Chapter 9.

## II. Vehicle Stop Checks

When not carrying out office-based tasks in the police station or talking to suspects, victims, or witnesses, officers spent the vast majority of their shift in a motor vehicle, patrolling areas proactively or travelling to and from addresses as tasked by their Sergeant or the Radio Control Room. Therefore, equally important to the power of stop and account was the power possessed by officers to 'stop check' (sometimes referred to as a 'routine road traffic check') vehicles and their occupants. Unlike the power to stop and account, the stop check power is enshrined in the statutory requirement that: 'A person driving a mechanically propelled vehicle on a road must stop the vehicle on being required to do so by a constable in uniform'.[38] The Road Traffic Act 1988, section 163(3) makes it an offence to fail to

---

[34] Territorial Support, Knapford, March 2015.

[35] Territorial Support, Knapford, March 2014.

[36] Neighbourhood, Brandam, January 2014. See also Loftus, *Police Culture* 123.

[37] Territorial Support, Knapford, March 2015; Territorial Support, Knapford, January 2016.

[38] Road Traffic Act 1988, s 165(1).

comply with an attempt by a uniformed officer to stop the vehicle.[39] There is no requirement that an officer possess any grounds of suspicion to stop a vehicle[40] and Bowling and Phillips argue section 163 stops are, 'used unfairly, have enormous community impact and yield little in crime detection or prevention.'[41] Once the vehicle has stopped, an officer possesses the power under section 164 to require the production of a driving licence from the driver, or under section 165 to obtain the name and address of the driver, and evidence of insurance documents or test certificates. Again, the officer does not need to show grounds for these requests, and it is an offence for the driver to fail to comply with these requests.

A stop check is therefore a more coercive tool than stop and account. Like stop and account, it places no restraints on an officer in terms of reasonable or even honest grounds of suspicion but, unlike stop and account, a failure to comply is a criminal offence. More proactive officers could spend an entire shift simply stopping vehicles to find out who their drivers were. They would also often use this opportunity to ask the details of the passengers, or more information about the driver or passengers (for example the purpose of their journey), although failure to disclose this additional information does not attract a legal sanction. In order to perform a stop check, the officer would put on their blue lights (and sometimes their siren) and follow the vehicle until it pulled over. If a vehicle refused to stop, the officer might choose to pursue if they were driving a suitable vehicle and were 'pursuit trained', otherwise they would radio in the details of the car that had 'made off' for other officers to look out for and hopefully stop.

As with stop and account, there is no requirement that a record is kept of stop checks, nor does PACE Code A currently apply to the use of section 163.[42] This means that, aside from the Human Rights Act 1998 and the Equality Act 2010, there are no statutory restrictions on the use of this power, despite the potential sanction attached to it. Further, the courts have defended the operation of section 163 in enabling officers to make random stops without any suspicion. In *Beard v Wood*[43] it was held that there was no need for an officer to suspect the driver had committed an offence, so long as she did so in good faith. In *Chief Constable of Gwent v Dash*[44] it was held that stopping cars at random (in this case to detect drink driving) was lawful. Crime detection was part of an officer's duty and it could not be said that they were acting capriciously or from indirect or improper motive. It is

---

[39] Section 163 does not apply to plain-clothed officers (*R (on the application of Rutherford) v Independent Police Complaints Commission* [2010] EWHC 2881 (Admin)).

[40] *Haashi (Shirwa Abdisayed) v HM Advocate* [2014] HCJAC 48 para 4.

[41] B Bowling and C Phillips, 'Disproportionate and Discriminatory: Reviewing the Evidence on Police Stop and Search' (2007) 70 *Modern Law Review* 936, 960–61.

[42] This was despite Home Office announcements in 2014 and 2016 that the requirement to record stop checks would be introduced.

[43] *Beard v Wood* [1980] RTR 454, considering the previous incantation of the power under the Road Traffic Act 1972, s 159.

[44] *Chief Constable of Gwent v Dash* [1986] RTR 41, upheld in *R (on the application of Beckett) v Aylesbury County Court* [2004] EWHC 100 (Admin) at para 13 per May LJ.

clear, therefore, that under what circumstances, and how frequently, officers use section 163 is not restricted by law in the absence of malpractice or discrimination. As a result, it is important to establish why officers choose to stop some vehicles and not others.

As with stop and account, officers were looking for something 'being out of place', 'not what you would expect to find here',[45] or 'drawing attention to itself'.[46] Again, officers often struggled to explain why certain vehicles had attracted their attention,[47] although sometimes a number-plate check or following the vehicle for a while would arrest the officer's suspicion. 'It's difficult to put my finger on exactly why I followed [the van] ... Intuition?'[48] Vehicles that were the 'type' to be used in crime were sometimes targeted, from battered white vans (burglary)[49] to 'sporty hatchbacks' or 'fast BMWs' (drug dealing).[50] Mirroring findings relating to stop and account, high-crime locations[51] or areas where 'Organised Crime Groups' (OCGs) have started moving to,[52] night-time shifts,[53] and the freedom the officer had to be proactive in their role all increased the rate of stop checks. After pub closing time on one shift, the observer noted, 'it just seems to be a fishing expedition at this time of night'.[54] On one Late shift, a single Territorial Support officer carried out 13 stop checks, three stop and accounts, and four stop searches.[55] Occasionally intelligence or suggestions from the Sergeant or Inspector could focus the attention of the officer on certain types of vehicles, for example when information suggested drug-dealers in a certain areas were travelling by mini-cab.[56] On other occasions, stop checks were carried out on vehicles matching the description of those reported over the radio for having been stolen, speeding, or containing suspected drunk-drivers. Officers were aware that the information provided might be wrong due to errors by a witness or a call handler, and so might also stop cars of a similar appearance, make, or model to that called in.

However, while for some officers the presence of one or more of these indicators would lead them to carry out a stop check, for other officers it would merely

[45] Response, Bree, September 2016.
[46] Response, Eriador, September 2017.
[47] This was less the case with Traffic officers, who would look for certain physical clues in order to perform stop checks: plates out of place, bald tyres, cracked light casings, and wear and tear to the vehicle. However, Traffic officers would also, on occasion, stop a vehicle driver on less easy-to-define behaviour.
[48] Response, Bree, September 2016.
[49] Territorial Support, Knapford, June 2014.
[50] Territorial Support, Knapford, September 2015; Territorial Support, Knapford, May 2015; Territorial Support, Lakeside, January 2015.
[51] Territorial Support, Knapford, September 2015.
[52] Territorial Support, Lakeside, January 2015.
[53] Territorial Support, Knapford, March 2014.
[54] Territorial Support, Knapford, March 2014.
[55] Territorial Support, Lakeside, January 2015. The totality of these stops uncovered only a single 'spliff'.
[56] Territorial Support, Knapford, June 2014; Territorial Support, Knapford, March 2014; Territorial Support, Lakeside, January 2015.

draw their attention to the vehicle and they would look to follow for a while. Sometimes this would be combined with a number-plate check over the radio, but often the officer would rely on their reading of what the occupants were doing once the police car or van was in their rear-view mirror. 'Unusual' movement or activity in the vehicle would most likely lead to a stop. For example, the driver of the car 'fidgeted with left hand',[57] or 'was arching his back a bit funny'.[58] It should be noted here that, as the police were normally tailing the vehicle, the actual *appearance* (particularly with regard to race) of the passengers was almost always unclear.

> Alf: Sometimes you'll get behind a vehicle and you'll see some lads, their heads moving, and them looking over (...) everything's unnatural, there's panic going on in the vehicle or there's something happening that they don't want you to deal with ... That's just like a trigger for us to say, 'they're uncomfortable now ... something not right'.[59]

On other occasions the movement of the vehicle itself would lead to a stop after the police came in to view. Accelerating,[60] turning off suddenly down a side alley,[61] or 'taking an usual route'[62] was likely to be interpreted as the driver hoping to 'shake off' the police and usually led to a stop check. As we will see below, on other occasions however, it was the mere presence together in a vehicle of a group of what, from their silhouettes, looked like young men, that would lead to a stop check of their vehicle, allowing questions to be asked of all the occupants. This inevitably led to what officers might call 'bad spots'. On one shift, a Territorial Support unit expressed embarrassment at carrying out three stop checks as the result of what they deemed to be 'bad spots' in 20 minutes. These included 'an OAP and a teacher', a 'family of four', and a woman.[63]

Finally, stop checks were likely to be carried out by officers on vehicles speeding,[64] driving carelessly, with non-functioning tail- or headlights,[65] or where the occupant was not wearing a seatbelt.[66] However while the outward reason for these stops was the same, the purpose varied. As has been noted elsewhere,[67] officers tend to avoid issuing tickets to 'ordinary people', preferring to give informal

---

[57] Territorial Support, Knapford, March 2014.

[58] Territorial Support, Knapford, January 2016.

[59] Territorial Support, Knapford, March 2015.

[60] Territorial Support, Knapford, March 2014.

[61] Territorial Support, Knapford, March 2014.

[62] Territorial Support, Lakeside, January 2015.

[63] Territorial Support, Knapford, March 2014.

[64] Neighbourhood, Shiloh, September 2015; Territorial Support, Knapford, July 2015.

[65] Territorial Support, Knapford, January 2016; Neighbourhood, Shiloh, September 2015.

[66] Territorial Support, Knapford, May 2015; Territorial Support, Knapford, July 2015; Territorial Support, Knapford, January 2016.

[67] R Grimshaw and T Jefferson, *Interpreting Police Work: Policy and Practice in Forms of Beat Policing* (London: Allen & Unwin, 1987) 162.

advice.[68] Officers usually explained their stop as being for reasons of safety, and their reason for taking no formal action because the occupants were 'decent people' (see below). In contrast, officers from proactive Territorial Support units often used minor traffic infringements as a pretext to carry out a stop check to identify the occupants of the vehicle. Where they were the 'criminal type', this check would allow them to gather intelligence (for example, who was now associating with whom) or disrupt the activity of an OCG (by issuing a traffic offence ticket or seizing the vehicle). This was not always the case, however, and some officers would be lenient in the face of minor traffic incursions to 'try and build bridges',[69] or gain the respect of those they had stopped: 'We're going to be in the area for some time, if you give them a [ticket] first time around, the relationship [is going to sour]'.[70] For one officer, letting a 'particularly nasty' OCG member off a ticket was part of a longer relationship between criminal and police officer which was beneficial to both: 'I must have arrested him five or six times for violent offences and not once have I had to fight or handcuff him'.[71]

# III.  Stop and Search

With the possible exception of arrest, the power of stop and search has probably attracted the most academic attention in studies of the police, providing, 'an excellent example of how excessive use of a police power can be dysfunctional or counterproductive'.[72] Stop and search has been a politically sensitive issue for senior police officers and politicians. This has been because: (a) stop and search is a coercive and intrusive power which deprives the suspect (albeit briefly) of their liberty;[73] and (b) it has disproportionately been used against ethnic minorities, particularly young black men.[74] Misuse of stop and search, particularly in deprived inner-city areas, was viewed as key causal factor of the early-1980s riots,[75] having already been identified as legally problematic by the Philips Commission, which reported in 1981.[76] While Waddington noted that stop and search 'epitomizes the exercise of police discretion',[77] in contrast with stop and account and stop checks,

---

[68] Despite their reputation for ticketing 'innocent citizens', and in the absence of targets, Traffic officers were no more inclined to give tickets than others.

[69] Response, Eriador, October 2017.

[70] Territorial Support, Knapford, July 2015.

[71] Territorial Support, Knapford, July 2015.

[72] Dixon, *Law in Policing* 79.

[73] PACE Code A 1.1; *Brazil v Chief Constable of Surrey* [1983] 1 WLR 1155.

[74] Bowling and Phillips, 'Disproportionate and Discriminatory'.

[75] Lord Scarman, *The Brixton Disorders 10–12 April 1981: Report of an Inquiry* (London, HMSO, 1981, Cmnd 8427).

[76] Royal Commission of Criminal Procedure, *The Investigation and Prosecution of Criminal Offences in England and Wales: The Law and Procedure* (London, HMSO, 1981, Cmnd 8092).

[77] Waddington, *Policing Citizens* 50.

there were significantly greater legal and policy restrictions placed on officers as to the circumstances in which a search could be made.

Our observations took place in the context of what officers perceived to be an 'attack' on their powers of stop and search, initially led by then Home Secretary, Theresa May. The Home Office highlighted statistics indicating the continuing racial disproportionality of the use of the power,[78] revised PACE Code of Practice A, and, in conjunction with the College of Policing,[79] introduced the *Best Use of Stop and Search Scheme*. The Scheme required that Criminal Justice and Public Order Act 1994 (CJPOA 1994), section 60 stop search notices (requiring no 'reasonable grounds' on behalf of the officer making the stop) could now only be issued by an officer above the rank of Chief Superintendent, that forces recorded a broader range of stop and search outcomes, introduced 'community trigger' complaint policies and local scrutiny committees, and introduced opportunities for lay observers to scrutinise patrol officers.[80] The stated intention behind these changes was to drive down the number of unnecessary stop searches and tackle the existing racial disproportionality.[81] Our data-gathering period would provide an opportunity to observe these changes in action.

PACE, section 1 sets out that a Constable may stop, detain, and search any individual or vehicle in a place to which the public have access for 'stolen or prohibited items'[82] if the officer has 'reasonable grounds for suspecting that he will find stolen or prohibited articles'.[83] Other stop and search powers also contain provisions for searches of individuals and vehicles based on reasonable suspicion, although for our purposes the most significant of these is the Misuse of Drugs Act 1971 (MDA 1971), section 23 which allows a search where the officer has reasonable grounds to believe they will find a controlled drug.[84] During our fieldwork, section 23 was utilised more than PACE, section 1. Under both powers, PACE Code A is clear that the officer searching must have both a genuine and reasonable belief they will find the prohibited item and that, 'Generalisations or stereotypical images that certain groups or categories of people are more likely to be involved

---

[78] Drawing upon statistics showing that black people were over seven times more likely, and Asian people more than twice more likely to be stop searched than white people. 2017 figures suggest that black British people were eight times, and those from all ethnic minorities four times, more likely to be stopped than white people: see www.gov.uk/government/statistics/police-powers-and-procedures-england-and-wales-year-ending-31-march-2017.

[79] Home Office/College of Policing, *Best Use of Stop and Search Scheme* (London, Home Office, 2014), available at assets.publishing.service.gov.uk/government/uploads/system/uploads/attachment_data/file/346922/Best_Use_of_Stop_and_Search_Scheme_v3.0_v2.pdf.

[80] Our role dovetailed conveniently for Force A in this sense. In March 2019, Home Office changes reversed this reform as part of its policy to reduce 'knife crime', reducing the level of officer who could authorise a s 60 stop to Inspector, and lowering the degree of certainty required: see www.gov.uk/government/news/greater-powers-for-police-to-use-stop-and-search-to-tackle-violent-crime.

[81] www.gov.uk/government/news/stop-and-search-theresa-may-announces-reform-of-police-stop-and-search.

[82] PACE, s 1(2)(a).

[83] PACE, s 1(3).

[84] MDA 1971, s 23(2).

in criminal activity'[85] cannot constitute reasonable grounds. However, reasonable grounds *can* arise from a conversation with an individual,[86] or from an individual's refusal to stop when asked by an officer.[87] In other words, an officer may draw grounds for suspicion from the physical or verbal responses of an individual who is asked to stop and account or is subjected to a stop check.[88]

Officers were almost unanimously of the view that stop and search was one of their most important powers in both detecting ('it is where most of our jobs come from')[89] and deterring crime (particularly knife crime)[90] and provided numerous examples of how they or colleagues had uncovered vast amounts of controlled drugs, bladed weapons, and even guns in personal and vehicle searches.[91] This contrasted with the more nuanced and critical view of the utility of stop and search provided by most academic research.[92] During our research, we witnessed many stop and searches, although the number of these reduced noticeably between 2014 and 2018. The majority of the searches we observed revealed nothing, but a significant minority led to the seizures of small quantities of drugs, almost always cannabis.

Broadly, there were two ways in which an officer would decide to conduct a stop search. In most cases, it would flow directly from a stop and account or a stop check. Sometimes the individual being stopped would either fail to explain away behaviour viewed by the officer as suspicious, or they would act in a way during the conversation that would arouse suspicion. More often, the individual or the vehicle they were in would smell of cannabis (or at least this would be the reason given for the subsequent MDA 1971, section 23 search). Less frequently, a stop search would be conducted on an individual because a member of the public had called in about suspicious behaviour that meant the officer's first action upon arrival was a stop search. On a few occasions, the officer was called by a Police Community Support Officer (PCSO) to carry out a stop search on a suspect they had apprehended but did not have the authority to search. The following section details the behaviour that would lead an officer conducting a stop and account/stop check to conduct a search and the operation of legal rules and Code of Practice or policy guidelines.

As might be expected, most officers required a higher standard of suspicious behaviour than they would for a stop and account/stop check. Looking 'out of

---

[85] PACE, Code A, para 2.2B(b).

[86] PACE, Code A, para 2.11.

[87] *R (on the application of Diedrick) v Chief Constable of Hampshire* [2012] EWHC 2144 (Admin) para 9.

[88] See A Sanders, *Criminal Justice*, 4th edn (Oxford, Oxford University Press, 2010) 92–96 for further discussion on the link between stop and account and stop search, and Bowling and Phillips, 'Disproportionate and Discriminatory' with regard to stop checks.

[89] Territorial Support, Lakeside, January 2015.

[90] Specials, Maron, July 2015.

[91] For example, Territorial Support, Lakeside, January 2015.

[92] M Tiratelli et al, 'Does Stop and Search Deter Crime? Evidence from Ten Years of London-Wide Data' (2018) 58 *British Journal of Criminology* 1212.

place', was rarely, if ever, seen as sufficient to warrant a search. In contrast, certain behaviour would almost always lead to a search. Running away when asked to stop and account was rare, but, if the suspect was subsequently caught, a search would always follow.[93] Smoking cannabis in public would usually lead to a search,[94] but not always. Some officers would throw the spliff in a bin, turn a blind eye, or even give a cheery 'Afternoon, boss!' as they passed.[95] Being in a vehicle which smelt of cannabis following a stop check always led to a search of the individual and the vehicle, even if the occupants claimed that the smell was from being in a smoke-filled house earlier. This was despite guidance from the College of Policing's Authorised Professional Practice on Stop Search that the smell of cannabis alone would not normally be sufficient to provide reasonable grounds for a stop search,[96] and that officers should also consider whether the smell could be attributed to the suspect, and the likelihood of finding the cannabis that the officer could smell. It should be noted that, when an officer gave 'smell of cannabis' as a reason to search following a stop check, the observer was often unable to verify this. Sometimes this may have been due to the observer being second on the scene after a vehicle window had been opened, but there were almost certainly situations when 'smell of cannabis' was given as a reason for a search when there was no smell. The practice of using an imaginary smell of cannabis to justify a stop search was confirmed by two of our participants independently.[97] If commonplace, it would not be identified by body-worn camera (BWC) footage and may be one factor behind the College of Policing's findings about the low detection rate in 'smell of cannabis' searches.[98]

While 'smell of cannabis' made up around half of the searches we saw, more subtle reasons were given by officers to explain their decision to stop and search:

> Alf: You do tend to use section 1 [*sic*] Misuse of Drugs because nearly everyone that you have been dealing with has either been using cannabis earlier or has been …
>
> Annie: It's on their clothes. They'll say it's because they had a spliff before they came out and it sticks on their clothes – they tend to wear the same thing over and over again. Some people, they just get so used to it they don't smell it, but obviously it's dead strong to us …

[93] Night-time Economy Team, Headquarters, October 2015; Response, Bree, September 2016.

[94] For example, Territorial Support, Lakeside, January 2015.

[95] Neighbourhood [Redacted] 2017.

[96] See www.app.college.police.uk/app-content/stop-and-search/legal/legal-basis/. See also P Quinton et al, *Searching for Cannabis: Are Grounds for Search Associated with Outcomes?* (Ruyton, College of Policing, 2017). All the officers we spoke with were aware of the College's position. See also whatworks. college.police.uk/Research/Documents/Stop_and_search_cannabis_Final_report.pdf.

[97] [Redacted] 2016.

[98] Quinton et al, *Searching for Cannabis*.

Researcher: What other suspicious activity might lead to a stop search?

Alf: Standing back. Shuffling with their clothing.

Annie: You're watching their hands …

Alf: Are they having a little look, wanting to see an escape route?

Annie: They're always watching [especially if another officer is looking for items they may have thrown away]. Sometimes they will be watching you more than you are watching them.

Researcher: What if they don't speak to you or give you lip?

Annie: I'd want to know why.

Alf: Yeah, what's the problem, if you've got nothing to hide why not be polite because we're there for their benefit. [He recounts stopping a man during a burglary investigation who was rude and asked 'why are you harassing me?'] And I was like, 'listen mate we're here for your benefit. Because while you're out now, do you want the thought that someone may be burgling your house? No, you don't. We're here because there is a problem in the area. I don't know if you are a burglar or have previous for burglary until I've stopped and spoke to you'.[99]

In contrast to Ericson's finding that police do not usually communicate their power and purposes,[100] we found it was common for officers to be clear about why they were stopping or searching, although sometimes they struggled to understand why this may upset the individual. This is illustrated by the following account of a stop search of one of two occupants of a car:

The passenger is annoyed: 'Why have you stopped me? I've done nothing wrong'. He claims they were just parked outside their 'nan's house' and this had been the third time they had been stopped [*sic*] this week.

Andy: 'We are in this area for a reason. We see a car parked in a dead-end with the window steamed up and two lads in it. We were going to have a word with you but then you were arsey to me so I asked more questions'. He says he can't explain why his colleague is searching the driver.

Passenger: 'Why aren't you searching me?'

Andy: 'I have no grounds to search you'.[101]

The following table illustrates the many and varied reasons observed or given by police officers to justify their decision to search an individual who was already subjected to a stop and account or a stop check. This is a comprehensive list of the

[99] Territorial Support, Knapford, March 2015.
[100] R Ericson, *Reproducing Order: A Study of Police Patrol Work* (Toronto, University of Toronto Press, 1982) 160.
[101] Territorial Support, Knapford, January 2016.

totality of the searches we observed that were not the result of 'smell of cannabis' or a CJPOA 1994, section 60 stop:

| Reason given | Search target/ Power | Found | Fieldnote |
|---|---|---|---|
| 1 male out in burglary hotspot. 'Known burglar'. Stopped for search for going equipped. | Stolen goods/ PACE, s 1 | N | Territorial Support 12/13 |
| 1 juvenile male on a bike and apparently accompanying a van. Driver of the van ran off. Officers stopped the boy, searched him and 'dosed' him with as many fines as they could think of. | Drugs/MDA, s 23 | N, but given tickets for £90 for no lights, cycling on pavement and no brakes | Territorial Support 12/13 |
| 4 men following PCSO report that drug deal was taking place | Drugs/MDA, s 23 | 1 small bag of cannabis | Neighbourhood 1/14 |
| 3 lads in 'the uniform', one looking very twitchy claiming to be autistic. Personal details not taken for the search form to be completed at a later date. | Drugs/MDA 1971, s 23 | N | Territorial Support doing NTE 1/14 |
| 3 lads, 2 on bikes. Given a 'pat down'. No details taken for records. | Drugs/MDA 1971, s 23 | N | Territorial Support doing NTE 1/14 |
| Man with a box who ducked behind a bus stop. Gave unconvincing explanation. | Stolen goods/ PACE, s 1 | N, but the stolen item in the suspect's hands was recovered | Territorial Support 2/14 |
| 3 males in van, picked up by Automatic Number Plate Recognition with a marker coming off motorway. | Drugs/MDA 1971, s 23 | N | Response 2/14 |
| 1 male and 1 female on a bus stole food from a service station. Bus driver wants them off. | Stolen goods/ PACE, s 1 | N | Response 2/14 |
| A couple: woman 'looking twitchy' and 'wanting to get off'. Man put a can in pocket when he saw the police. | Drugs/MDA 1971, s 23 | N | Territorial Support 3/14 |
| 1 male and car. In a car that fits a description and behaving 'a bit shifty'. | CJPOA 1994, s 60 | Class A drugs. Arrest | Territorial Support 3/14 |

*(continued)*

*(Continued)*

| Reason given | Search target/ Power | Found | Fieldnote |
|---|---|---|---|
| 2 males, one without seatbelt in a van in 'rag order'. Nothing in the van but suspect they are stealing. £300 in Scottish notes. | Stolen goods/ PACE, s 1 | N, tickets for seatbelt and for vehicle defects | Traffic 3/14 |
| 1 male. 2 in a van. Passenger has a case of beer in the footwell. Known to police. | CJPOA 1994, s 60 | N | Territorial Support 3/14 |
| 1 male and car searched, female passenger in car not searched. Lied about not being known to the police. | CJPOA 1994, s 60 | N, but issued an order to produce his insurance certificate | Territorial Support 3/14 |
| 1 male, young lad. Made off when he saw police and threw a grinder into the back of a lorry. | Drugs/MDA 1971, s 23 | N | Territorial Support 3/14, s 60 in place |
| Being unable to explain presence of tools in van due to language | Weapons/ PACE, s 1 | N | Territorial Support 6/14 |
| Man 'put something in his pocket or checked his pocket' and 'looked fidgety' when questioned. | Drugs/MDA 1971, s 23 | N | Territorial Support 6/14 |
| 1 young male cycling on pavements and known for TWOCing in the past but now going straight. | Drugs/MDA 1971, s 23 | N | Territorial Support 7/14 |
| 3 lads suspected of homophobic abuse, one appearing 'wired'. | Drugs/MDA 1971, s 23 | Cannabis and grinder. One arrested for Public Order Act 1986, s 4A offence | Territorial Support on NTE 8/14 |
| 1 lad searched from among a group running away as police vehicle approaches. Quick check of ID and a search of a bag. Not recorded. | Drugs/MDA 1971, s 23 | N | Territorial Support on NTE 8/14 |
| 1 lad, black, known to the officer in connection with drugs. Nothing beyond that as grounds. But officer had just sworn out a warrant on an address the lad was connected to. | Drugs/MDA 1971, s 23 | N | Neighbourhood 9/14 |

*(continued)*

**(Continued)**

| Reason given | Search target/ Power | Found | Fieldnote |
|---|---|---|---|
| 5 lads smoking weed in a tunnel under the motorway. | Drugs/MDA 1971, s 23 | N | Neighbourhood 11/14 |
| 1 man walking drunkenly visibly emptying his pockets. Find cannabis on the ground but nothing on him. | Drugs/MDA 1971, s 23 | N | Neighbourhood 11/14 |
| 2 males carrying binbag full of knock off gear bought on gumtree. Searched for evidence of stolen items or going equipped. Bag taken and held pending proof of purchase of 'Hogo Boss' (counterfeit) gear. | Stolen goods/ PACE, s 1 | N | Territorial Support 11/14 |
| 2 lads running away from prison walls after reports of items being thrown over. Claim they were playing by the walls. Didn't throw stuff over. Done for littering. | Drugs/MDA 1971, s 23 | N but ticket for littering. | Territorial Support 11/14 |
| 1 male driving slowly past a reported break in. Stopped. Lots of cash on him, but has an explanation. | Stolen goods/ PACE, s 1 | N | Territorial Support 11/14 |
| Woman whose jaw was 'moving uncontrollably'. | Drugs/MDA 1971, s 23 | N | Territorial Support 1/15 |
| 1 male, known to the police. Reveals he has cash on him. | Drugs/MDA 1971, s 23 | N | Territorial Support 1/15 |
| 1 male driver of an Audi. Right car, right look. Has £200 cash. | Drugs/MDA 1971, s 23 | N | Territorial Support 1/15 |
| 1 male looking 'jumpy' carrying bag. Looks like a 'baghead'. Wants to make off, arouses suspicion. | Drugs/MDA 1971, s 23 | N | Territorial Support 2/15 |
| 3 lads in a car 'known' as dealers for an OCG. 1 without a seatbelt. | Drugs/MDA 1971, s 23 | N | Territorial Support 2/15 |
| 1 male, made off when he saw officers. Stopped with a car key at his feet and by a car they belonged to. Denied it was his. | Stolen goods/ PACE, s 1 | N | Territorial Support 2/15 |

*(continued)*

*(Continued)*

| Reason given | Search target/ Power | Found | Fieldnote |
|---|---|---|---|
| 2 searched on a bus ticket operation. Forged bus tickets and fake ID suspected. | Stolen goods/ PACE, s 1 | Stolen ID card. | Territorial Support 5/15 |
| 3 young males in hatchback car tagged for involvement in a historical burglary | Drugs/MDA 1971, s 23 | N | Territorial Support 5/15 |
| Intelligence the individual is a drug dealer | Drugs/MDA 1971, s 23 | N | Territorial Support 5/15 |
| 5 searched. 4 lads stood by a car and leaning in to the driver. 1 lad believed to have been seen throwing a snap bag away as the police arrived. | Drugs/MDA 1971, s 23 | N | Territorial Support 5/15 |
| 1 lad wearing daft clothes walks to the officers and puts his arms up for a search. So they search him. | Drugs/MDA 1971, s 23 | N | Territorial Support 5/15 |
| 2 lads and a car, passenger not wearing a seatbelt. They get out as police stop the car and walk towards them to be searched. Grounds for a search not clear. | Drugs/MDA 1971, s 23 | N, OSCO for seatbelt | Territorial Support 5/15 |
| 1 lad searched. His mate made off on a bike, probably with whatever drugs the officers suspect he had. | Drugs/MDA 1971, s 23 | N | Territorial Support 5/15 |
| 1 male fitting a description searched following reports of a knife. No others in the group were searched. | Weapon/ PACE, s 1 | N | Response 6/15 |
| Getting out of a car straight away following a stop check | Drugs/MDA 1971, s 23 | N | Territorial Support 7/15 |
| 3 lads ran off as police approached. Hanging around in a dispersal zone. Two others got away. | Drugs/MDA 1971, s 23 | N | Response 7/15 |
| 1 male on a bike makes off. Fits description of male trying car doors in a pub car park. | Going equipped/ Stolen goods/ PACE, s 1 | N, but arrested for dangerous cycling | Response 7/15 |

*(continued)*

*(Continued)*

| Reason given | Search target/ Power | Found | Fieldnote |
|---|---|---|---|
| 3 males and 1 female and a car. Parked at back of shops, one lad smoking threw away his spliff. Search of ground found spliff. All denied it, so all searched. Officer searching was probationer, so needed practice. | Drugs/MDA 1971, s 23 | N, aside from the spliff on the ground | Response 9/15 |
| Man hid in pub when police van appeared. Had bag designed for shoplifting. | Stolen goods/ PACE, s 1 | N | Territorial Support 9/15 |
| 1 male known to the police for dealing ran off down road. | Drugs/MDA 1971, s 23 | N | Night-time Economy Team 10/15 |
| 1 male and 1 female. In car, put seatbelt on as officers approached. Red eyes, but said they had been swimming. Daughter in the back. Not happy at the attempt to lie about the seatbelt. | Drugs/MDA 1971, s 23 | Cannabis Fixed Penalty Notice | Territorial Support 11/15 |
| 2 males in van, 'that's pothead's driving'. Search of van and occupants. Quad bike in the back. | Drugs/MDA 1971, s 23 | N | Territorial Support 11/15 |
| Man in a van containing clothes, a laptop, and an old police baton | Stolen goods/ PACE, s 1 | N | Territorial Support 1/16 |
| Driver parking in dead end: 'Sweating and nervous'. | Drugs/MDA 1971, s 23 | N | Territorial Support 1/16 |
| Intelligence that male was a drug dealer. | Drugs/MDA 1971, s 23 | N | Territorial Support 1/16 |
| 1 woman suspected to be awaiting a drug supply run. Known user. Search partly an excuse for her to talk and offer intel without looking suspicious. | Drugs/MDA 1971, s 23 | N | Territorial Support 7/16 |
| 2 lads on bikes going home from work at 2am appear to throw something when they see the police. Search of the grass verge. One bag of cannabis found on one lad. | Drugs/MDA 1971, s 23 | Bag of cannabis. Cannabis warning | Territorial Support 7/16 |

*(continued)*

*(Continued)*

| Reason given | Search target/ Power | Found | Fieldnote |
|---|---|---|---|
| 1 male in van drives off at sight of police and tries to claim he wasn't driving. No licence, no insurance and confesses to a knife in the doorwell. | Weapon/ PACE, s 1 | N, but weapon already volunteered and two tickets issued | Territorial Support 9/16 |
| Male ran away when stop and accounted. | Drugs/MDA 1971, s 23 | N | Response 9/16 |
| 1 male, driving car erratically. Stopped and confesses to possession. Car and he are searched, test done for drug driving (clear). | Drugs/MDA 1971, s 23 | Class A drugs. Arrested and house searched. | Territorial Support 11/16 |
| 4 men standing by stolen car. | Unclear what grounds. Unrecorded. | N, but bag of cannabis in car. | Response [Redacted] 2017 |
| PCSOs apprehended homeless man with history of burglary in back garden of a property. | Burglary equipment/ PACE, s 1 | 1 small bag of cannabis | Neighbourhood 12/17 |
| 1 lad and car. Two passengers made off on foot. Suspected drug dealers. | Drugs/MDA 1971, s 23 | N | Territorial Support 12/17 |
| 1 young lad. Put down a can of petrol when he saw the police. Searched for drugs, but really suspected of using scrambler bikes. | Drugs/MDA 1971, s 23 | N. Seized can of petrol | Territorial Support 3/18 |
| 1 male at a cash machine with a mate. Mate not searched. Male is jumpy and a known user. Assume he is getting money for his drugs but search him anyway. | Drugs/MDA 1971, s 23 | N | Territorial Support 3/18 |
| 1 male in car with faulty brake light, smell of weed. Find wad of cash. | Drugs/MDA 1971, s 23 | N | Territorial Support 4/18 |

In addition to these searches, another 39 individuals (from 21 different encounters) were searched on the basis that the officer said that they could smell cannabis either on them or from their vehicle. A further five individuals were searched under the CJPOA 1994, s 60, which does not require a reason to be given, and where no reason was given.[102]

We cannot extrapolate from this data to show general trends, and do not claim it is representative, but our data is illustrative of four features that broadly mirror nationwide statistics on stop and search. First, that over the research period, there were relatively few stop and searches given the high number of stops overall. Although a stop and account or stop check was almost always the first stage in a stop search, most led to the individual being sent on their way with no search. Second, it illustrates a noticeable drop-off in the number of stop and searches, which we return to in Part V below.

Third, it shows the relatively low number of detections of prohibited or stolen items, particularly those being searched for. From the table above we can see that of the 102 individuals we observed being searched, items were only found on eight of the suspects. Five of these finds were small amounts of cannabis, two were amounts of class A drugs, and one was a stolen item. Of the 39 individuals that were searched following a stop because the officer reported there was a smell of cannabis, two were found with small amounts of cannabis, one with a large amount of cannabis, and one with Class A drugs. Of the five section 60 searches, no items were found. In sum, of the 146 individuals we saw being searched, only 12 stolen or prohibited items were found,[103] of which seven were small amounts of cannabis for personal use. We witnessed no searches where knives were found in pockets, money in suitcases in car boots, or guns under car seats, despite being told of these finds by some of our participants.

Finally, the data illustrates the difficulty in predicting whether stop searches would be carried out, based on often very minor behavioural triggers that individual officers responded to differently and which the same officer may often also respond to differently depending on her role, shift, or even the time of the day:

> The reasons given for stop searching and stop and accounting seem to change. So, drug dealers are searched not because they are nervous or twitchy but because they are comfortable when pulled over by officers whereas ... for others, people looking twitchy is very much a sign of guilt and that if you had nothing to hide you wouldn't be acting that way.[104]

Suspects avoiding a stop search typically were able to respond in a composed (and usually deferential) manner to a police stop and give a good account of who they

---

[102] We should note that the table above includes stop and searches carried out when s 60 powers were in place, but officers nevertheless gave grounds for the search.

[103] This does not include items that were already in view prior to the search (eg a stolen item in the arms of the suspect, or a spliff that was being smoked). It also does not include an unclaimed bag of cannabis in a stolen car.

[104] Territorial Support, Knapford, March 2014.

were and where they were going or why they were parked there.[105] While admitting that you were 'known to the police' did appear to increase the chance you would be searched, it was by no means the most important factor. Once again, officers struggled to put their finger on exactly what would dispel their suspicions, but they tended to talk about the idea of 'normality' and of 'fitting in' with officer's expectations.

> Researcher: So let's flip it the other way 'round. If you have stopped and accounted someone, what sort of things could they do which might dispel suspicions and you would basically send them on their way?
>
> Alf: Erm … Natural
>
> Annie: Yeah, if they were just normal … Maybe depending on what dealings they've been having with the police previously …
>
> Alf: Like those two we stopped and chatted to at the side of the road earlier. The moment we got out we could see that they were kids and one had a shirt and tie on. Although he was nervous … there was a different nervous to him … a nervous polite, do you know what I mean? You could … by the way his demeanour was that … he didn't look like he had nothing to hide … he was interacting with us normal, as any normal teenager would … and there was nothing to say in his body language and his demeanour to say 'I'm feeling scared, I've got something here that I shouldn't have'.
>
> Annie: Their attitude … it's how they speak to us, it's how they are.[106]

## IV. Discrimination and the Targets of Police Engagement

Early on in *The Case for the Prosecution*, McConville et al note that, 'Police powers are not exercised randomly or representatively across society. They bear most heavily on young working class males, especially young black males'. They go on to note that the 'demeanour', which we have seen can elevate a stop and account/ stop check into a search, is 'socially and racially patterned'.[107] Waddington also warns that police discretion can become a 'cloak' for 'prejudice and discrimination', particularly against the poor, ill-educated, young, and ethnic minority residents of deprived neighbourhoods.[108] In 2017, David Lammy, the MP for Tottenham and campaigner against racial discrimination in British society, stated that 'The disproportionality that I found throughout the criminal justice system begins with stop and search'.[109] Our research was not with the Metropolitan Police Service, who

---

[105] Territorial Support, Knapford, July 2015.
[106] Territorial Support, Knapford, March 2015.
[107] M McConville et al, *The Case for the Prosecution: Police Suspects and the Construction of Criminality* (London, Routledge, 1993) 17.
[108] Waddington, *Policing Citizens* 37–39.
[109] *The Guardian* (26 October 2017) www.theguardian.com/law/2017/oct/26/stop-and-search-eight-times-more-likely-to-target-black-people.

from Brixton, to Stephen Lawrence, to Mark Duggan, have a seemingly unshake-able reputation for the worst excesses of racial discrimination in policing, and we cannot claim our findings here are representative of all police forces. However, we would argue that disproportionality and discrimination occurs much earlier than this. It may occur when an officer decides to patrol a working class area with a high ethnic minority population, rather than a white middle-class area. It may occur when an officer decides to respond to a more 'exciting' or urgent call coming from the same area, rather than dealing with a domestic abuse or safeguarding incident elsewhere. Our research also suggests that a wider and more significant form of discretion exists in the largely unfettered freedom an officer has to decide whether or not to conduct a stop and account or a stop check. Given the findings of other researchers and commentators from across the country,[110] it is likely that this conclusion will be evident elsewhere.

The policing of racial minorities has 'attracted enormous attention' from researchers,[111] and there is a long history of discrimination and harassment against ethnic minority groups.[112] In 1997, Holdaway argued that, '[r]acial prejudice and discrimination have been found to be abiding elements of the occupational 'culture' of the police rank and file,[113] and the McPherson report more than a decade later also noted that rather than 'institutionalised racism' being the sole problem, discriminatory stop and searches also resulted from the racial prejudices of individual officers.[114] Loftus's post-McPherson ethnography of the police found the 'stereotyping of black and minority ethnic men as inherently criminal' by offic-ers was evident on many occasions, but that officers were by no means 'culturally homogeneous in their response to minority ethnic communities'.[115]

Given most of the previous research, one of our most significant observations was the lack of overt racial or religious discrimination from frontline police officers. In six years and over 200 shifts, we did not see any evidence of officers dispropor-tionately targeting minority groups for stops, searches, or arrests in contrast with white people. Loftus's research identified that, 'anxiety about being labelled racist sometimes led to the avoidance of proactive encounters with members of ethnic minority groups'.[116] We suspected a similar reticence on behalf of some of our volunteers to stop and account those from ethnic minorities, although the offic-ers gave other reasons for their decisions. For example, one researcher watched

---

[110] For example, Bowling and Phillips, 'Disproportionate and Discriminatory'.

[111] M Rowe, *Policing, Race and Racism* (Devon, Willan, 2004); Waddington. *Policing Citizens* 49.

[112] Loftus, *Police Culture* 141; B Bowling and C Phillips, *Racism, Crime and Justice* (Harlow, Pearson Education, 2002).

[113] S Holdaway, 'Constructing and Sustaining "Race" within the Police Workforce' (1997) 48 *British Journal of Sociology* 19, 22.

[114] K Stenson and P Waddington, 'MacPherson, Police Stops and Institutional Racism' in M Rowe (ed), *Policing Beyond McPherson: Issues in Policing, Race and Society* (London, Routledge, 2013) 128, 132.

[115] Loftus, *Police Culture* 143–44.

[116] Loftus, *Police Culture* 125.

a Territorial Support unit that had conducted numerous stop and accounts/stop checks and three searches earlier in the evening, drive past a black man smoking what appeared to be a spliff without comment,[117] and another team stop and account every group of young men they came across with the exception of the only group of young black men. The researcher noted that 'the team are deliberately staying away from stop and accounting black people'.[118] On another occasion, following a response to a fight between different school gangs, the officer declined to stop and search a group of young black men who appeared to have been part of the gang who had travelled into the locality to take part in the fight, despite radio reports that weapons were used and the fact that the officer did not believe the story given to him for their presence in the area.[119] However, disproportionality of stop search in this division had been flagged up earlier in the month at a force-wide committee. Ethnic minorities were sometimes pulled over in stop checks, but it was normally impossible to tell the ethnicity of vehicle occupants when the decision to stop was made (and 'bad spots' leading to stops included cars with black families as much as white).[120]

> Bertie spins the van round. 'There's a lad worth a stop'. He is a young lad, black, one of the few black faces we have seen today. He is known to Bertie. He pulls him up, half expecting him to try to run. He is a bit taken aback but ok. 'Why are you stopping me?' Bertie explains. 'Intel that you have been dealing drugs'. 'Me?' 'And why are you hanging around the corner shop?' 'Just somewhere we meet'. Bertie gives him a quick pat down, but nothing too intrusive. Bertie asks if he wants a copy of the stop form, but he doesn't. As we head off, I ask about it. Bertie had been quite assertive, using physical presence, but emphasized that he was 'treating the lad with respect'. He told the lad to get his hands out of his pockets – 'it makes me nervous'. He invaded his body space a bit and the lad backed off, but nothing more than that. I mention that we sometimes suspect that officers have ignored black lads when we are around. Bertie hadn't. He hadn't thought about it. He knows the lad and he is always worth a stop.[121]

Incidents of *indirect* discrimination on the grounds of nationality were occasionally observed, although some of them may have been justifiable and proportionate under the Equality Act 2010. In one incident, two Eastern European men were searched when they could not give an account for the presence of tools in their van due to their lack of spoken English,[122] and, in one force, Traffic officers were instructed to stop check lorries with foreign number-plates to look for road

---

[117] Territorial Support, Knapford, February 2014. One possible alternative explanation for this sudden change in behaviour is that this was towards the end of the shift and the team wanted to get back to the station to complete their paperwork.

[118] Territorial Support, Knapford, February 2014. At a later interview the explanation given was that they were not dressed like they would be involved in criminal activity.

[119] Response, Weathertop, January 2018.

[120] Territorial Support, Knapford, March 2014.

[121] Neighbourhood, Arlesdale, September 2014.

[122] Territorial Support, Knapford, June 2014.

safety infractions.[123] However, during the six years of the research, the observers did not see a single instance of what they interpreted to be direct racial discrimination in the use of street powers by frontline officers.

We do not claim that our findings indicate that concerns about the racist use of discretion by frontline police generally are overstated. It may be that the forces in question differed in their training or that attitudes to the social acceptability of racial 'banter' differed at police stations in these cities, in contrast to other parts of the country.[124] We must of course also be mindful of the impact of the researcher's presence on the research participants and their colleagues. A stranger in the office, particularly one working with senior management, will inevitably lead to behaviour and language being altered. On frequent occasions, for example, officers indicated that, had we not been present, they would have sworn (although most of the officers we were with were happy to swear regularly in our presence). Given that our observations took place during the controversy about disproportionality in stop and search (and at a time of severe cuts in police numbers), officers would have been particularly aware of the sensitivities around this area and the potential risks to their career. Finally, given that we were observing volunteers, it is likely that those who volunteered were more confident that their views and behaviour were 'on-message' with force policies on equality and diversity. Nevertheless, in line with one of the overall themes in this book, we feel comfortable in speculating that attitudes to outward displays of racism and religious intolerance – at least in the two forces under observation – are likely to have changed over time, and probably post-MacPherson, to make it less acceptable. Of course, our research focused on frontline officers. We are not suggesting that there were not wider structural problems within the police forces or the wider justice system that bore down more heavily on ethnic minorities than the white majority.

However, the forces and their frontline officers were not compliant with the Equality Act 2010 with respect to other protected characteristics. Direct discrimination on the grounds of both gender and age was commonplace. The Equality Act 2010 permits the former only in a narrow range of specialist occupations or situations which were not relevant here, whereas the latter is only permitted where the measure or practice is necessary and proportionate. A combination of the two characteristics – being young and male – dramatically increased the chance of a stop and account, and, following on from this, a stop and search.

> Researcher: What are the kinds of triggers when it comes to you seeing suspicious activity?
>
> [Redacted]: Age. Appearance …[125]

---

[123] Traffic, Knapford, June 2015.

[124] This would be in line with Stenson and Waddington's contention that there were likely to be geographical differences in the level of racial prejudice in the police across the country (Stenson and Waddington, 'MacPherson').

[125] [Redacted] 2015.

Throughout the research, officers expressed the opinion that young men were more likely to be involved in criminal activity and there was no doubt that this demographic was targeted for stops and for searches disproportionately. For example, four young men in a car together were considered, 'the type to be smoking cannabis together or being involved in burglaries'.[126] Young males together late at night would always attract attention in high-crime areas, but also young men together during the day would raise the question 'why aren't they at work?' and may also lead to a stop.[127] One of our first conclusions was that,

> There's no question that younger people are getting stopped and questioned more than older people and there's no doubt that men are getting stopped and questioned more than women are ... and often a stop and search flows straight from that stop and account.[128]

On several occasions, officers conducted stop checks on hatchbacks or high-powered vehicles only to immediately lose interest when they saw that the driver was a woman or an elderly man. Sometimes upon seeing this, the officer would not even speak to the individual and would just wave them on.[129]

> Constantly the discussion is 'who's in that car?' And if the answer is 'Oh no, it's just a woman' the [officers] don't stop it, or they will follow someone and it will turn out to be a woman so they won't stop it. Whereas, if it is a man [driving a car that has caught their attention], they will do ... maybe 60 to 70% of the time.[130]

Early in the research, prior to the crackdown on the use of section 60 searches, it was not uncommon for a section 60 notice to be put in place instructing officers to search males between the ages of 15 and 35 in that locality, regardless of grounds for suspicion.[131] The focus of street powers on young men has been noted by a number of studies,[132] and it is clear that this remains an entrenched situation.

It was predominantly working class males who were stopped, on account of heavy police patrolling and section 60 notices being largely in place for deprived areas with high-crime rates. Loftus argues that class issues tend to have been forgotten when we look at disproportionality in policing; the working class can be considered a harassed and victimised group and so long as, 'the white residuum operates as unproblematic terrain for the police use of discretionary powers and authority', studies of police needs to recognise this.[133] Waddington also noted that the distribution of policing resources led to an increased impact upon the young

---

[126] Territorial Support, Knapford, March 2014.
[127] Territorial Support, Knapford, September 2015.
[128] Territorial Support, Knapford, March 2014.
[129] Territorial Support, Lakeside, January 2015.
[130] Territorial Support, Knapford, June 2014. Also Neighbourhood, Siloh, May 2015.
[131] Territorial Support, Knapford, March 2014.
[132] M Brogden et al, *Introducing Police Work* (London, Unwin Hyman, 1988), especially 102–12; R Ericson and K Haggerty, *Policing the Risk Society* (Oxford, Oxford University Press, 1997) 260.
[133] Loftus, *Police Culture* 160.

and the working class (in addition to ethnic minorities).[134] Our research found that what might be described as working class fashion (on young men) was a trigger for police attention.[135] However, it was largely a product of a police focus on public spaces where young working class males were likely to be present,[136] and sweeping up any young men in that area, that led to working class males being targeted. Wider police discretion, in terms of decisions about where to patrol and who to talk to, were therefore more significant than the 'invocation' discretion once the officer was faced with a suspect.

Officers did not normally talk about class, but they did draw a differentiation between 'decent people' (sometimes 'decent folk', 'law-abiding', 'good people', or 'taxpayers') and the 'criminal type' (sometimes 'shit'). This mode of police thinking that has been well-documented by previous research.[137] Drivers who 'looked like decent people' were less likely to be pulled over, even if their vehicle had a light out, whereas groups of young men in street clothing would be stopped.[138] Neighbourhood officers in one station talked disparagingly about Traffic officers because they gave tickets to 'decent people', although our observations with Traffic officers suggested that this was largely a myth. 'Penalising good people' through a failure to use their discretion to turn a blind eye was, for them, a failure of policing.[139] When a Territorial Support team was tasked to take part in a nationwide operation against use of mobile phones in cars, they expressed concerns they would have to take action against 'decent people'.[140] Following a stop, being perceived as 'decent people' would also lower the chance of receiving a traffic ticket or being searched. They were more likely to be believed than criminals: 'I don't need to go and have a look'.[141]

## V. The Evolution of Stop and Search?

We therefore identified substantial evidence of long-running and entrenched patterns of policing where street powers are used disproportionately against young working class men. We have also noted the continued distinction, with very real consequences, between decent people and the criminal type. However, while these themes endured, our research into police stop and search powers also identified significant change across the six years of the fieldwork. This was not

---

[134] Waddington, *Policing Citizens* 45.
[135] Territorial Support, Knapford, March 2014.
[136] See also McConville et al, *Case for the Prosecution* 17.
[137] Dixon, *Law in Policing* 315; Waddington, *Policing Citizens* 40–41.
[138] Neighbourhood, Shiloh, May 2015.
[139] Territorial Support, Brandam, January 2014.
[140] Territorial Support, Knapford, May 2015.
[141] Response, Eriador, September 2017. Although we also saw a few instances of an officer not bothering to give a ticket even to a couple of vehicle occupants identified by the officer to be 'horrible people' (Territorial Support, Knapford, July 2015).

necessarily a change in attitude, but a change in the way in which powers were applied. It was a change identified by both the observers, and by the participants. When we first entered the field in October 2013, we noted the high number of stop and accounts, stop checks, and stop searches. On the last of these, 'Once you have been stop and accounted, you don't need to do much to elevate that to a stop search – moving your hands suddenly, acting nervous, smelling of weed … would all get you searched …'[142] In contrast, our later observations (sometimes with the same officers or teams) saw significantly fewer stops and, when those stops took place, they were much less likely to lead to a search.

> Phil points out a man with a bag on [the] street. He is going to stop and account but, after a chat with Andy, who says, 'no, he's alright', doesn't stop him. I ask if three years ago they would have stopped him. Phil: 'Yes, that's the case … We're stopping less people'.[143]

Observations of three shifts in a deprived and high-crime area in the first half of 2018 saw not one stop and account or stop check.[144] In particular, officers expressed concerns that stops might lead to complaints, and that they could not rely upon the force to support them. Turning a blind eye was becoming a safer option in the eyes of some officers.[145]

Stop searches were also reducing dramatically. One of our participants explained that he had carried out only one stop search in 12 months, prompting his colleague to say he had conducted two. Both stop searches had been successful, which was 'good, but if I had done 20 stop searches and found three items, meaning I had caught another bad guy' he believes he 'would have got into trouble'.[146] It was a similar pattern across forces and roles: 'I think our main role, in terms of stop search and disrupting people, has declined in the last 18 months, two years', explained one Territorial Support officer.[147] 'A few years ago I'd have searched him', explained Kenny as he lets a man with a history of bike theft cycle off following a stop check.[148] The dramatic reduction in stop searches was also identifiable from force-wide and nationwide figures, where the number of reported PACE, section 1 searches tumbled from 1,229,324 in England and Wales in 2010/11 to 303,228 in 2016/17.[149]

What was driving this change? Participants identified four reasons why they and their colleagues were using stop search less. First, officers noted a pressure to reduce the number of searches, particularly of ethnic minorities. This was a political priority, clearly voiced by the then Home Secretary, Theresa May, that

---

[142] Territorial Support, Knapford, March 2014.
[143] Territorial Support, Knapford, January 2016.
[144] Neighbourhood, Weathertop, January 2018; Neighbourhood, Withered Heath, March 2018; Neighbourhood, Dunland, June 2018.
[145] Neighbourhood, Shiloh, September 2015.
[146] Response, Bywater, June 2017.
[147] Territorial Support, Knapford, January 2016.
[148] Response, Bree, September 2016.
[149] Home Office, *Stop and Search Statistics, Year Ending March 2017.*

was cascaded down through the police forces we were observing. Many officers felt the pressure to reduce stop and search was wrong, but few wanted to resist the new guidance.[150] The College of Policing's guidance that the 'smell of cannabis' was, on its own, no longer sufficient grounds for a search also provoked discussion.[151] Was the intention to, in effect, decriminalise the use of cannabis? It was in this context that, for the first time, some officers admitted to us that they had sometimes claimed there was a 'smell of cannabis' to justify a search when there was none:[152] 'I used to say I smelt cannabis'.[153] Officers were aware that refusal to toe the line in Force B risked censure and additional training. It was being 'drilled into' officers that searches should no longer be carried out as a result of 'gut instinct' or a suspect's previous history.[154] Second, officers were unsure that they would be supported by their supervisors in the event of complaints. Rumours of a 'three strikes and you're out' policy were common, suggesting that any officer who conducted three unsuccessful searches might be subject to discipline. Others believed that Professional Standards[155] would also be involved in such circumstances.[156] This appears to have been a result of news reports of such a scheme in Northamptonshire,[157] but they persisted in Force A for some time. Third, in each force, the recording of searches was changed and became more burdensome. In Force A, the paper form was replaced by an electronic record that required up to 30 minutes to complete, particularly for those officers not using the power frequently. Even experienced officers took more than ten minutes.[158] This acted as a disincentive for officers being stretched by austerity and no decline in demand.[159] Sergeants complained that their officers were no longer conducting stop searches in order to avoid the associated administration,[160] and one officer complained it had taken 60 minutes to fill out the paperwork for a search of a car and two individuals, when previously they would have used a single form.[161]

The fourth reason for the decline in searches, arising at the same time as this 'attack' on stop search, was the roll-out of BWCs across both forces. The policy

[150] Response, Bywater, June 2017.

[151] Quinton et al, *Searching for Cannabis*.

[152] [Redacted] 2016.

[153] [Redacted] 2015.

[154] Response, Bree, September 2016.

[155] The Professional Standards Department (or Board) are a team tasked with the investigation of complaints against and of wrongdoing by police officers. In popular media, they are often referred to as Internal Affairs.

[156] Territorial Support, Brandham, October 2016; Mental Health Triage, January 2016.

[157] 'Northamptonshire police ban stop and search by officers who abuse powers' *The Guardian* (18 August 2015), available at www.theguardian.com/law/2015/aug/18/police-force-bans-stop-and-search-officers-who-abuse-powers-adam-simmonds.

[158] Response, Hackerbeck, September 2015.

[159] Night-time Economy Team, Knapford, October 2015.

[160] Football Ops, October 2015.

[161] Mental Health Triage, Maron, January 2016.

at both forces was that all stop and searches needed to be recorded on BWCs, although at Force B, over 12 months into the policy being enacted, only 50% of recorded searches were being recorded in some divisions. From our observations, however, nearly all searches were recorded. Officers perceived that BWCs were another disincentive to search. They were aware that a sample of the footage was checked and knew colleagues who had been censured for not carrying out the search correctly. As Phil noted, BWCs had been the main driver for the drop off in searches which had in turn 'killed' the proactive effectiveness of his Territorial Support unit.[162] Henry believed that BWCs deterred searches without proper grounds: 'I don't know what we are meant to be doing now. I don't know if we are meant to be proactive or what?' Later in the shift, his team stopped and accounted a group of young men they considered to be part of a local OCG:

> One of the lads nods at his BWC with a grin: 'That's ruined it for you lot, hasn't it?' Later, in the privacy of the van, the officers discuss this. One officer laughs as the comment is recounted, but Mish says grimly 'He's right though, isn't he?'[163]

Importantly, there is nothing to suggest that the changes we observed with regard to stop and search, and to a lesser extent stop and account/stop checks, are irreversible. It was clear that many frontline and senior officers resented the restrictions and deterrents to the use of the powers.[164] However, in Force A, efforts to reverse the decline were met by scepticism. Efforts to encourage more searches were interpreted as a return to performance management and targets.[165] Only a significant investment in refresher training for all officers re-established a shared sense of what senior officers expected of the frontline. Towards the end of our research, statistics on stop and search in one of our forces spiked. Senior officers put this down to a combination of an HMICFRS inspection and to a new tranche of recruits who were required to complete at least one stop and search in order to pass their probation. It was not clear that either of these factors would have a sustained effect on the use of the powers.

At the same time, we do not suggest that the reductions in searches have solved the problem of racial disproportionality, which appears to remain entrenched despite the changes.[166] However, the changes in officers' practices with regard to stop and search that we witnessed were stark, and swift. This leads us to question the claims of earlier researchers who argue that the police are culturally resistant to change.[167] In particular, the argument that 'police culture' structures discretion

---

[162] Territorial Support, Knapford, January 2016.

[163] Territorial Support, Knapford, September 2015.

[164] Eg London Mayor Sadiq Khan *The Independent* (10 January 2018), Metropolitan Police Commissioner Cressida Dick *The Guardian* (8 August 2018), Chief Constable of Merseyside Police Andy Cooke *The Times* (4 September 2018).

[165] Territorial Support, Brandham, October 2016.

[166] In 2016/17, stops of white people reduced 28%, while for minority ethnic people the reduction was only 11% *The Guardian* (26 October 2016).

[167] Loftus, *Police Culture*; Sanders et al, *Police Powers*.

rather than supervision or the law[168] does not tally with our experiences when we consider the use of police stops.

The inability of the law to regulate how the police use their discretion when it comes to stops and searches was highlighted by a number of studies analysing the effectiveness of PACE. Dixon refers to the 'limits of legalism' in this context, and noted that some officers express bravado about being able to get around laws and rules designed to control their discretion.[169] McConville et al. too note the inability of the law to manage police behaviour and how officers were able to work around legal regulation through application of the 'Ways and Means Act'.[170] Reiner refers to the 'law of inevitable increment – whatever powers the police have, they will exceed by a given margin'.[171] With regard to searches, our research supported these views to a certain extent. We witnessed *some* officers carrying out *some* searches that were, in our view, not compliant with the rules on reasonable suspicion. This was particularly true of MDA 1971, section 23 searches where it was claimed that there was a 'smell of cannabis'. Further, the rate of these unlawful searches is also probably higher than we observed given the inevitable distortion of the field that our presence caused, and the type of officer who volunteered to participate in the study. We also observed stop searches that were unlawful in a different way, for example a case where reasonable grounds were present, but the search was not recorded in any way and would not have appeared on the statistics:

> The officers have been hunting a car on false plates for a number of days. They have found it alongside four young white males who were known to the officers as OCGs. A number of police vehicles surround the vehicle and I am asked to stay in the car. I wait a couple of minutes but then go to see what's happening. The four lads are handcuffed and being searched, one complaining his cuffs were too tight. 5–6 officers are involved (...) Nothing was found on the lads but a small bag of cannabis was found in the car. When asked about the search and the subsequent lack of recording, one officer explained: 'They offered themselves to be searched. The lad I was searching turned out his own pockets ... It's a good way to avoid filling in the forms'. This was not totally correct as I saw the officer reaching into the pockets of a suspect and asking what certain items were. BWCs were left on standby for the duration.[172]

It is likely that this type of hidden search was occurring more regularly away from the researcher's gaze, but we neither saw nor heard anything to suggest it was an endemic problem. The law was clearly not stopping all illegal searches but, in the vast majority of cases, it was in play in an officer's mind and, as Herbert suggests, such restrictions are not unimportant in shaping police behaviour.[173] Our findings

---

[168] McConville et al, *Case for the Prosecution* 18.
[169] Dixon, *Law in Policing* 303–304.
[170] McConville et al, *Case for the Prosecution* 182–84. Also, Waddington, *Policing Citizens* 136.
[171] R Reiner, *The Politics of the Police*, 4th edn (Oxford, Oxford University Press, 2014) 173.
[172] [Redacted] 2017.
[173] S Herbert, 'Police Culture Reconsidered' (1998) 36 *Criminology* 343.

suggested that the law and guidelines relating to PACE searches in particular were more than merely 'presentational rules' which 'exist to give an acceptable appearance to the way the police work is carried out'.[174]

However, it was not a change to the law that was driving down the use of stop searches during the course of our fieldwork. The main factor behind the change was the national policy environment which affected the climate in which officers were expected to act. This was reinforced by Inspectors and Sergeants in briefings and in the ongoing feedback provided on their 'jobs' by Sergeants. 'What sarge will say' was often in the minds of officers when making operational decisions. We are, therefore, not as sceptical as Jefferson and Grimshaw, who suggest that constabulary independence negates attempts to control police operational discretion.[175] We saw policy changes (whether real or perceived) to be the key driver of change. These influences undermined even senior officers' efforts to counteract the national political climate in Force A. At the same time, and as we will see in the next chapter, force policies could cause confusion, and the way in which they 'cascaded' down the chain of command was sometimes problematic. For stop and search in particular, pressures and guidance resulting from the Best Use of Stop Search combined into de facto force policies that had the same effect at both forces – a belief that stop and search was being discouraged. This was exacerbated by other practical and bureaucratic pressures upon officers, including increased paperwork and rules on using BWCs. The result was that, for most officers, PACE, section 1 and MDA 1971, section 23 searches started to be used only in exceptional situations. Officers responded to this pressure differently, but even those who protested most vociferously against the policies ultimately bowed to them.

[174] Dixon et al, 'Consent and the Legal Regulation of Policing' 347.
[175] Grimshaw and Jefferson, *Interpreting Police Work* 274.

# 7

# Arrest and Detention

Any study of police street work is obliged to address the power of arrest. Arrest is a highly coercive power[1] that has been the subject of numerous legal challenges. It is a particularly sensitive issue for the police given that arrest is almost always followed by a significant period of detention and a restriction on an individual's normal right to liberty under the European Convention on Human Rights (ECHR) Article 5. As with stop and search, debates about the police discretion to make an arrest have focused, to a large extent, on disproportionality, particularly with regard to race. Mirroring the discussion in the previous chapter, racial disproportionality was not something we observed, although this is not to suggest that it did not occur when we were not present. We should also not ignore the national statistics on arrest, which suggest that people from black and mixed ethnic groups were more than twice as likely to be arrested as those from the white population.[2] However, in line with previous research on the police,[3] the defining feature of our work with frontline officers across all ethnic groups in this regard was the *absence* of arrest from everyday police work.[4] Officers would regularly recount arrests they had previously made, but in the period of our work, it was unusual for an arrest to be made in a 10-hour shift. Indeed, one of the observers went over a year without observing an arrest. Understanding the relative absence of arrest is fundamental to understanding police discretion in the use of their street powers because 'police decisions not to invoke the criminal process, except when reflected in gross failures of service, are not visible to the community'.[5] This chapter considers police understanding of their arrest powers, how discretion was used when deciding whether or not to make an arrest, and the level to which Custody Sergeants intervened to prevent unlawful detention. It concludes by making some observations about the decline of arrest during our period of fieldwork.

---

[1] A Sanders et al, *Criminal Justice*, 4th edn (Oxford, Oxford University Press, 2010) 141.

[2] N Uhrig, *Black, Asian and Minority Ethnic Disproportionality in the Criminal Justice System in England and Wales* (London, Ministry of Justice, 2016).

[3] Eg E Bittner, *Aspects of Police Work* (Boston, Northeastern University Press, 1990) 32; D Black, 'The Social Organization of Arrest' (1971) 23 *Stanford Law Review* 1087, 1093.

[4] Black goes as far as to suggest that, 'Perhaps a study of arrest flatters the significance of the everyday police encounter' (Black, 'Social Organization of Arrest' 1092).

[5] J Goldstein, 'Police Discretion' (1960) 69 *Yale Law Journal* 543, 552.

# I. Police Understandings of the Power of Arrest

It is long established in common law that a police officer has more powers than a member of the public to make a summary arrest.[6] The Police and Criminal Evidence Act 1984 (PACE), Code G, para 2.4 states that the decision whether or not to arrest is 'an operational decision at the discretion of the constable'. The law on arrest is permissive only,[7] providing situations when an officer *may* arrest but not requiring an arrest under any situation. Police powers to arrest without a warrant are now set out in PACE, section 24(1)–(2). In addition to being able to arrest any individual about to commit an offence or in the act of committing an offence, an officer may arrest anyone she has reasonable grounds for suspecting is about to commit an offence, is committing an offence, or has committed one. In order to arrest on suspicion, the officer must have reasonable (rather than just honest)[8] grounds to believe the suspect is guilty of an offence ('did they have reasonable cause for suspecting that the respondent was guilty of the offence')[9] or is about to commit one. This must be determined objectively, based on the information available to the officer and without regard to their unsupported beliefs.[10] The fact that there were other options available to the officer rather than arrest does not make that arrest unlawful.[11]

These long-standing principles were complicated further by reforms to PACE brought in by the Serious Organised Crime and Police Act 2005, section 110, which abolished the previous rules categorising offences into 'arrestable' and 'non arrestable', and extended the power of summary arrest to all offences, however minor. The pay-off for this extended power was that, in addition to possessing reasonable grounds to suspect the arrestee of an offence, the officer now also needed to identify one of the reasons for arrest set out in the amended PACE, section 24(5). The reasons include: enabling the suspect's name or address to be ascertained; preventing the suspect absconding, causing physical injury to him/ herself or another, causing loss/damage to property, committing a public decency offence, or unlawfully obstructing a highway; protecting a child or vulnerable person; and allowing the 'prompt and effective investigation of the offence'.[12] In relation to section 24(5)(e) (allowing the 'prompt and effective investigation of the offence'), Code G notes that this is applicable where further investigation of the suspect's involvement in the offence 'would be frustrated, unreasonably delayed or otherwise hindered and therefore be impracticable'.[13]

---

[6] *Dallison v Caffery* [1964] 2 All ER 610.

[7] D McBarnet, 'Arrest: The Legal Context of Policing' in S Holdaway (ed), *The British Police* (London, Edward Arnold, 1979) 24.

[8] *Dallison v Caffery* [1964] 2 All ER 610 at 368 per Lord Denning.

[9] *Castorina v Chief Constable of Surrey* [1988] NLJR 180 (CA).

[10] ibid.

[11] *Holgate-Mohammed v Duke* [1983] 3 All ER 526 at para 216 per Sir John Arnold P.

[12] Section 24(5).

[13] PACE, Code G 2.9.

In addition to the arrest reasons, an arresting officer also needs to reasonably believe that it is *necessary* to arrest for the reason stated.[14] The suggestion that this might require an officer to show that an arrest was necessary because there were no other means of achieving one of the section 24(5) arrest reasons[15] was quickly debunked by the Court of Appeal in *Hayes v Chief Constable of Merseyside*.[16] In *Hayes*, Hughes LJ declared that it was only necessary for the arresting officer to give 'a cursory'[17] or 'fleeting'[18] consideration of alternatives (most likely requiring a suspect to voluntarily attend a police station for interview at a later date). It was not the case that 'there must be no feasible or viable alternative or that arrest must in every case be a matter of last resort'.[19] The Court here acknowledged that 'it is not the case that a voluntary attendance is always as effective a form of investigation as interview after arrest'.[20] The test requires officers to genuinely believe that the arrest is necessary and to base the decision to arrest on reasonable grounds on the information known at the time.[21] *Hayes* is now well-established in terms of the meaning of necessity in this context, having been applied in a number of subsequent cases,[22] and also in the revised PACE Code G,[23] which came into practice two years prior to our fieldwork commencing. The Code makes further requirements of officers, demanding that they also consider their obligations under the Equality Act 2010 not to discriminate on any protected ground.[24] The Code also requires that officers exercising their power of arrest should apply it in a proportionate manner, having considered the right to liberty and security under the ECHR, Article 5,[25] although it has been noted in both the Divisional Court and Court of Appeal that the necessity test essentially already performs this human rights function.[26]

The additional requirements demanded of an officer before a summary arrest is made did not prevent the Law Society, Bar Council, and Liberty expressing

---

[14] PACE, s 24(4).

[15] See R Austin, 'The New Powers of Arrest: Plus ça Change: More of the Same or Major Change?' (2007) *Criminal Law Review* 439.

[16] *Hayes v Chief Constable of Merseyside* [2012] 1 WLR 517.

[17] Following Sir Brian Kerr LCJ in *Re Alexander's Application for Judicial Review* [2009] NIQB 20 at para 19.

[18] ibid, 39.

[19] *Hayes* at para 32. This is reiterated in subsequent amendments to Code G (Note 2.C), and the ACPO Position Statement on arrest necessity (November 2012): see library.college.police.uk/docs/APPREF/ACPO-Position-Statement-Necessity-to-Arrest.pdf.

[20] *Hayes* at para 42.

[21] ibid, paras 40–42.

[22] *Lord Hanningfield of Chelmsford v Chief Constable of Essex Police* [2013] 1 WLR 3632; *Richardson v Chief Constable of West Midlands Police* [2011] 2 Cr App Rep 1, and *B v Chief Constable of Northern Ireland* [2015] EWHC 3691 (Admin); *R (on the application of L) v Chief Constable of Surrey* [2017] EWHC 129 (Admin).

[23] PACE, Code G 1.3.

[24] PACE, Code G 1.1.

[25] PACE, Code G 1.2.

[26] *Shields v Chief Constable of Merseyside Police* [2010] EWCA Civ 1281; *B v Chief Constable of Northern Ireland* [2015] EWHC 3691 (Admin).

serious concerns about the effect this would have on civil liberties and the ECHR, Article 5.[27] These concerns were shared by a number of academics who have argued that the changes extended rather than restricted police power,[28] prioritised crime control efficiency over suspect rights,[29] and that *Hayes* has developed section 24 beyond its legislative intention, changing 'necessary' to mean 'convenient'.[30] We share the concerns about how 'necessity' has developed post-*Hayes*, as we have argued elsewhere:

> Any application of the proportionality test should include an assessment of whether the arrest is necessary, requiring consideration of whether there is a less restrictive alternative. (…) given that officers should already be considering the *reasons* for arrest, it is difficult in practice to see how a 'cursory' consideration of necessity would go beyond the subjective deliberation as to what reason exists for potentially making a summary arrest.[31]

It is clear, following *Hayes*, that arrest *reasons* and arrest *necessity* overlap to the extent that it can be difficult to determine where consideration of the former ends and the latter starts. It is hardly surprising, therefore, that frontline officers are struggling to apply the tests correctly, despite a number of training packages for new recruits and serving officers.

Data on the understanding that officers had of arrest necessity could sometimes be gathered through watching arrests or the booking-in of prisoners at the Custody Suite. However, arresting officers rarely volunteered information about why they felt that it was necessary to arrest without being directly asked, and the necessity reason logged by the Custody Sergeant did not always match the thought process of the arresting officer at the moment of arrest. Further, as was consistent throughout our study, as much could be learned from the decisions of officers not to take action. It therefore became common for the observer to ask about arrest necessity, either after an arrest had been made, or when the officer had decided on an alternative course of action. These alternatives included requesting voluntary attendance (VA) for an interview at the police station at a later date, issuing a domestic violence protection notice (DVPN), fixed penalty notice/cannabis warning or traffic ticket, issuing informal 'advice' (usually a 'telling-off'), or simply ignoring the offence completely. However, it became apparent, from the responses given to this question, that many officers had not considered the necessity for arrest at all, instead focusing on the reasons for arrest. Questions about arrest necessity

---

[27] House of Commons Research Paper 04/89 2/12/04.

[28] E Cape, 'PACE Now and Then: Twenty-One Years of "Rebalancing"' in E Cape and R Young (eds), *Regulating Policing: The Police and Criminal Evidence Act 1984 Past, Present and Future* (London, Bloomsbury, 2008) 202.

[29] Sanders et al, *Criminal Justice* 143.

[30] E Cape, 'Arrest: Power of Summary Arrest – Reasonable Grounds for Believing that Necessary to Arrest Person in Question' (2012) *Criminal Law Review* 35.

[31] G Pearson et al, 'Policy, Practicalities, and PACE s 24: Police Understanding and Subsuming of Necessity in Decision-Making on Arrest' (2018) 45 *Journal of Law and Society* 282, 288.

often led to the officer stating that their necessity was to ensure a prompt and effective investigation (the section 24(5)(e) arrest reason), or to protect an individual from harm (section 24(5)(d)).

Even the kind of cursory or fleeting consideration of alternatives to arrest envisaged in *Hayes* or *B* was often missing, or at least escaped translation into words. For example, when called to a property following a complaint that a husband had punched his wife, the responding officer immediately arrested for assault under the Offences Against the Person Act 1861, section 47, explaining to the suspect that 'my arrest necessity is to protect a vulnerable person'. This explanation for the necessity grounds was subsequently given to the Custody Sergeant. The problem here was that: (a) the explanation given was the arrest *reason* not the *necessity*; and (b) the officer and Sergeant were both aware that, since the complainant was unwilling to make a statement, the suspect would be released back to the home address in a matter of hours following the decision to take no further action ('to NFA'). At the time of arrest, there was no suggestion that alternatives (which could have protected the wife for a longer period) were considered. For example, a DVPN could have been served forcing the suspect to leave the property.[32] This pattern was observed in many contexts, with officers simply using a section 24(5) reason to arrest also as their necessity, and missing opportunities to reduce the identified risk (for example, by asking the suspect to leave a property, or by confiscating prohibited items)[33] and request VA at a later date. Similarly, officers who arrested, giving the section 24(5)(e) 'prompt and effective' reason as both their arrest reason and their necessity, were taking risks with the legality of the arrest. The Divisional Court in *B v Chief Constable of Northern Ireland* held that necessity 'requires more than merely desirable or more convenient to the arresting authority'[34] and that for section 24(5)(e) to be satisfied, the arrest must be necessary for the investigation to be both prompt *and* effective.[35] In this sense, 'effective' was to be interpreted as, 'tending to achieve its purpose' rather than merely being efficient or cost-effective.[36] An officer who uses 'prompt and effective' as a default reason for an arrest without considering possible alternative methods of protecting evidence or securing an interview may struggle in a court of law to explain how the investigation may have been thwarted without the arrest.[37]

> Researcher: Even if you've got a *reason* to arrest, for example to protect a vulnerable person, that's not the same as arrest necessity.

---

[32] Neighbourhood, Dunland, June 2018.
[33] Territorial Support, Brandham, November 2014.
[34] *B v Chief Constable of Northern Ireland* para 26.
[35] ibid, para 27.
[36] ibid, para 28.
[37] Though the Court of Appeal has ruled that only nominal damages will be awarded for an arrest that is only technically unlawful on procedural rather than substantive grounds (*Parker v Chief Constable of Essex* [2018] EWCA Civ 2788).

Aidan: No, it *is* arrest necessity. You could arrest someone purely to protect a vulnerable person. So I could arrest somebody in theory for littering if it was to protect a vulnerable person, and hold them in custody (…) that is, absolutely, that's Code G.[38]

Given the complexity of the law and the overlap caused by the judgment in *Hayes*, confusion is probably not surprising.[39] The uncertainty may also be exacerbated by shifting policy pressures on officers, for example the need to take 'positive action' following domestic violence, which we will consider in Part V. However, this confusion has very significant implications for both the individual liberty of suspects and the ability of the police service to initiate formal action against offenders. Officers focusing on the *reason* rather than the *need* to arrest are less likely to consider the increasing number of alternatives to arrest, which may in many cases provide a better solution for the suspect, the complainant, and the officer (in terms of their time and availability for other jobs). However, although this will play a role in unnecessary arrests being made, it is not the case that officers are making large numbers of lawfully-dubious arrests by use of the 'Ways and Means Act'.[40] Equally significant, because they are not considering alternatives to arrest, officers may sometimes choose to take no formal action at all because of the various practical pressures placed upon them. Only in the latter stages of our research was VA being used more frequently, although this shift appeared to be more the result of longer waits at Custody and the opening of new 'VA suites'.

# II. Determinants of the Use of Police Discretion to Arrest

It has long been established that, in the exercise of their discretion whether or not to arrest, legal determinants, such as those set out in PACE, section 24(4)–(5) and Code G, are often not at the forefront of an officer's mind. Research dating back to the 1960s identified that, in the United States, there were many significant non-legal reasons determining the likelihood that an arrest would be made,[41] much of which focuses on the 'significant effect' of situational factors.[42]

---

[38] Response, Eriador, November 2016.

[39] General confusion amongst officers about the meaning of 'necessity' in the test of proportionality has been noted elsewhere (K Bullock and P Johnson, 'The Impact of the Human Rights Act 1998 on Policing in England and Wales' (2012) 52 *British Journal of Criminology* 630, 637).

[40] P Waddington, *Policing Citizens: Authority and Rights* (London, UCL Press, 1999) 136.

[41] W LaFave, *Arrest: The Decision to take a Suspect into Custody. The Report of the American Bar Foundation's Survey of the Administration of Criminal Justice in the United States* (Boston, Little Brown, 1965).

[42] R Worden, 'Situational and Attitudinal Explanations of Police Behaviour. A Theoretical Reappraisal and Empirical Reassessment' (1989) 23 *Law and Society* 667, 701.

Previous research has noted a plethora of reasons why an officer may choose to make a summary arrest, including previous convictions, disorder undermining police authority, general suspiciousness (being 'out of place'), intelligence, workload and 'quality' of arrest, pressure from an influential victim,[43] and a refusal to defer to police authority.[44] Our observations suggested that all of these indicators of an increased risk of arrest were still relevant. However, different roles, and different officers within these roles, were likely to be influenced to a greater or lesser extent by them. There was no 'one size fits all' equation which could be applied to a scenario to determine whether an arrest would be made. Moreover, for the overwhelming majority of officers, arrest reasons and arrest necessity were, to a greater or lesser extent, subsumed by a host of personal, practical, and policy reasons.

## A. Personal Morality, Role-Specific Determinants, and Suspect Demeanour

Personal or role-specific determinants were always significant in terms of whether an arrest would be made or not. Certain officers were simply more willing to make arrests than others, although it was not always easy to ascertain why this was the case. Sometimes, it appeared that confidence on the part of the officer was an important factor but, sometimes, the confidence that appeared to come from a time-served officer also led to a cynicism that would lead officers to avoid an arrest because they felt that it was pointless. A belief that there was insufficient evidence (often due to a complainant refusing to give a statement), or that the Custody Sergeant or Crown Prosecution Service (CPS) would simply 'NFA' the case led more experienced officers to believe that their time was better spent elsewhere than in a Custody Suite holding cell.[45] At other times, we saw that the officer's individual personality could play an important role in a decision not to make an arrest, even when it appeared justified and proportionate. Officers would sometimes look to bend rules and policy, or interpret offences less seriously where they felt that they would be expected to arrest, but did not feel it was morally right. We saw this on numerous occasions with regard to low-level domestic abuse, particularly where the perpetrator was young and lacking in previous convictions.[46] Suspects who were apologetic and helpful in answering an officer's questions reduced their

---

[43] M McConville et al, *The Case for the Prosecution: Police Suspects and the Construction of Criminality* (London, Routledge, 1993).
[44] Black, 'Social Organization of Arrest' 1099.
[45] Neighbourhood, Abbey, April 2016.
[46] Response, Wilderland, September 2016.

chance of arrest.[47] Many officers would also 'give a break' to elderly or vulnerable suspects who, for want of a better explanation, they simply felt sorry for:

> [The officers] responded to a report that a man was on the street brandishing a make-shift spear and shouting threateningly. They arrived at the address to find an 80-year-old man sat on a settee, who had attached a knife to the end of a pole. He was agitated but not threatening and had clear mental health problems. The makeshift weapon was seized but no action was taken. 'What if it was your grandad?' asked Maz.[48]

> A lone male on the street is smoking something. He ducks into a pub as he sees the van. Officers jump out of the van to pursue him. In the pub, there is a plastic bag lined with tinfoil – apparently this is to enable shoplifting of clothes (...) While held in the van, he admits he was doing shoplifting. [According to the officers he] was an aspiring, young, fit OCG who had been 'off the radar' for years. He is now thin and ill and hooked on heroin, crying in [the] van. The officers who knew him before are shocked and genu-inely upset. They could have charged him with Going Equipped to Steal. Compassionate discretion seems to dominate their decision not to take any action, although one later suggests that, in the age of targets, they would have arrested him.[49]

The latter example was particularly surprising as the officers were from a Territorial Support Unit, one of the more proactive roles when it came to using street powers, including arrest.

The role that the officer was performing was a key determinant of how they would use their discretion. Territorial Support officers frequently expressed the view that 'taking people off the streets'[50] in the short-term was part of their job, while Response officers would often claim that 'policy' forced them to make arrests. In contrast, Neighbourhood officers were more likely to attempt informal resolutions, knowing they had to maintain a working relationship with arrestees and their friends and family. Nevertheless, while role was important, individual working personalities remained influential. The proactive officer may go out of her way to make arrests, while the sympathetic officer, in contrast, may be prepared to re-interpret or turn a blind eye to offences. Most officers fell on a sliding scale between these two extremes, but with two overriding considerations dominating their arrest discretion: (a) to avoid 'in the job' trouble[51] (and therefore wishing to do things 'by the book'); and (b) to avoid unnecessary work, which, given the paperwork and waiting around that attached itself to an arrest, was a considerable disincentive to arrest (or indeed request a VA). Where mandatory arrest was seen as force policy (see domestic violence, below), refusing to make an arrest had the

---

[47] Territorial Support, Knapford, March 2014; Response, Farthing, January 2017.

[48] Mental Health Triage, Maron, September 2015.

[49] Territorial Support, Knapford, September 2015.

[50] Territorial Support, Knapford, February 2014; Territorial Support, Knapford, July 2015.

[51] M Chatterton, 'The Supervision of Patrol Work Under the Fixed Points System' in S Holdaway (ed), *The British Police* (London, Edward Arnold, 1979); P Waddington, *Liberty and Order: Policing Public Order in a Capital City* (London, UCL Press, 1994).

potential to create both in job trouble and also additional work for the officer in defending their position afterwards.

In contrast to officers feeling sympathetic towards a suspect, where a suspect was rude, aggressive, or otherwise challenged an officer's authority, this would increase the risk of an arrest (or indeed other formal disposal). However, this was not standard across all officers. Some officers were more easily provoked, whereas others had remarkably thicker skins.[52] The idea that 'contempt of cop' (this was not a phrase we heard officers use) increases the chance of arrest has been established in studies of American policing.[53] Studies in the UK have also suggested that suspects challenging or humiliating an officer in front of members of the public are more likely to be arrested,[54] and Buvik, carrying out research in Norway, talks about the phenomenon of '[t]alking yourself into jail'.[55] We noted that insulting words or behaviour increased the risk of arrest, but this was by no means common. Abusive words or aggressive behaviour, by contrast, substantially increased the risk of an arrest, although it also brought into play the possibility of an arrest for breach of the peace in addition to the original suspected offence. As one officer explained, having arrested an offender who had sworn at them, 'I treat everybody the same, but not when they don't treat me the same'.[56] Those under the influence of alcohol who swore at officers were likely to be arrested for 'drunk and disorderly' whereas, if they swore at other members of the public, verbal advice was more likely.[57] 'Fronting up' to an officer was the ultimate challenge to her authority and would also most likely result in an arrest.[58]

However, although role-specific and individual interpretations were important determinants of whether an arrest would be made, there were other understandings that were to a large extent shared across roles, stations, and forces that could act as predictors of whether an arrest would be made or not. We have discussed these situational variables in more detail elsewhere,[59] but the remainder of this section provides an overview of the non-legal reasons we observed to dominate an officer's arrest discretion, in addition to individual or role-specific factors. Here our observations were similar to those with regard to police stops and searches,

---

[52] See also K Buvik, 'The Hole in the Doughnut: a Study of Police Discretion in a Nightlife Setting' (2016) 26 *Policing and Society* 771.

[53] T Barker, *Police Ethics: Crisis in Law Enforcement* (Springfield IL, Charles C Thomas, 2011) 31; Black, 'Social Organization of Arrest' (especially 1099); F Cooper, 'Masculinities, Post-Racialism and the Gates Controversy: The False Equivalence Between Officer and Civilian' (2011) 11 *Nevada Law Journal* 1.

[54] See also Waddington, *Policing Citizens* 154; Worden, 'Situational and Attitudinal Explanations of Police Behaviour' 688.

[55] Buvik, 'The Hole in the Doughnut'.

[56] Territorial Support, Brandham, January 2014.

[57] Night-time Economy Team, Knapford, October 2015.

[58] Territorial Support, Knapford, February 2014.

[59] Pearson et al, 'Policy, Practicalities, and PACE'.

and indicated considerable shared understandings between different officers, different roles, and different divisions and forces.

## B. Decent Folk versus Criminals

The first of these shared factors was the division between 'decent people' and the criminal type. If an officer considered that a suspect was a 'suspected OCG'[60] or a 'prolific offender' they would be far more likely to make an arrest. In contrast, 'decent people' were far more likely to get a break, and not only for minor offences such as cannabis possession.[61] This was different reasoning from the personal sympathies noted above (although there may have been an unspoken overlap) and was because the suspect fell outside the criminal type categorisation popular amongst officers. So, for example, a young male with no previous convictions, who was found in possession of a knuckle-duster and seemed genuinely distressed when he was searched, was given verbal advice in front of his mother: 'There was no way I was going to take him into custody'.[62] This example is illustrative of an important by-product of the reasoning that we saw from officers in their arrest decision-making. The decisions were often explained in an 'all or nothing' fashion: either the suspect should be arrested, or merely given verbal advice. In this case, a VA might have been more appropriate, but there was no evidence that it was given even a 'fleeting' or 'cursory' consideration as required by PACE, section 24. A second example was of a driver who had a police-style baton in the doorwell of his van. He was again only 'given an advisory' because he did not belong to the criminal type category: 'Had he been a young lad like the type we are after ...' the officer claimed they would have made an arrest. For the same offence, a 'suspected OCG' would have 'definitely' been taken into custody: 'If you're a career criminal, are you going to benefit from advice from the police? I don't think you ever would ... If they are habitual offenders, then I don't think dealing with them by verbal advice would be right'.[63] A corollary of this is that crimes against 'decent people' by the 'criminal type' were likely to be treated more seriously than crimes within communities seen by many officers as 'shit'. Here officers were more likely to walk away once the situation was temporarily defused, even in one example of an affray involving a weapon. On this occasion another officer did make an arrest because he predicted that the dispute would escalate, but he had no doubts that it was a 'shit job': 'I think that [the Custody Sergeant] thought it was "shit on shit", as in, why should we give a fuck?'[64]

---

[60] Territorial Support, Knapford, February 2014.
[61] Territorial Support, Knapford, March 2014.
[62] Territorial Support, Knapford, July 2015.
[63] Interview, Territorial Support, Knapford, March 2014.
[64] Neighbourhood, Withered Heath, March 2018.

## C. Public Expectations and Geographical Determinants

Another situational factor that played a role in whether an arrest was more or less likely was where the suspected offence took place and what action the officers thought might be expected of them by members of the public in the vicinity. Sometimes this reflected the officer's own feelings – sympathetic or otherwise – about the suspect, discussed above. Would members of the public think that taking a child or an elderly person into custody would be disproportionate or unfair?[65] Sometimes this would depend less on the nature of the suspect and more on the environment. The fact that cannabis was being smoked at a shrine for a recently-murdered gang member overrode the fact that suspected 'OCGs' were smoking cannabis openly in front of officers.[66] Conversely, an individual snorting what appeared to be a prohibited substance in a phone box was arrested. The fact that it was in a public area was at the forefront of the officer's mind: 'It was opposite a college and a set of traffic lights [...] People saw her doing it and the public wouldn't have understood a VA'.[67] In another example, an officer was faced with two young men who were verbally abusive and physically obstructive to police officers attempting to respond to another incident. Some members of the public present were recording the incident on their mobile phones.[68] In both of these cases, there was, in the mind of the officer, a public expectation of arrest which tipped the balance towards this response.

## D. Tactical, Operational, and Workload Pressures

In addition to these public-facing situational and environmental considerations, there were a host of backstage[69] pressures that influenced an officer's decision whether to arrest. These included tactical and operational pressures, workload, and consideration of colleagues. The clearest tactical pressure to arrest was seen from the work of a Territorial Support unit, who frequently used arrest to achieve both short- and long-term tactical aims. Their primary tactic was to disrupt gang activity. In the short term, this meant taking as many suspected OCG members into custody as they could,[70] even if there was little realistic hope of charge or prosecution. In the longer term, this fed into the strategy of discouraging gangs from using firearms because they knew if would lead to their operations being disrupted in the future. Taking a suspected 'OCG' off the street for the night

---

[65] See also Waddington, *Policing Citizens* 686.
[66] Territorial Support, Knapford, July 2015.
[67] Territorial Support, Knapford, September 2015.
[68] Response, Eriador, September 2017.
[69] We do not use this in the same sense as Goffman as there was very much a police audience being played for (E Goffman, *The Presentation of Self in Everyday Life* (Harmondsworth, Penguin, 1971)).
[70] For example, Territorial Support, Lakeside, January 2015.

was considered a 'result',[71] even if she was subsequently released without charge. The overriding impression from our time with the Territorial Support units was that arrest and detention was a 'practical peacekeeping method that has only in its most outward aspects the character of a legal action',[72] and that taking the suspect off the streets in the short term was the only end in the officer's mind. However, if the officer had evidence for a charge, then this might also lead to bail conditions being imposed, which could further disrupt the gang's activities.[73] We also observed arrest being used tactically to allow officers to carry out searches of premises without revealing their intelligence source.[74]

As we saw in Chapter 5, workload and time pressures were always at play and officers were aware of the practicality of taking a prisoner into custody. For example, officers in public order situations will often not be able to make arrests for fear of reducing the operational capability of their Police Support Unit.[75] What was more evident from our observations of everyday policing were the individual pressures on officers that could dissuade them from making an arrest, even when the officer could lawfully do so under PACE, section 24(5). Officers were always aware of how much time remained of their shift. If there were only a couple of hours remaining, an arrest was less likely for all bar the most serious of crimes or most wanted suspect (there was a kudos in being able to capture such individuals). As we have explained, when Custody Suites were busy, officers could be faced with up to three hours waiting in a holding cell, which would take them beyond the length of their shift. Officers would instead tend to look for reasons *not* to arrest in these situations.[76] Even early on in a shift, the long wait and the paperwork accompanying an arrest acted as disincentives to arrest. At one force, cutbacks in personnel had impacts not only upon the availability of Custody Suites and Custody staff, but also on specialist units tasked with processing prisoners, again disincentivising arrest.

> 'You've seen how it is'. Davo explains the lack of officers who responded to the [Grade One Domestic Abuse] call and refers back to an earlier conversation we had about them being understaffed. Davo doesn't think they can afford to be off the streets [by taking the suspect into custody] for that long when there are so many calls coming in.[77]

Officers were also mindful of whether delivering a prisoner into custody would make them unpopular with the Custody Sergeant, who could either

---

[71] Territorial Support, Knapford, February 2014.

[72] E Bittner, *The Functions of the Police in Modern Society* (University of Minnesota, National Institute of Mental Health, Center for Studies of Crime and Delinquency, 1970) 113.

[73] Night-time Economy Team, Knapford, October 2015.

[74] Territorial Support, Maron, January 2015. McConville et al note that many reasons for arrest could be found in police 'working rules', including the gathering of intelligence (*Case for the Prosecution* 99).

[75] G Pearson and A Sale, 'On the Lash: Revisiting the Effectiveness of Alcohol Controls at Football Matches' (2011) 21 *Policing and Society* 1. A Police Support Unit (or PSU) is a unit of officers trained in public order tactics.

[76] Night-time Economy Team, Knapford, October 2015.

[77] Response, Ettenmoor, October 2016.

cause embarrassment to the officer by refusing to take the suspect into custody (although as we will see below, this was rare), or order the arresting officer to stay with a vulnerable prisoner in an observational capacity in the cell. In one example, both Triage and Response officers refused to arrest an individual with a registered personality disorder who had waved a carving knife threateningly at officers, requiring them to forcefully disarm her. The Triage officer explained that, in their view, none of the Response officers wanted to spend time in Custody with the suspect waiting for 'her bloods to be checked' before she could be charged or de-arrested.[78]

However, other practical pressures pushed officers away from requesting a VA, which in some cases led to arrests that were not necessary. Many officers avoided VAs, perhaps because they did not want the workload stored up for a subsequent shift (expressing a preference for being able to 'write off' jobs rather than having to go back to them). Furthermore, the feeling amongst officers was that, where VAs were served on the 'criminal type', they were unlikely to attend as agreed. This would entail the officer spending time locating them.[79] The impact of their decisions on their colleagues was another pressing concern, with officers not wishing to gain a reputation for 'landing work' on others that they should be doing themselves. Almost all officers had an awareness of colleagues who avoided work, especially that which led to significant administration (for example by avoiding responding to domestic abuse calls unless absolutely necessary).[80] A senior officer in the Special Constabulary argued that VAs should be avoided because they placed a workload on other officers:

> If we were going to VA, when would they next come in? When would we next be on duty? It's more complicated for us to VA. (…) What you don't want to be doing is handing workload over to a normal bobby. There's nothing worse than them coming in on a Saturday morning and seeing a job that the Specials have left them … I would rather take somebody in and have them released the following day on bail (…) than to land it with one of my colleagues with a VA or whatever.[81]

## III. Force Policy and Domestic Abuse

We have seen that there are a plethora of drivers behind police decisions to arrest or – more usually – not to arrest, and that these drivers tend to subsume the legal tests for whether or not an arrest should be made, set out in PACE, section 24 and

---

[78] Mental Health Triage, Maron, January 2016.
[79] However, following *B v Chief Constable of Northern Ireland*, likely delays in processing a suspect do not necessarily make an arrest lawful. The 'prompt and effective' test from s 25(5)(e) requires that the arrest is necessary to make the investigation *effective*, not just prompt (paras 26–28).
[80] Response, Bree, September 2016.
[81] Interview, Specials, Maron, July 2015.

Code G. These drivers include the personal characteristics, beliefs, and policing style of the individual officers, tactical and role-specific influences, understandings about the nature of crime, criminals, and 'decent people', context-specific situational factors, and workload and co-worker pressures. However, while some of these were observable to varying degrees throughout our fieldwork, there was a more formal influence on the decision whether or not to arrest that was highly significant in changing the way in which officers used arrest in certain circumstances. In the previous chapter, we identified the influence of national political discourse and policy changes on decisions to stop and search. Similarly, with regard to arrest, we also saw policy changing the behaviour of officers, albeit not uniformly across the board. Again, here we are using a broad definition of policy[82] to include direction, guidance, and supervision which is communicated to officers from Sergeants or Inspectors. Usually, this cascades down from a force-wide policy, which may itself derive from national directives or guidance from the Home Office or College of Policing, or from changes to the law or Codes of Practice. However, it is the *local application and supervision* of policy which we observed to have a greater influence on changing police behaviour rather than its source or higher authority. This could particularly be observed with regard to force policies on domestic violence, which were interpreted in different ways as they cascade down to different stations, shifts, and roles, and which were then applied differently by frontline officers depending on this interpretation and explanation by their line-managers in briefings. Despite force-wide training packages, force policies did not always lead to uniformity in approach. Changes to practice were subject to both the vertical fragmentation (changes in policy as it cascades down through the ranks) and horizontal fragmentation (differences in policy interpretations across the ranks).[83] Those changes that did occur, though, could be both rapid and potentially dramatic.

With specific regard to arrest, force policies should not curtail the operational freedom of an officer to decide whether or not to make an arrest. So long as the officer is acting in good faith and in the course of her duty, this should remain subject to PACE, section 24. *R (Tchenguiz and R20 Ltd) v Director of the Serious Fraud Office*[84] appears to have established the rule from *O'Hara v Chief Constable of the Royal Ulster Constabulary*.[85] Instruction from a senior officer (in this case to 'arrest that man') is not sufficient to satisfy reasonable grounds for arrest. It is also clear from the case that the arresting officer must continue to make her

---

[82] In contrast to the narrower definition of 'an authoritative statement signifying a settled practice on any matter relevant to the duties of the Chief Constable' in R Grimshaw and T Jefferson, *Interpreting Police Work: Policy and Practice in Forms of Beat Policing* (London, Allen & Unwin, 1987) 204.

[83] The concepts of vertical and horizontal fragmentation are discussed in more detail in Chapter 10.

[84] *R (Tchenguiz and R20 Ltd) v Director of the Serious Fraud Office* [2013] 1 WLR 1634.

[85] *O'Hara v Chief Constable of the Royal Ulster Constabulary* [1997] 1 All ER 129. Confirmed by the European Court of Human Rights in *O'Hara v UK* (2002) 34 EHRR 32. See also *Parker v Chief Constable of Essex* [2018] EWCA Civ 2788.

own decision as to the necessity of the arrest, independent of the wishes of an instructing senior officer. There is no reason to assume why force policies would not also fall under the *O'Hara* rule, as they operate in a similar fashion. In practice, however, force policies curtail the operational freedom of officers, who are aware that acting in breach of this policy may lead to censure by their Sergeant or Inspector and, in some cases, this might lead to retraining.

Two operational policies that affected the likelihood of arrest were with regard to possession of small amounts of cannabis and to accusations of domestic violence. As we saw in the previous chapter, small amounts of cannabis were uncovered on a fairly regular basis following searches of individuals or vehicles. With the exception of arrests for OCG disruption purposes, officers usually preferred not to take an individual into custody on this basis. Force policies on 'cannabis warnings', which followed from national ACPO guidance,[86] directed officers away from arrest and towards warnings and penalty notices. However, the guidance stated that for offenders who had received two previous warnings, a third should not be given and instead the police should 'consider the options available for prosecuting the suspect and arrest may then be necessary to enable the prompt and effective investigation of the offence or of the person's conduct'.[87] This was not, however, how the policy worked in practice. Vertically and/or horizontally it had mutated, for many officers, into something else. Instead, officers complained that the policy on repeat drug offenders 'took away' their 'discretion' not to arrest.[88] In one incident, the officer explained that they felt that a charge was pointless because the court would only impose a small fine. Nevertheless, they believed that the policy for third-time offenders was that of mandatory arrest ('they have to be taken in').[89] A policy developed at national level to prevent Custody Suites being clogged with minor drug offenders therefore transformed into one that had the potential to lead officers to arrest, with no consideration of other alternatives.

A second example comes from the College of Policing's Authorised Professional Practice (APP) on Domestic Violence. This states that 'Police officers have a duty to take positive action when dealing with domestic abuse incidents'. This positive action is primarily in response to the ECHR, Article 2 right to life and is that 'officers take positive action to make the victim and any children safe … Officers must be able to justify the decision **not** to arrest where the grounds exist and it would be a necessary and proportionate response'.[90] APP then goes on to list a

---

[86] ACPO, *Guidance on Policing Cannabis – Use of Cannabis Warnings* (London, ACPO, January 2007). ACPO stands for the Association of Chief Police Officers, which has now been replaced by the National Police Chiefs Council (NPCC).

[87] ACPO, *Guidance on Policing Cannabis* 2.4.5.

[88] Territorial Support, Knapford, September 2015.

[89] Interview, Territorial Support, Knapford, March 2014.

[90] College of Policing APP, *Major Investigation and Public Protection: Domestic Abuse: Arrest and Other Positive Approaches*, available at www.app.college.police.uk/app-content/major-investigation-and-public-protection/domestic-abuse/arrest-and-other-positive-approaches/.

number of 'benefits of arrest' (although no drawbacks). Unsurprisingly, the APP was reflected in policies at both forces but, although officers can access the APP directly online, our observations found this to be rare. Officers instead relied on short training packages, briefing reminders, or discussions with their colleagues, the Sergeant or, less regularly, the Inspector. As a result, the domestic abuse APP guidance also became distorted, with different officers interpreting it and using it in different ways. Inspectors and Sergeants offered versions of the guidance with often significantly differing interpretations of what it said and what it expected of them and their officers. At this level, we should not be surprised to see an interpretation of the policy that is risk averse. This was interpreted again by officers, during briefings and through training packages, and then applied in often time-pressured decisions. At some point in the process, for many officers, the APP requirement for positive action had morphed into a policy of mandatory arrest. Even officers who seem to have read the original guidance picked up on the line that, '[o]fficers must be able to justify the decision **not** to arrest where the grounds exist', ignoring the end of the sentence: 'and it would be a necessary and proportionate response'.

A fairly typical example came from a Grade One response to a 999 call from a wife who said her husband had hit her and tried to strangle her. The disturbance was over by the time we arrived but, after a quick chat with the complainant, the husband was arrested for a section 47 assault. The officer explained to the prisoner that 'arrest necessity is to protect a vulnerable person'. On the way to the Custody Suite she explained to the researcher that 'the policy is to arrest', but that because the wife had refused to provide a statement, her experience was that the CPS would not prosecute, meaning that the Custody Sergeant would NFA and release the suspect immediately. That an arrest was still made despite this knowledge goes to show the power of (misinterpreted) force policy.[91] Following a short interview under caution, in which the suspect gave 'no comment' answers to all questions, this was exactly what occurred. Less than three hours after the arrest, the officer drove the husband back to his wife's house. It was clear from this vignette that: (a) there had not been even a cursory consideration of alternatives (for example an emergency DVPN notice); and (b) the arrest could not have been necessary to protect the complainant because the disturbance had already ended before the officer arrived and the suspect was returned to the property only a few hours later.[92]

Officers were commonly of the opinion that the policy had taken away their discretion in 'domestics' and most considered it unnecessary, ill-judged, and often disproportionate (although a handful expressed a strong alternative view). Nevertheless, with few exceptions, even officers who objected to the policy

[91] Worden, for example, identifies the influence of expected legal outcomes in terms of whether officers are likely to make an arrest ('Situational and Attitudinal Explanations of Police Behaviour' 689–90).
[92] Neighbourhood, Dunland, June 2018.

144 Arrest and Detention

preferred to follow it rather than 'fight the system'[93] by not making an arrest following a response to a domestic incident:

> For the last five years at least the DV policy is that, if you attend a domestic incident, positive action must be taken which effectively … it doesn't explicitly say that in the policy but it is certainly enforced culturally, from the senior management team, that (…) domestics must result in arrest except in exceptional circumstances.[94]

Following this interview, the officer was called to a Grade Two domestic: a boyfriend and girlfriend who lived separately. The young male had sent abusive texts and then pushed the complainant during an altercation at her mother's house. As we drove to the address, the officer was visibly agitated:

> [He] is drumming his fingers on the steering-wheel, saying that force policy says he has to make an arrest because it has been [recorded] as domestic abuse (…) But you can see that he doesn't want to (…) You can see that he is stressed. He is saying things like 'I'm not given a choice'. He could see that I was watching to see what decision he would make.[95]

It was another example of how policy was ill-serving officers in terms of their compliance with PACE, section 24. Positive action would have been satisfied by asking the male for his copy of the key for his girlfriend's mother's house, after which he could have VA'd the male. Ultimately, this was a rare occasion when the officer's own moral code overrode his interpretation of force policy. The incident was 'cuffed in a spectacular manner'[96] as the officer ignored the offences committed (despite both parties making allegations and there being physical evidence of threatening text messages and criminal damage). Assisted by his decision not to switch on his body-worn camera (again in contravention of force policy), the officer closed the incident by reporting back that there had been a mistake and no crimes had been committed. This was one of a number of observed incidents in a short period whereby different officers were cuffing crimes in order to avoid making arrests that they believed to be required by policy but which they felt were disproportionate.[97] The cuffing of domestic incidents fits into the longer overall pattern observed in earlier research which has revealed dismissive police attitudes to domestic violence perpetrators.[98] However, the two incidents described in this section detail how, in different ways, the APP guidance was both overriding

---

[93] Response, Ettenmoor, January 2017.
[94] Interview [Redacted No 1 2016].
[95] Fieldnotes [Redacted No 1 2016].
[96] Fieldnotes [Redacted No 1 2016].
[97] Fieldnotes [Redacted No 2 2016; Redacted No 3 2016].
[98] S Holdaway, *Inside the British Police: A Force at Work* (Oxford, Basil Blackwell, 1983); C Hoyle, *Negotiating Domestic Violence: Police, Criminal Justice and Victims* (Oxford, Oxford University Press, 1998); L Westmarland, *Gender and Policing: Sex, Power, and Police Culture* (Cullompton, Willan, 2001); A Myhill and K Johnson, 'Police Use of Discretion in Response to Domestic Violence' (2015) 61 *Criminology and Criminal Justice* 3.

officer consideration of what is a legal arrest and also, in terms of protecting at-risk individuals, had the potential to exacerbate, rather than reduce, the risk posed to the victim.

## IV. The Role of the Custody Sergeant

The preceding sections of this chapter have identified that there are a host of personal, role-specific, environmental, and workload reasons why an arrest may be made and that these subsume the test for arrest necessity set out in PACE, section 24(4), and clarified in *Hayes*, which was meant to counter-balance the 2005 increase in the power of arrest. Prior to making an arrest, an officer should give at least a cursory consideration of the alternatives before deciding that an arrest is necessary for one of the reasons set out in section 24(5). However, we observed that officers typically failed to differentiate arrest reason and necessity, or simply did not consider alternatives to arrest due to other factors driving their use of discretion. Post-*Hayes* at least, it is difficult to argue against the view of Sanders et al that the necessity rule is purely presentational, 'giving the appearance of due process while doing nothing to promote its substance'.[99] An officer's argument post-arrest that they gave cursory consideration to a VA but dismissed it is difficult (although, as case law shows, not impossible) to impugn in court without evidence that the consideration did not take place.

Here, the role of the Custody Sergeant could potentially provide a check on unlawful arrests. The Custody Sergeant's role under PACE is to take responsibility for authorising detention following an arrest. PACE, section 37(1) requires the Custody Sergeant to 'determine whether he has before him sufficient evidence to charge that person with the offence for which he was arrested' and to release the suspect if the grounds for detention cease to apply. There is no statutory obligation on a Custody Sergeant to ensure that the arrest was made for a lawful section 24(5) reason or was necessary under section 24(4). Nevertheless, our observations indicated that Custody Sergeants both asked for, and were required to make a record of, the arrest reasons and of the necessity.[100] However, this did not act as a check against unnecessary arrests. Although Custody Sergeants did typically understand section 24 more than most arresting officers, they rarely asked about any alternatives to arrest. Furthermore, although they asked arresting officers about reasons for arrest, this was largely a matter of completing the electronic records associated with detention. Occasionally arresting officers would stumble when asked about arrest reason, in which case the Custody Sergeant might suggest a reason.

---

[99] Sanders et al, *Criminal Justice* 144.

[100] This is not to suggest that they had no interest in the law on *detention*. As Skinns notes, Custody Sergeants had a 'profound regard' for legal rules (L Skinns, *Police Powers and Citizen Rights: Discretionary Decision Making in Police Detention* (London, Routledge, 2019) 112).

On other occasions, particularly when the prisoner was aggressive and taken straight to a cell, the Sergeant would fill out the form with the reason they thought was most appropriate.[101] In both of these scenarios, the reason for arrest suggested or input by the Custody Sergeant was usually 'prompt and effective', without any further discussion or explanation of how the arrest would allow a more effective investigation than a VA. For a number of months, in one Custody Suite a piece of A4 paper was sellotaped to the custody desk, setting out the possible reasons for arrest under section 24 to assist arresting officers when asked their arrest reason.[102] In short, our time in the Custody Suites (unsurprisingly given their statutory role) only rarely found Custody Sergeants challenging arresting officers on the legality of their arrest, but it did uncover further evidence that many officers were not considering the necessity of their arrest and that some had not even considered their statutory reason for arrest.

In line with findings from most other research, decisions by Custody Sergeants not to book prisoners into Custody were rare,[103] even when they outwardly disagreed with the arrest. We saw only a handful of examples of Custody Sergeants declining to take a prisoner into custody,[104] usually because the prisoner was a juvenile[105] or otherwise vulnerable. Indeed, Custody Sergeants seemed most preoccupied not by the legal rights or wrongs of a detention but in ensuring that none of their charges died or came to harm in custody.[106] In line with the findings of other researchers into custody prior to the 2005 changes to the arrest regime, although Custody Sergeants very rarely refused to authorise detention, they occasionally offered 'words of advice' to the arresting officer to try and dissuade them from similar future arrests.[107] On other occasions, feedback from the Custody Sergeant was less formal but still clear, and also tended to reflect the understandings of frontline officers about 'decent people' and the criminal type:

> Arrest for affray with a weapon: [The prisoner] is 'an unpredictable smack user' with a history of violence. There are two witnesses (…) Arrest necessity is to 'to protect individuals'. The Custody Sergeant is world weary and unimpressed. He questions the arrest

---

[101] This allowed for what Dixon has called a 'reinterpretation' of arrests to satisfy the audience of the records (D Dixon, *Law in Policing: Legal Regulation and Police Practices* (Oxford, Clarendon, 1997) 272).

[102] Custody, Tidmouth, November 2013.

[103] J Long 'Keeping PACE? Some Front Line Policing Perspectives' in E Cape and R Young (eds), *Regulating Policing* (Oxford, Hart Publishing, 2008) 91, 95; McConville et al, *Case for the Prosecution*; C Phillips and D Brown, *Entry into the Criminal Justice System: A Survey of Police Arrests and Their Outcomes* (London, HMSO, 1998); L Skinns, *Police Custody: Governance, Legitimacy and Reform in the Criminal Justice Process* (London, Routledge, 2011).

[104] It is impossible to know whether the researcher's presence made Custody Sergeants more likely to act 'by the book' and refuse detention, or less likely to embarrass officers in front of an external observer.

[105] Eg Response, Kirk Machan, July 2015. This was an arrest for dangerous cycling but the officer's real reason was to disrupt a gang suspected of breaking into cars.

[106] Custody, Tidmouth November 2014.

[107] I McKenzie, 'Helping the Police with their Inquiries: the Necessity Principle and Voluntary Attendance at the Police Station' (1990) *Criminal Law Review* 22; Long, 'Keeping PACE?' 95.

because no charges were pressed. Rich: 'I think that [the Custody Sergeant] thought it was "shit on shit", as in, why should we give a fuck?' If it had been on an ordinary street and happened to a 'decent' member of the public, he wouldn't have thought it was a shit job.[108]

# V.  The Decline of Arrest

At the time of writing, the number of arrests is decreasing dramatically. From a peak of 1,475,266 in 2007/08, Home Office figures indicated that they dropped to 1,069,000 in 2012/13 before a gradual decline down to 671,126 in 2018/19. This has been despite a similarly dramatic *increase* in police recorded crime 2014–2019.[109] Similar reductions in the numbers of arrests were recorded in both areas under research. It is impossible to identify a single factor behind this. The Home Office suggested the reduction of arrests was partly explained by greater use of other disposals, particularly aimed at reducing the number of young people entering custody.[110] However, Home Office figures have also revealed the extent to which the number of police officers has reduced in recent years, with the number of officers in 'visible frontline' roles reducing by more than ten per cent between 2015 and 2018. In this period, the number of Neighbourhood police officers fell by a third, from 23,928 in March 2015 to 16,557 in March 2018.[111] These reductions were seen in both force areas, with recruitment freezes and the moving of officers from Neighbourhood roles into Response. While we cannot see how the reductions in police numbers would not have an impact on arrest figures, there appears to be more to this story, particularly as arrests were dropping prior to the most severe cuts to the police service. Officers we observed all told a similar tale: they and their colleagues were arresting less regularly than in previous years.

One of the factors identified by officers at both forces was the phasing out of targets for arrests, stop searches, and crime detections.[112] A review by the Police Superintendent's Association in 2015 found that, 'most forces have generally moved away from the use of hard numeric targets, with a few exceptions. Target setting, however, appears to be not uncommon at sub-force level by those in supervisory roles'.[113] 'Hard' performance indicators of this nature were in place in some roles at one force after our fieldwork had started, whereas at the other

---

[108] Neighbourhood, Withered Heath, March 2018.

[109] Home Office, *Arrest Statistics Data Tables: Police Powers and Procedures Year Ending 31 March 2019* available at www.gov.uk/government/statistics/police-powers-and-procedures-england-and-wales-year-ending-31-march-2019.

[110] *The Telegraph* (26 October 2017).

[111] *The Independent* (26 August 2018).

[112] The powers to set performance targets under the Police Act, s 38 were abolished in 2012 (Police Reform and Social Responsibility Act 2011, s 81(a)).

[113] I Curtis, *The Use of Targets in Policing* (2015) 4 available at www.policesupers.com/wp-content/uploads/2015/12/Review_Targets_2015.pdf.

force they had been scrapped several years previously. The arrest targets 'had a huge impact on whether arrests were made or not', explained one officer in Force B, who said he had been instructed by an Inspector to make more arrests because the division was not meeting its targets.[114] A colleague recounted the 'old system' of targets for crime detections and arrests, and how a Superintendent put pressure on officers to arrest and even had a white board at the station with each officer's statistics on it.[115] At Force A, Henry explained that under the old 'PI or Target culture', officers in one Territorial Support Unit were expected to make a minimum of seven arrests a month. In contrast he noted that, 'I have made four arrests this month, and I consider that high'. Under the old regime some officers would feel the need to 'top up' their arrests so that they did not miss their targets, often at the football:

> We would look at a [football] crowd and identify targets to arrest if they did *anything* [his emphasis]. If someone was noisy or annoying … and you'd would look at him and say 'I'll have him' and just wait and then go and arrest. And that would be your arrests for the month.[116]

This was also Maz's experience. Arrest targets had been abolished and officers had 'got their discretion back'. But in her previous role in Force A, there had been pressure to both arrest and conduct stop searches: 'a tick's a tick', it didn't matter how it was obtained.[117]

Therefore, once again, it was force policies that were driving behavioural change in frontline policing. But how does this square with our observation that the change in the law with regard to arrest necessity appears not to have led to the type of human rights-led consideration of alternatives that was envisaged? It may be that asking officers to conduct such a complex decision-making process when making sometimes split-second decisions is unrealistic. It may be that training, or application of the changes to PACE through force policy has not been clear or robust enough, or has been diluted as it cascades down to Inspectors and Sergeants. Or it may be that the pressures on officers identified above simply mean that they cannot prioritise PACE. Nevertheless, there was evidence that *some* officers were aware of how the arrest decision-making process should have changed and that some had changed their approach to arrest as a result.

One officer reflected on how an online training course had assisted his understanding. Whether or not to arrest had been 'more of an instinctive reaction' before, but that:

> [the force] are much more stringent on the necessity criteria these days … More so the last couple of years. We have to consider the necessity criteria and consider whether we should be taking away someone's liberty (…) So you were (…) going into custody

---

[114] Response, Eriador, September 2017.
[115] Neighbourhood, Dunland, June 2018.
[116] Football Ops, October 2015.
[117] Mental Health Triage, Maron, September 2015.

with the same person, and it's the old 'prompt and effective investigation of the offence', and the custody officer is like, 'happy days', 'great', and all that, and booked them in. Then the Home Office … came back to us and said … what it's about is avoiding taking people's liberty unnecessarily and we need to have more than just this 'prompt and effective'. And, if you ask bobbies now, they will probably say arrest rates have gone down, probably like, 80% … Because bobbies being bobbies, it's the path of least resistance (…) Current climate, you're more inclined to sit back and think about it before (…)[118]

It is possible that the 2005 changes are playing some role in the overall fall in arrests nationally. Although we could not detect this in the forces we were studying, training and policy varies from force to force. Whether this is true or not, we do not consider that it is time yet to give up on the idea of implementing the arrest necessity criteria in a manner that makes officers more likely to consider alternatives.

Our research suggests that, if our findings are representative, arrest in England and Wales is not working as intended. First, when judged against its objectives as a crime control and investigation tool, it is limited. Officers on the one hand feel they are being pushed into making what are often pointless arrests by force policy and, on the other, are disincentivised to make arrests by the practical and procedural barriers placed before them. We did of course observe necessary arrests (in terms of protecting vital evidence or protecting individuals from imminent harm), but over the period of our research these were a minority when contrasted with arrests made for other reasons. The key point here is that the pressures officers were placed under were not just affecting whether an arrest was made, but also whether the suspect was subjected to a formal criminal justice procedure at all. At one end of the scale, we witnessed a number of arrests that were unlawful when judged against PACE, section 24. At the other, we saw officers who felt that an arrest would be disproportionate, misreporting testimony and ignoring physical evidence, in order to cuff crimes that had occurred. Many officers, at both ends of this scale, tended to view an arrest decision as an 'all or nothing' decision in terms of a criminal justice response to the crime. Unless penalty notices were available (eg for cannabis possession and traffic offences), 'arrest' and 'taking formal action' often became one and the same thing. Officers who decided not to arrest often decided not to take any formal action at all and would use 'words of advice' or simply turn a blind eye. The result of this is that many offences are not being recorded and some incidents were being 'de-crimed'.[119] At a time when more and more offences are being 'crimed', it is no surprise that rates of charge are reducing.[120] The current system, therefore, sees some who should not be arrested

---

[118] Interview, Neighbourhood, Shiloh, September 2015.

[119] This phenomenon has been noted in respect of domestic violence (Myhill and Johnson, 'Police Use of Discretion').

[120] The proportion of crimes resulting in a charge or summons has reduced from 15% in 2015 to 8% in 2019 (Home Office, *Crime Outcomes in England and Wales: Year Ending March 2019*).

ending up in police custody with little hope of charge, and some of those who could be charged escaping the criminal justice system completely.

Second, we also need to judge arrest against the wider *stated* objectives or rhetoric of the law that we may find in traditional versions of the rule of law. These include procedural or formal equality[121] and impartial enforcement,[122] in other words the principle that *like cases must be treated alike.*[123] Here again the use of arrest falls short, although we would argue that this is due to the way the legislation is applied, rather than the fact it contains the type of wide discretion that McBarnet would counsel makes the rhetoric of the law and the law on paper always likely to be at odds.[124] In practice, however, our fieldwork was littered with instances of the power of arrest being applied more forcefully against certain – usually economically weaker – elements of the community. Young people, males, and those living in disadvantaged communities were far more likely to find themselves in custody. This was not just because policing resources were being targeted at those areas, but because many frontline officers and Custody Sergeants shared similar views on the utility of custody for the criminal type in contrast to 'decent people'. Although we did not identify discrimination against ethnic minorities in our fieldwork, it does not take much of a stretch of the imagination to see how this inequality before the law may also affect racial minority populations in other force areas.

---

[121] See J Jowell and D Oliver, *The Changing Constitution* (Oxford, Clarendon, 1994). Not to be confused with substantive equality (R Cotterrell, *Law's Community: Legal Theory in Sociological Perspective* (Oxford, Clarendon, 1996)).

[122] P Hewitt, *The Abuse of Power – Civil Liberties in the United Kingdom* (London, Martin Robertson, 1982).

[123] HLA Hart, *The Concept of Law* (Oxford, Clarendon Press, 1993).

[124] D McBarnet, *Conviction: The Law, the State and the Construction of Justice* (London, Palgrave MacMillan, 1981) 156.

# 8

# Legitimacy and Accountability

The consideration of stop and search and of arrest in the preceding chapters gave rise to discussions of legitimacy and accountability. The patterns we have identified in the use of powers prompt questions about equity and discrimination, questions that have been raised consistently and widely for the past 40 years and more.[1] This chapter considers the arguments about legitimacy and accountability, and the importance of both if we are to accept and embrace the wide powers of discretion that police officers possess. It focuses on the problem that officers are mindful not so much of accountability to the public, but of accountability to their superiors. It asks whether such accountability can ever lead to police forces being seen as legitimate by the communities they police, particularly in 'over-policed' working class communities or those with disproportionately high ethnic minority populations.

## I. Understanding Legitimacy and Accountability

The subject of legitimacy has largely been the preserve of political science and philosophy and has been concerned with the state and with institutions.[2] It has been identified as the solution to a simple problem: 'to find a basis of loyalty that is voluntary but not purely instrumental; that does not depend only on rational self-interest or purely on personal preferences'.[3] Securing the active cooperation of the citizenry, rather than compelling it through coercion or incentivising it through rewards, represents the ambition of the modern state. This ideal is realised through democratic processes that, while they may not secure the results we individually want, are generally accepted as a means of collective expression.

---

[1] M Simey, *Democracy Rediscovered: A Study in Police Accountability* (Liverpool, Liverpool University Press, 1988); P Day and R Klein, *Accountabilities – Five Public Services* (London, Tavistock, 1987); D Oliver, *Government in the UK – the Search for Accountability, Effectiveness and Citizenship* (Milton Keynes, Open University Press, 1991).

[2] D Beetham, *Legitimation of Power* (London, Macmillan, 1991).

[3] M Zelditch, 'Theories of Legitimacy' in JT Jost and B Major (eds), *The Psychology of Legitimacy: Emerging Perspectives on Ideology, Justice and Intergroup Relations* (Cambridge, Cambridge University Press, 2001) 37.

As they have emerged in policing, questions of legitimacy have largely been framed by Beetham's work. However, Beetham is concerned with questions at the level of a state and with distinguishing philosophical from political science conceptualisations to reach what he considers is a definition fit for the social sciences. Power is legitimate for him when:

    i. it conforms to established rules;
    ii. the rules can be justified by reference to beliefs shared by both dominant and subordinate, and
    iii. there is evidence of consent by the subordinate to the particular power relation.[4]

Beetham is not concerned with specific powers, let alone police street powers. In using this apparently simple model, we have then to question its value as we scrutinise the use of power in a particular context.

The focus of discussion has, on the whole, overlooked the first two questions. Authorised by Parliament and, thus, largely in accordance with beliefs held by the majority, the police organisation, in its current form, and the specific powers to stop and search or to arrest are deemed broadly legitimate in literature on the use of those powers. Discussions of legitimacy move smoothly into ones of accountability, scarcely considering the consent of the subordinate. Indeed, the law assumes that consent of the subordinate is given through Parliamentary processes. If the law is legitimate, is it used appropriately? If not, how can its misuse be challenged?

Where accountability is considered in a criminal justice setting, it does not stray too far from the conventional debates about the concept that have emerged since the late 1980s.[5] A traditional model of accountability emphasises the role of democracy and of the law as the expression of the will of the majority, with the rights of the individual guaranteed by the courts.[6] This model is of course highly idealised,[7] with criminological and socio-legal literature in particular long highlighting that the rule of law has a tendency to legitimise rather than constrain power,[8] and that the courts typically work in favour of the already-privileged.[9] In contrast to the flawed traditional model, forms of accountability associated with the New Public Management have emphasised efficiency at an organisational level and choice as the guarantee of quality and service for the individual. While this does not fit so easily with policing, we can still see the influence of this

---

[4] Beetham, *Legitimation of Power* 16.

[5] Oliver, *Government in the UK*; S Weir and D Beetham, *Political Power and Democratic Control in Britain* (London, Routledge, 1998).

[6] Day and Klein, *Accountabilities*.

[7] J Stewart, *The Rebuilding of Public Accountability* (London, European Policy Forum, 1992).

[8] D McBarnet, *Conviction: The Law, the State and the Construction of Justice* (London, Palgrave MacMillan, 1981).

[9] N Lacey et al, *Reconstructing Criminal Law*, 4th edn (Cambridge, Cambridge University Press, 2010) 77.

model in the pluralisation of policing and in forms of reporting and accounting.[10] Through the New Labour years in the UK, experiments with a partnership model of accountability, working with communities and other agencies to share responsibilities, emerged.[11] Drawing upon ideas such as public value,[12] this collaborative approach to problems, to governance and to accountability remained largely peripheral, affecting only some neighbourhoods and some aspects of policing. Police and Crime Commissioners have reintroduced a degree of democratic oversight, though at the same time emphasising the operational independence of the police.[13] However, we should not overemphasise the degree to which one form of accountability has replaced another. Rather, we might think more in terms of the accretion of different, and sometimes contradictory, modes, increasing the forms of reporting and accountability rather than simply changing them. And much as with discussions of legitimacy, those of accountability tend to consider the subject at the aggregate level. They acknowledge the impact of scrutiny and of performance indicators on the conduct of policing, but less so on the actions of individual officers.

## A. Experiencing Legitimacy and Accountability

Formal systems of legitimacy and accountability can, then, appear remote from both the experiences of the police and of the public. They are concerned with legalities and statistics representing aggregates rather than with the immediate interactions between police and citizens. For many officers, the legitimacy of their actions is not to be questioned by the public. Classically, this is expressed in the simple notion that, if someone is innocent, then they have nothing to worry about.[14] All officers, but Traffic officers in particular, have a ready answer to the question, 'haven't you anything better to do?' One officer, Toby, challenged in precisely these terms responded, 'seems not', and proceeded to write the OSCO out as slowly as he could.[15] The consent of those being policed, of the subordinate in Beetham's terms, was not something that could impinge upon the immediate interaction. Indeed, observing embarrassing clips of officers posted on YouTube or other social media, some remarked that where they were made to look foolish was when they allowed someone to undermine the legitimacy of their actions. An officer, recorded entering a flat on finding the door open, looked foolish as he

---

[10] R Reiner, *The Politics of the Police*, 4th edn (Oxford, Oxford University Press, 2014).

[11] J Newman, *Modernising Governance* (London, Sage, 2001).

[12] M Moore, *Creating Public Value: Strategic Management in Government* (Cambridge, MA, Harvard University Press, 1995).

[13] E Turner, 'PCCs, Neo-liberal Hegemony and Democratic Policing' (2014) 13 *Safer Communities* 13.

[14] Territorial Support, Knapford, March 2015.

[15] Traffic, Knapford, July 2014.

retreated without a good response to the questions of the tenant. In discussing in a briefing how the situation might have been better handled, an Inspector suggested a defence he might have offered. What was not questioned was whether the officer acted legitimately or not.[16]

If legitimacy is not readily questioned, by the public or by the police, accountability appears ever present. Officers are accountable both for what they do and for what they do not do. Much of what officers do consists of taking personal details, documenting decisions, and submitting the reports that are required to conclude particular incidents. We noted above the influence of the Radio Control Room on the actions of officers and of the need to complete DASH forms. It is in situations like these that officers perceive their discretion to have been curtailed. Whether this is the case or not, the recording and the subsequent justification for actions in reports does then tend to influence the ways in which officers will approach a case. The recording of interactions, whether on BWCs or in written reports, is as much about accountability for actions as it is about any other purpose. Yes, there is an evidentiary aspect. But, in the majority of cases concerning mental health, domestic violence, or people missing from home, the records are there more for the purposes of ex post audit of risk management in the event that something goes wrong.

Where officers acted in ways that might be open to question, they were wise to immediately record their version of events, at the very least in their pocket notebooks (PNBs). Observing a Neighbourhood officer on one occasion, a colleague spent much of the start of the shift writing a statement about an incident that occurred two years previously. Looking back at his PNB, he had recorded the times and the officers involved in the operation. He had even recorded the time he went for his meal break. What he had failed to record was that he had raised objections to the decision of a superior officer to seize a dog with the intention of putting it down. Without that note in his PNB, he is in the same boat as the Inspector who gave the order, having to justify himself in statements.[17]

## B. Searches and the Use of Force

Particular decisions were subject to specific reporting. A stop and search encounter had to be recorded on a form, as we have noted. The format changed with time and with technological developments, including the linking of BWC footage to an electronic record of a search, and required officers to explain their grounds for conducting the search. In our observations, officers were easily capable of explaining themselves in ways that were acceptable on the forms. Indeed, regardless of

---

[16] Territorial Support, Maron, November 2015.
[17] Neighbourhood, Abbey, November 2016.

changes to policies and recording practices, an experienced officer who wanted to search a person could always present credible grounds on the forms.[18]

During the course of our observations, and following a review of the data available,[19] police forces began to record their use of force (such as the use of restraint techniques, handcuffs or PAVA spray). Brief reports were expected from officers to justify their decision to use force and the data is now also published.[20] We would note, however, that in the course of our observations, handcuffs and leg or arm restraints were very rarely used. Officers did use physical force, but only rarely did that use appear excessive. One officer, concerned that his decision to PAVA spray a man and his son in their own property (a property the officer had instructed them not to enter because of a serious fire hazard), wrote a lengthy explanation of his actions. Using the National Decision Making model (NDM), he detailed the information he considered, the assessment he made, the powers and policies relevant, the options available and explained the actions taken. The report detailed human rights considerations and common law duties that, in the matter of seconds that the decision actually took, were almost certainly not at the forefront of his mind. The NDM, instead of guiding a decision, acted as a framework for his ex post justification of a split-second decision.[21] Whether that decision was legitimate or not, the reporting and accountability systems were used to justify the actions of the officer.

The recording of use of force was in addition to existing requirements to detail the circumstances in which a Taser[22] was used. Any occasion on which a Taser was drawn required a full account from the officer concerned. This appeared to weigh more heavily on those officers trained in the use of this equipment than simply the report of the use of force. Whether the Taser was fired or not, the act of drawing it was a decision that had to be fully justified.

> Simon has arrested a male for an assault on him and for damage to property. He was violent, spitting and lunging from a first floor window. He brandished a hammer, but it looked like he might have something else in his hand. As an observer, I had stood back from this incident and could not see clearly, but his right hand was holding something. Whatever it was, Louise drew her Taser. On the way to Custody, having restrained and arrested the male, Louise and Simon compare notes. She thought he might have a knife as well as the hammer. Simon doesn't contradict her, but he doesn't mention a knife. It was something shiny. Louise asks me what I had seen. I don't know, but whatever it was, the male appeared intent on hurling himself at the officers from

---

[18] Territorial Support, Peel Godred, July 2016.

[19] National Police Chiefs' Council, *National Use of Force Data Review Project* (NPCC, 2015) available at www.npcc.police.uk/documents/reports/2016/Use%20of%20Force%20Data%20Report.pdf.

[20] Home Office, *Police Use of Force Statistics, England and Wales: April 2017 to March 2018* (London, Home Office, 2018) available at assets.publishing.service.gov.uk/government/uploads/system/uploads/attachment_data/file/764894/police-use-of-force-apr2017-mar2018-hosb3018.pdf.

[21] Neighbourhood, Abbey, June 2016.

[22] Taser is a brand name that now stands as the term used to refer to any brand of conducted electrical weapon used by the police.

the first floor window. As Simon books the arrested male into Custody, I sit in the Writing Room with Louise. She wants to get a head start on the paperwork. In particular, she wants to write up her decision to draw her Taser. She phrases and rephrases her statement. She has reviewed the BWC footage, but that shows the ground floor of the house and some shaky images of the male as she raises her Taser. It doesn't show what she saw. After more than 30 minutes, she is happy with her opening three or four sentences. With more than three hours of the shift remaining, she anticipates spending the rest of it writing.[23]

These written reports are prepared in anticipation of internal and external scrutiny, of complaints and of subsequent legal action. Officers frequently expressed concerns about complaints and litigation. These were, to our knowledge, quite rare phenomena, but they loomed large in the thinking of officers. In the case of wrongful arrest we detailed above (see Chapter 2, text to notes 54 and 55), the officer was anxious about the potential for a payout to the individual concerned and wrote up the incident in some detail. He ensured he had a copy of the 'mugshot' his Sergeant had handed him at the start of the shift and wrote up an account of his actions in response to the direction to arrest the wrong brother.[24] No litigation followed, but the sense that it might was evident. During the course of the research, and as powers were being curtailed by the Best Use of Stop and Search,[25] officers spoke more and more of stopping people as something that would give rise to complaints. That most complaints relating to stops were concerned with incivility and not with the misuse of the powers did not alter the perception that they were more exposed.[26] This concern with civility in interactions with the public then leads to a more current theme in policing research, one that has tended to eclipse questions of accountability.

## C. Procedural Justice

Drawing more on social psychology, the literature on procedural justice asks what makes people comply with the law and with police officers, beyond simple compulsion, even when the outcomes are ones they do not support, did not expect, or did not hope for. Distinguishing the rational from the normative, Tyler[27] expands on the notion of procedural justice to explain why it appears that the way a person is treated can have more influence over their assessment

[23] Response, Ffarquhar Road, September 2015.
[24] Territorial Support, Brandham, November 2013.
[25] See Chapter 6 for a fuller discussion.
[26] Territorial Support, Brandham, October 2016.
[27] T Tyler, 'A Psychological Perspective on the Legitimacy of Institutions' in JT Jost and B Major (eds), *The Psychology of Legitimacy: Emerging Perspectives on Ideology, Justice and Intergroup Relations* (Cambridge, Cambridge University Press, 2001); T Tyler, *Why People Obey the Law* (Princeton, Princeton University Press, 2006).

of an encounter than whether the result met their own needs. Procedural justice theory suggests that it is more important to citizens that they are treated fairly than that the outcomes satisfy their interests. Encounters with police officers are, then, opportunities to build trust, to act without evident bias, to treat citizens with respect and to allow them voice in the manner in which power is exercised. The quality of interactions has a beneficial effect in further increasing trust in the police, compliance, and active cooperation regardless of the outcome of the particular incident.[28]

This virtuous cycle has a negative side. Evidence, including that cited above, suggests that poor interactions with police officers are more damaging than any positive ones, undermining efforts to improve relationships over months in a matter of seconds.[29] However, what represents a 'good' encounter or a 'bad' one is not always clear or, indeed, agreed. Waddington et al[30] used focus group discussions of a videoed encounter to illustrate the variety of ways in which the public view and interpret the same behaviour. Worden also problematises the 'good' versus 'bad' encounter dichotomy, noting that the public often see procedural justice where it is lacking, or a lack of it where officers are acting deliberately 'by the book' to ensure fair procedure is being followed.[31] Furthermore, it is not clear how precisely to engender the sorts of behaviour in officers that will generate the trust anticipated by theories of procedural justice. In part, it is a matter of training.[32] But Haas et al also suggest that internal procedural justice, that is fair treatment and trust between officers and supervisory ranks, may facilitate procedural justice on the streets.[33]

---

[28] C Donner et al, 'Policing and Procedural Justice: a State-of-the-art Review' (2015) 28 *Policing* 153; K Murphy, 'Does Procedural Justice Matter to Youth? Comparing Adults' and Youths' Willingness to Collaborate with Police' (2015) 25 *Policing and Society* 53; K Murphy et al, 'Promoting Trust in Police: Findings from a Randomised Experimental Field Trial of Procedural Justice Policing' (2014) 24 *Policing and Society* 405; MD White et al, 'Exploring Procedural Justice, Legitimacy, and Willingness to Cooperate with Police across Offender Types' (2016) 43 *Criminal Justice and Behavior* 343; JM Gau, 'Consent Searches as a Threat to Procedural Justice and Police Legitimacy: an Analysis of Consent Requests during Traffic Stops' (2012) 24 *Criminal Justice Policy Review* 759; JM Gau, 'Procedural Justice, Police Legitimacy, and Legal Cynicism: a Test for Mediation Effects' (2015) 16 *Police Practice and Research* 402; M Dai et al, 'Procedural Justice During Police-Citizen Encounters: the Effects of Process-based Policing on Citizen Compliance and Demeanor' (2011) 39 *Journal of Criminal Justice* 159; L Mazerolle et al, 'Procedural Justice and Police Legitimacy: a Systematic Review of the Research Evidence' (2013) 9 *Journal of Experimental Criminology* 245.
[29] For examples, see M Hough et al, 'Procedural Justice, Trust, and Institutional Legitimacy' (2010) 4 *Policing* 203.
[30] P Waddington et al, 'Dissension in Public Evaluations of the Police' (2015) 25 *Policing and Society* 212.
[31] R Worden and S McLean, *Mirage of Police Reform: Procedural Justice and Police Legitimacy* (Oakland, CA, University of California Press, 2017).
[32] WG Skogan et al, 'Training Police for Procedural Justice' (2015) 11 *Journal of Experimental Criminology* 319.
[33] NE Haas et al, 'Explaining Officer Compliance: the Importance of Procedural Justice and Trust Inside a Police Organization' (2015) 15 *Criminology and Criminal Justice* 442.

These two last observations raise a further aspect of legitimacy, that of the individual, the person exercising authority. While Beetham,[34] as a political scientist, is concerned with systems and processes, we might also ask whether the individual is legitimate. Kerman suggests:

> influence in authority, by contrast [with ordinary influence], falls into the domain of *obligation*: people accept influence insofar as they see the influencing agent as having the right to make certain demands or requests and see themselves as having the obligation to adhere to them. The authority's ability to exert influence depends on his or her perceived legitimacy.[35]

The uniform and other paraphernalia of the role of police Constable are outward indications of legitimacy. But manner, confidence, knowledge and other factors also affect the way an officer comes across on the street.[36] In contrast, Neyroud and Sherman might argue that only an officer fully engaged with the latest science in policing carries the necessary professional legitimacy.[37] Either way, whether it is a craft or a science, the procedural justice literature does raise questions about what it is officers should be doing in encounters with citizens.

Procedural justice is a relational concept. It is about interactions and interpretations. The experience of being heard and treated with respect are important aspects of the idea. However, much of the research undertaken on procedural justice considers evidence of trust and confidence in the police as expressed in surveys.[38] These provide an indication that the police do indeed act in accord with the beliefs of the majority and have consent to do so.[39] Miller and D'Souza, for example, consider the evidence of the impact of searches on public confidence

---

[34] Beetham, *Legitimation of Power*; D Beetham, 'Revisiting Legitimacy, Twenty Years on' in J Tankebe and A Liebling (eds), *Legitimacy and Criminal Justice* (Oxford, Oxford University Press, 2013).

[35] HC Kerman, 'Reflections on Social and Psychological Processes of Legitimization and Delegitimization' in JT Jost and B Major (eds), *The Psychology of Legitimacy: Emerging Perspectives on Ideology, Justice and Intergroup Relations* (Cambridge, Cambridge University Press, 2001) 54–55.

[36] M Rowe et al, 'Learning and Practising Police Craft' (2016) 5 *Journal of Organizational Ethnography* 276.

[37] P Neyroud and L Sherman, 'Dialogue and Dialectic: Police Legitimacy and the New Professionalism' in J Tankebe and A Liebling (eds), *Legitimacy and Criminal Justice* (Oxford, Oxford University Press, 2013).

[38] Dai et al, 'Procedural Justice during Police-Citizen Encounters'; J Jackson and B Bradford, 'What is Trust and Confidence in the Police?' (2010) 4 *Policing* 241; NM Riccucci et al, 'Representative Bureaucracy in Policing: does it Increase Perceived Legitimacy?' (2014) 24 *Journal of Public Administration Research and Theory* 537; NA Theobald, and DP Haider-Markel, 'Race, Bureaucracy, and Symbolic Representation: Interactions between Citizens and Police' (2009) 19 *Journal of Public Administration Research and Theory* 409.

[39] JM Coicaud, 'Crime, Justice, and Legitimacy: A Brief Theoretical Inquiry' in J Tankebe and A Liebling (eds), *Legitimacy and Criminal Justice* (Oxford, Oxford University Press, 2013); J Sunshine and TR Tyler, 'The Role of Procedural Justice and Legitimacy in Shaping Public Support for Policing' (2003) 37 *Law and Society Review* 513; Jackson and Bradford, 'What is Trust and Confidence?'; J Jackson et al, 'Why Do People Comply with the Law? Legitimacy and the Influence of Legal Institutions' (2012) 52(6) *British Journal of Criminology* 1051; Hough et al, 'Procedural Justice, Trust, and Institutional Legitimacy'.

in the police, using survey data compared with searches conducted in the previous year.[40] They ask, what is the relationship between increases or decreases in visible policing (as represented by searches conducted on the street) and expressions of confidence in the police? Whether these searches were legitimate, or even legal, is not questioned. In their brief discussion of the Scarman Report on the use of stop and search powers, Bottoms and Tankebe similarly consider consent but assume that, because something is legal, it is also legitimate.[41] They suggest that the widespread use of a legal power was ill-advised rather than illegitimate. But, we might argue, we know it was an illegitimate use of the powers because it was one of the factors that led to a riot, a very visible demonstration of the withdrawal of consent.

Perhaps the clearest example of the limitations of research on procedural justice to consider questions of legitimacy and legality is Hough's discussion of five incidents of officers stopping and searching young people, from which he develops a simple typology.[42] In the first example, officers search some young black males who were 'hanging around outside the newsagent'. They are known to be part of a gang, showing their colours (though what evidence against them the police may have is unclear). But it is a gang that has not been causing any trouble for some time. Commenting on this incident, Hough declares:

> [O]nce police officers commit themselves to the assertion of authority over anyone who challenges their authority, they sharply limit their options in the case of challenge. This is, of course, one of the classic dilemmas about wielding power or exercising legitimated authority.[43]

But this is precisely the point. The decision was not legitimate. Not only did it not comply with the law, it is questionable whether it accorded with the beliefs of the dominant. And, according to Beetham, the visible refusal of consent alone is grounds to question its legitimacy. The third account offered by Hough concerns three young black men stopped for 'walking together at a strange time of the day'.[44] It was 17:30, not 04:00, though this would not have made the search legitimate in itself. Indeed, these sorts of encounters are at the heart of the problem with police powers. The dominant may confer upon officers the power to act on their behalf and the legal authority to do so. But those powers must also be exercised in accord with the beliefs of the dominant and with the consent of the subordinate. At the same time, research suggests that the dominant appear to gain in

---

[40] J Miller and A D'Souza, 'Indirect Effects of Police Searches on Community Attitudes?' (2016) 56 *British Journal of Criminology* 456.

[41] A Bottoms and J Tankebe, 'Beyond Procedural Justice: a Dialogic Approach to Legitimacy in Criminal Justice' (2012) 103 *The Journal of Criminal Law and Criminology* 119, 139.

[42] M Hough, 'Procedural Justice and Professional Policing in Times of Austerity' (2013) 13 *Criminology and Criminal Justice* 181.

[43] Hough, 'Procedural Justice' 188.

[44] Hough, 'Procedural Justice' 190.

confidence, though only marginally, in the knowledge that the streets are being actively policed, while those being searched, that is the subordinate, lose trust and confidence in the police to a much greater extent. Even if we assume all those searches were legal, in terms of efficiency, itself a legitimating principle, the use of powers such as stop and search is of doubtful value at best.[45]

# II.  Legitimacy in Practice

To develop these points further, we will consider two incidents in some detail. They concern two stop and search encounters, each very different in nature. We will interrogate both cases to understand the nature of legitimacy and accountability.

## A.  Three Lads on Board

The first of the incidents occurred in March 2014, before the Best Use of Stop and Search had been announced. The observation was conducted with Territorial Support officers operating out of Knapford police station.

> 18:50 As Alf and Annie leave the station, they get a call. Plain clothes officers have pulled over a taxi on the main road not far from the station. There are three young males on board and they need a hand searching them. They suspect possession of cannabis. Alf and Annie speak to the taxi driver. He knows nothing. He just picked them up and is taking them to town. The lads are young and white. They are polite and seem relaxed, but they are confused. One of the plain clothes officers is definite he smelt cannabis on one of the lads. He searches them at the side of the road, checking their pockets. He asks the lad repeatedly: 'have you got any gear on you?' 'No'. Alf asks the other two males: 'Tell us. We just want honesty. It will be easier on you if you do'. They continue to deny it. They admit having smoked some earlier in the evening, but they haven't got anything with them. 'Are you sure? If you deny it, we are going to have to search you at the station. Tell me now'. They continue to deny it.

> The two plain clothes officers drive to Cronk Custody while the three lads are put in the back of a van. They are not in the cages, but on the seats. They are treated politely, but they are astonished at what is happening. They are each to be searched, one by one, in a cell. While they wait in the van, the officers chat to them about football. They are at University and are visiting friends. 'We won't be coming back!' 'You shouldn't be smoking weed then, should you lads?' They accept they did smoke some, but they swear they have nothing on them. 'How many times have we heard that, though? Some people lie to the police!' 'You shouldn't smoke weed and this wouldn't happen'.

---

[45] B Bowling and C Phillips, 'Disproportionate and Discriminatory: Reviewing the Evidence on Police Stop and Search' (2007) 70 *Modern Law Review* 936; P Quinton et al, *Does More Stop and Search Mean Less Crime? Analysis of Metropolitan Police Service Panel Data, 2004–14* (London, College of Policing, 2017).

One by one, they are taken to the cell and searched. The Sergeant is there now and is quiet. He seems uncomfortable. Having found nothing on the first two, the plain clothes officers return for the last male. He asks: 'is this necessary?' The officers are apologetic now, unable to row back from a decision they appear to be regretting. Alf and Annie offer to drive the three males to their destination. They don't want to know. All three are clean. The plain clothes officers appear a little shamefaced.[46]

We have already noted the controversies around the smell of cannabis as the grounds for a search.[47] At the time of this incident, such concerns were not ones publicly debated. In formal terms, their actions were legal and accountable. In procedural terms, the males were treated politely and were given an opportunity to be heard. But they were not heard, and nothing they could have said or done would deflect the officers from their purpose. The legitimacy of the search is also open to question. For the three males, it was clearly illegitimate. We might even question whether the majority would support the use of these powers in this way. The plain clothes officers stopped a taxi with three males who matched their model of the type they should be interested in. All their briefings and intelligence reports directed their attention towards such people. The smell of cannabis was little more than an excuse to search the lads, to take their details and to log the 'intelligence'. The decision of the plain clothes officers was one that all other officers appeared to support, at least in front of the three males and the observer. However, the body language and dialogue suggested that not all officers were happy, and the Sergeant was definitely not. The use of powers in this fashion was precisely the issue that gave rise to efforts to curtail them and to make their use more accountable.

## B. Standing Lad

The second of the two incidents occurred in June 2015, after the introduction of Best Use of Stop and Search. The observation was conducted with Response officers operating out of Ffarquhar Road police station.

> The officers have recently escorted a student suffering from an overdose of some sort to the hospital and are awaiting an update. The Radio Control Room pass on a report from a security guard at a local leisure centre. The security guard says that he has seen a group of young people in a small local park. He believes one of them, a male, is holding a knife and he has provided a description of the clothing worn by this one male – dark blue top, black trousers or tracksuit bottoms.
>
> 20:50 Simon goes around the ring road and approaches the park along one of the arterial routes. On the way, the Radio Control Room asks the officers to check a second report nearby. This concerns young males firing paint ball pellets at passing cars.

---

[46] Territorial Support, Knapford, March 2014.
[47] P Quinton et al, *Searching for Cannabis: Are Grounds for Search Associated with Outcomes?* (London, College of Policing, 2017).

They prioritise the knife. Simon skirts around the second job in his approach to the park where the male with a knife has been reported.

The second officer is a Probationer. He has still to complete aspects of his development portfolio, evidencing his competence. This might be an occasion for a search of open ground.

21:00 They arrive at the park. The Probationer gets out at the first entrance, off the main road. Simon continues around the perimeter to a second entrance. Obscured by buildings, the van cannot be seen as it pulls up. And behind this second entrance, at a distance of perhaps 100 metres, looms the leisure centre. Both officers walk into the park, which is largely empty, and approach seven lads and one girl. They all appear to be White British and about 14 or 15 years' old. They are gathered around a raised concrete platform, all seated save for one. None make any move to leave or, indeed, any move at all. The lad who is standing fits the description given. He has a blue top and dark tracksuit bottoms. None of the others fit this description. Simon talks to them, explaining why they are there. The atmosphere is relaxed at first. Simon then points out that the standing lad matches the description they have been given. It becomes clear that the Probationer is going to search him. He has his body-worn camera switched on and clearly explains who he is, where he is based, the powers under which he is conducting the search, and the process for a complaint. The search does not proceed beyond outer garments. The Probationer clearly follows the mnemonic, GO WISELY, though not in this order.

However, the standing lad demands to know why he is being accused. 'You are not being accused of anything. You are being searched because you match a description'. The standing lad doesn't see the distinction. He doesn't understand why he is being searched while his friends look on. Again, he asks, why is he being accused? This conversation continues in the same vein.

Neither officer searches any of the others present. They take no more names and details. The other lads and the girl begin to leave. We don't learn how they perceive this incident. As they leave, the standing lad stops questioning the Probationer, but he is not happy. The officers have found nothing on him. While the Probationer takes down the details he needs to complete the stop form, a copy of which they offer him, the standing lad spots the observer, standing back but within hearing. He wants to know who they are. The Probationer is surprised by this change in tack and just says 'Ask him!' 'I am from the University and I am watching these officers to see what they do and how they act'. 'What do you think of this then?' 'The officers are doing their job. But I can understand why you don't appreciate it'. 'Yes! I don't appreciate it'.

At the conclusion of the encounter, the standing lad is confused. He has been politely treated, but he doesn't really understand why he has been singled out. His friends have gone and he is alone. He is not sure whether he wants a copy of the stop form. He is upset, though, and leaves.

21:18. The officers head off. They search for the lads firing paintballs, but there is no sign of them or of any paint or damage in the vicinity.[48]

---

[48] Response, Ffarquhar Road, June 2015.

This incident, of no more than 20 minutes, reveals so much about such encounters. While research focuses upon the decision to search, the background reveals the wider considerations that envelop it. The officers were going from one job to another and had another waiting to go to next. One was a probationer who needed to complete records of his experience. They focused on this call because of the report of a knife from a member of the public, a security guard. They had to take this seriously. In discussion with the observer, they explained that they had to search the lad who fitted the description. If something had happened later that evening, they would not have been able to justify not searching him. Neither of them expected to find anything and so they didn't consider searching any of the others or of searching the park for a discarded knife. They had other jobs to go to.

Officers to whom we have described this scenario have found reasons to do any number of different things. Some suggested they would search all the young people, including the girl.[49] Others would have detained them while the area was searched. Others would not have searched anyone and instead have asked them if they knew of any kids with knives. Many officers countered with a question. What if there were no powers to search? Should they have been arrested? These responses express something of the police experience of stop and search. You are damned if you do, and damned if you don't.

In thinking about legitimacy, the decision to search the standing lad was legitimate in terms of the law and of public support. However, it did not have the consent of the subordinate, the standing lad himself. His departing friends might have understood the situation, but we do not know. In thinking about accountability, a stop and search form (a paper version at this time) was completed and given to the lad. The incident was recorded on BWC and would be available to review in the event of a complaint. It would also be available, alongside a copy of the stop form, to a panel of lay people tasked with reviewing such incidents as a result of the Best Use of Stop and Search scheme. Indeed, the incident was directly observed by a lay observer, in this case an academic. Finally, the statistical record would show this as another unsuccessful search. However, these checks and records do not make transparent or accountable the real grounds for the decisions the officers took. Their concern was as much about the 'what if' questions. What if they chose not to search and the lad did have a knife? The prospect of explaining this to supervisors was the more pressing concern. Turning to think about procedural justice, it would be important to gain a better understanding of the experience of the standing lad and of his friends. Observing the encounter, it was apparent that the standing lad did not understand why he was being searched and why the

---

[49] While policy in this police force allowed male officers to search female suspects, so long as that search did not proceed beyond outer garments, most officers would call for the assistance of a female officer. Time and availability then become factors affecting the decision to search female suspects.

others were not. The probationer might have explained the situation more clearly, a skill that perhaps comes with experience.[50]

## C. Consequences

The officers played different roles in these two vignettes. Response and Territorial Support duties will focus officer attention in particular ways. Proactive officers, those looking for people in particular places or at particular times, will seek to find grounds to intervene. Without grounds, in their way of thinking, they cannot do their job. To paraphrase Alf and Annie, crime is all around you, you just have to go and find it.[51] For Response officers, there was enough pressure on time without going looking to create more. Reports from the public could not be ignored, but they did not carry great weight. They were off to attend to a further report from the public, of paintballs that also proved to be a red herring. Rather than being proactive, their concern was much more with the interpretation of their actions in hindsight. In each case, and regardless of Best Use of Stop and Search, the most imminent form of accountability was to supervisors: the Sergeant in the first instance, and some officer in some unknown future reviewing the case with the benefit of hindsight in the second. If there were to be any meaningful consequences for the officers, it was from supervision that they could expect them.

However, there are further consequences of systems of accountability. Recording the two instances above for the purposes of accountability entails a record against the name of the individual. They have a life on police records as a result. Seen subsequently, the details of the original encounter are lost, unless an officer digs deeply into the records. A cursory glance at an individual's file instead reveals a history of contact with the police. All such contacts are evidence of suspicion and, therefore, of guilt. After all, there is no smoke without fire. Someone with a lengthy record of encounters who has not been caught with anything has been lucky. Next time, they may not be so lucky. If crime is out there, it is more likely to be found on someone who has already acquired a police intelligence record than on someone who is 'clean'.[52] As we saw in Chapter 6, when officers encounter citizens in a place or at a time that raises suspicions, their most common opening gambit was: 'are you known to the police?' A positive answer would dramatically increase the likelihood of the stop and account escalating to a search. It is to the recording and the use of this information that we turn in the next chapter.

---

[50] Rowe et al, 'Learning and Practicing Police Craft'.

[51] Territorial Support, Knapford, March 2015 (see Chapter 6, n 34 above).

[52] M Rowe and T Søgaard, '"Playing the Man, not the Ball": Targeting Organised Criminals, Intelligence and the Problems with Pulling Levers' (2020) *Policing and Society* available at doi.org/10.1080/10439463.2019.1603226.

# III.  Reflections

Before doing so, we might reflect on understandings of legitimacy and account-ability in the use of police street powers. For all the emphasis on legal compliance and on reporting of the individual use of powers, such as force, arrest, or stop and search, the focus of officers' concerns were internal to the police organisa-tion. There was little evident concern about complaints themselves. Ruffling a few feathers or being a bit robust with some young men might give rise to complaints. What was of concern was the reaction of their supervisors. Complaints were commonly dismissed swiftly, with evidence often provided by BWC[53] or, on some occasions, the presence of an observer.[54] However, some officers experienced more than their share of complaints and clearly felt the wrath of their Sergeant and Inspector. The form of discipline that might be imposed could vary from not being asked to do overtime or special duties, such as policing a football match, or it might include being given the jobs that nobody wants, including constant obser-vation of a person in custody or standing guard at a crime scene.[55] This is not to say that policies and procedures had no effect on officer conduct. We have noted the impact of changes to stop and search and to arrest that occurred during the period of our observations. But we would argue that legal and political forms of accountability and questions of legitimacy did not directly impinge upon officers' considerations. They were very much factors that were mediated by supervision. Where officers did not believe their immediate superior would support them in the event of a complaint, they were likely to avoid controversial, legally dubious, or otherwise risky contact with the public. Where that supervision was robust in supporting officers in their decisions about the use or otherwise of street powers, those officers were freer to act as they saw fit.

Instead, the demands of scrutiny and accountability, the paperwork, form-filling and report writing were all experienced as a burden and a distraction from the job as officers saw it. This is much as we might expect, and it is a phenom-enon remarked upon in many public service agencies. But the accretion of forms and of risk assessment tools can undermine their purpose. They cease to be about making an officer accountable for their decisions. They can tend to direct officer behaviours in ways that cannot be simply predicted, as we noted in the previous chapter with respect to policies on domestic violence. They can also encourage resistance or the deliberate undermining of the intent. Whatever the response of officers to the pressures to be accountable and legitimate, the ways in which offic-ers responded was well understood by Sergeants and Inspectors. We each observed officers checking decisions and actions with the Sergeant, or sometimes a more seasoned officer, commonly over the radio but sometimes in person. We noted

[53] Territorial Support, Knapford, May 2015.
[54] Neighbourhood, Arlesdale, October 2014.
[55] Territorial Support, Brandham, October 2016.

Sergeants questioning and challenging the decisions of officers, though never in front of the public and very rarely in front of us as observers. The role of the Sergeant has been noted by Her Majesty's Inspectorate of Constabulary[56] and by the College of Policing.[57] Yet the role and influence of the Sergeant, and of the Inspector, on the actions and decisions of officers, and of their sense of what it is to be accountable, remains an underexplored topic.

---

[56] Her Majesty's Inspector of Constabulary, *Leading from the Frontline: Thematic Inspection* (London, HMIC, 2008).

[57] College of Policing, *Leadership Review: Recommendations for Delivering Leadership at All Levels* (London, College of Policing, 2015).

# 9

# Monitoring, Technology, and Recording of Crime

If, as we suggest, Sergeants and Inspectors loom large in any understanding of police accountability, this influence is increasingly mediated by technologies. The introduction of radios and vehicles to routine patrol work has made the old beat system, patrolled on foot and very directly supervised by a Sergeant, not only a thing of the past but something it is difficult to now envision. Even though much of the work of police officers described by studies in the 1970s and 1980s remains familiar, the emergence of mobile computing, hand-held devices, and body-worn cameras (BWCs), among other technologies, have had profound effects on the ways officers approach and respond to incidents. This chapter focuses on the roll-out of these technologies and the use and sharing of intelligence. It considers the challenges officers face in terms of using the new technology and questions whether the new kit really assists frontline policing or just provides a mode of performance management. It considers the procedures around crime recording and the way the recording of crime for purposes of accountability affects the work of police officers. First, however, we will consider the role of technology in supervising the work of frontline officers.

## I. Remote Supervision

We have noted in Chapter 4 the absence of visible supervision of much of the work of frontline police officers. This is in stark contrast to the image of the Sergeant in the inter-war years, checking up to see that officers were sticking to their beats.[1] At the same time, we have also indicated, in Chapters 6, 7, and 8, the importance of immediate supervision in influencing officer understandings of force policies and of the ways in which it is appropriate to use discretion. This oversight is now, largely, conducted from a distance. Indeed, in some instances, officers might not see a Sergeant in person during a shift.[2] In other instances, 'their' Sergeant, that is

---

[1] M Brogden, *On the Mersey Beat: Policing Liverpool between the Wars* (Oxford, Oxford University Press, 1991).
[2] Response, Westmarch, January 2017.

the person responsible for an officer's welfare and development, might even be on a different shift pattern.[3] These practices have been shaped, over the past 50 years and more, by the emergence of radios and the ubiquitous use of police vehicles. More recently, the role of Sergeant has been shaped by the computers and related technologies that dominate policing, and so many other occupations. While Sergeants have not been the main subjects of our observations, and so we observe their work indirectly, it is apparent that some supervise with their keyboards.

> 19:45 Reports of a collision. A PCSO has been knocked off his bike in Lakeside. James, as a Traffic Officer (or, officially, Roads Policing), has been assigned to the motorways, but no Sergeant is attending. He is furious. He sets off for Lakeside. 'It doesn't matter that it is a PCSO. He is still one of us'. He backs up the first officer on the scene and helps take statements. But he remains furious with the Sergeants, two of them, seated behind their desks back at Knapford.[4]

From our observations, we can note James' anger, but we cannot know what those two Sergeants were engaged in, some 30 miles away. From other observations, we know that they might have been dealing with other incidents, coordinating resources to assist or simply monitoring progress. Clearly, there is a good deal of the role of Sergeant that concerns staffing, training, annual leave, and so forth. Much of this is managed through computer systems, all with strange acronyms that we became familiar with over time. The supervision of officers on the street could take the form of monitoring of force systems and the radio. On returning to the station, whether for a break, to complete paperwork or at the end of the shift, Sergeants would frequently comment on particular cases and incidents. They were not at the scene, but they had followed events on the computer log. They might comment on the decisions made or ask about other options considered. They might then also view footage recorded on BWC. As supervision, this is largely ex post, akin to an audit of the actions of officers.[5] Much supervision is thus mediated by technology. The Radio Control Room would draw particular cases to the Sergeant's attention, giving the log reference number, and asking for it to be signed off. Sergeants also check the actions officers have taken to find missing persons, using another system that tracks these cases.[6]

This mode of supervision reflects the influence of information technology on policing more generally. For Ericson and Haggerty, the role of 'police culture' in shaping the actions and decisions of officers is overstated. Instead, they suggest that the actions and decisions taken by officers are informed more by systems and technologies for recording and reporting: 'Police work is not ad hoc and situational but prospectively structured by the categories and classifications of risk communication and by the technologies for communicating knowledge internally

---

[3] Response, Arlesdale Green, February 2018.
[4] Traffic, Knapford, April 2014.
[5] M Power, *The Audit Explosion* (London, Demos, 1994).
[6] Response, Ffarquhar Road, September 2015.

and externally.'[7] Knowing what the system expects, the questions that will automatically arise when writing up an incident, officers act in anticipation of those reports and questions. They form the basis on which many Sergeants will judge the decisions taken, and so police officers quickly learn to create a record that is auditable.[8] We noted, in the previous chapter, the importance of making a written entry in an officer's personal notebook. This is a strange hangover in an increasingly electronic world. Most reports relating to incidents were submitted through force systems, whether that be case management packages or intelligence databases. After a search warrant, officers would each write their own version of events and log any items seized. For some time, the office would become a quiet space, the silence only interrupted by the tapping of keyboards and officers checking the start and finish times to ensure the reports all tally with the PACE record.[9]

Report writing, using words in a carefully-judged manner, forms a key part of the job. In the previous chapter, we noted the close attention an officer gave to writing up her decision to draw her Taser. But even the most mundane actions and decisions might draw attention. On one shift, an officer was not able to drive because of an accident involving a police van:

> He was turning right and the vehicle he was in has a sensitive collision recording device. As he hit the kerb, it went off. He should then take it straight to the fleet maintenance team to be checked out and cleared for a police vehicle accident. But a four-car crash on the bypass came out. He judged this more important. More than 90 minutes later, he had forgotten the collision and returned to the station. It was picked up on the next shift. A Sergeant noted it and reported the 'accident'. It is not an accident, but it is dragging on as a consequence. And nobody wants to take the sensible decision. An officer in the corner of the room comments on the language of policing. He suggests the van didn't 'hit' the kerb. Saying it 'kissed' the kerb might be the better way of expressing it. Just as he would 'invite a man to take a seat' in the back of a van.[10]

Learning how to write up incidents occupied a good deal of the time of any tutee.[11] Anyone familiar with police reports will recognise the peculiar language, the words carefully chosen and the habit of putting all proper names and addresses in capital letters. Pre-empting queries and enquiries from supervision, and potentially from the Crown Prosecution Service (CPS), is perhaps one of the key skills of any police officer. Increasingly, these reports are structured in software packages, directing officers to respond to tick boxes, to enter specific details and to attach supporting materials, whether documents, photos, or body-worn video (BWV) clips. Many of the pro forma questions arise as a consequence of the decision

[7] R Ericson and K Haggerty, *Policing the Risk Society* (Oxford, Oxford University Press, 1997) 33.
[8] Power, *Audit Explosion*.
[9] Territorial Support, Maron, February 2016.
[10] Neighbourhood, Abbey, June 2016.
[11] Response, Hackerbeck, September 2015; Response, Trollshaws, September 2016.

made, in the Radio Control Room, to 'crime' a case in a particular way. Omitting elements might be cause for questions, whether from the Sergeant or the Radio Control Room. Thus, much as Ericson and Haggerty suggest, this work is driven by decisions to categorise an event or a person in a particular way.

# II. Categorisation

The National Crime Recording Standards, since their development,[12] have come to direct the work of Response officers in ways perhaps not always intended. Far from being simply a tool for the accurate recording of offences, the standards are now affecting the ways officers respond to and record incidents. Mention of an offence in a report will require that offence to be cleared up, in some way. A decision to take no further action (to 'NFA it') required justification and would need signing off by the Sergeant. A quality audit of records might pick up the offence and raise a flag if it had not been resolved. One officer deliberately avoided mention of any damage in resolving a report of a dispute at a hostel. If she had recorded the broken mug, it might have raised a criminal damage flag.[13] Once a case has been categorised, the reports and forms that are expected to follow multiply. For any case of domestic abuse, DASH[14] reports will be required on all persons who might be deemed vulnerable, even if the officers assess the incident differently to the initial report and evaluation by the Radio Control Room:

> 19:17 Officers respond to a call about domestic violence. A kid has said something at school that suggests there may be violence in the home. The report is passed out now, while things are relatively quiet. On the way to the address, Spencer asks his Tutee what they will need to do on this job. DASH forms? For the mother and child?

> 19:25 Arrive at the address. The door is answered by a man. He gets his partner down and the two are then separated. Spencer goes into the kitchen with the man and the Tutee takes the woman to the lounge. The kid is upstairs. The woman has no complaints to make. She says her partner's ex is being a pain, threatening and harassing him and them. She turned up outside and shouted at the house. This has caused some tensions and they have argued over it. They are in the courts soon to get a restraining order.

---

[12] Public Administration Select Committee, *Caught Red-handed: Why We Can't Count on Police Recorded Crime Statistics* (London, House of Commons, HC760, 2014); Home Office, *Crime Recording General Rules* available at assets.publishing.service.gov.uk/government/uploads/system/uploads/attachment_data/file/845360/count-general-nov-2019.pdf; M Maguire, 'Criminal Statistics and the Recording of Crime' in M Maguire et al (eds), *The Oxford Handbook of Criminology*, 5th edn (Oxford, Oxford University Press, 2012); M Maguire and S McVie, 'Crime Data and Criminal Statistics: a Critical Reflection' in A Liebling et al, *The Oxford Handbook of Criminology*, 6th edn (Oxford, Oxford University Press, 2017).

[13] Response, Kirk Machan, September 2015.

[14] The Domestic Abuse, Stalking and Harassment and Honour-based Violence (DASH) risk assessment tool rates cases as representing high, medium or low risk based on the number of risk factors identified.

But she is adamant there has been no domestic violence. Her story then matches with what Spencer gets from the male partner. Both also have a beef with the way they have been treated by the police. In the harassment case, they have been treated as if they were guilty because he is on probation and has a tag. But, this evening, they are not hostile. The kid wanders in and seems fine.

20:45 Back at the station, Spencer struggles with the DASH form. They are online now. It asks about the 'perpetrator' and asks 'why was an arrest not made?' Later, it asks 'does the victim deny the assault?' How does he answer this? Yes? No?[15]

The danger came more from the man's ex-partner, but the forms didn't allow for this nuanced assessment. Spencer resolved the issue by completing the DASH forms and cross-referencing to the intelligence report, but he wasn't confident this would be understood. Then again, officers were used to making multiple DASH reports on the same people after repeated incidents. The purpose of these forms, where they went and who read them appeared largely a mystery to many Response officers.[16] There appeared to be little follow-up. That they needed doing once the case had been categorised was unavoidable. They remained on each officer's 'to do' lists until they were completed.

In contrast to what we might expect, much of this work of categorisation was not in the hands of the officers tasked to respond to emergency calls. Instead, call handlers in the Radio Control Room taking reports from the public identified the offences alleged. Once a job had been 'crimed', that is an offence had been identified, officers would be required to treat the case as if that offence had occurred. Ironically, a crime witnessed or suspected by a police officer is now less likely to be recorded as such than one phoned in by a member of the public, regardless of their knowledge of the criminal law, or even their sobriety or state of mind. Citizen reporting of crime and of offences is notoriously unreliable,[17] it nevertheless drove the actions of officers and could leave them struggling to handle cases on the basis of what they encountered at the scene.

This appeared particularly so in cases involving domestic disputes, perhaps because the police are called at a point of distress and perhaps because call handlers are conscious that they should not downplay the potential seriousness of such calls. The expectation is then on officers to take positive action, however that is interpreted, on the basis of the reports received. We have observed numerous calls which, when given out over the radio, required a Grade One response under blue lights. On arrival, the situation was far from what was expected. A case passed on as involving the illicit filming of underage sex turned out to be nothing of the kind.

---

[15] Response, Arlesdale Green, February 2018.

[16] J Medina et al, 'Cheaper, Faster, Better: Expectations and Achievements in Police Risk Assessment of Domestic Abuse' (2016) 10 *Policing* 341; E Turner et al, 'Dashing Hopes? The Predictive Accuracy of Domestic Abuse Risk Assessment by Police' (2019) 59(5) *British Journal of Criminology* 1013.

[17] D Simon, *In Doubt: the Psychology of the Criminal Justice Process* (Cambridge, MA, Harvard University Press, 2012).

A domestic security camera had caught a young couple together, unaware that they had set off the motion sensitive camera. Because there was the implication of underage sex, the case was crimed as a rape and further targets required that such cases be recorded and crimed within an hour of the initial call.[18] Reports of a knife being used to threaten a woman in a domestic dispute turned out to have confused two elements. The woman had picked up the knife and threatened to stab her partner. He had responded, 'if you do, I'll stab you back'. He had not, at any point, had hold of the knife.[19] In each of these cases, the officers had to spend time in changing the 'crime' already recorded. Unable to do it themselves, the change request was referred to be reviewed by an Inspector and then passed on to a central team.

We have noted these consequences of the NCRS elsewhere in our observations. In the search for an 'accurate' record of crimes reported to or identified by the police, the standards have altered the nature of the work. Recording systems began to determine the decisions and courses of action available to officers in advance of their attending an incident. The Radio Control Room staff would then expect to see the appropriate follow-up actions on each case, whether it was DASH forms or the seizure of a vehicle, and would chase the officers concerned until all such actions were complete and the case could be closed off. For many of those we observed, this constrained their discretion. For others, it required some further ingenuity in order to allow them to circumvent the system and carry out their duties as they thought appropriate. Once again, how officers made sense of the NCRS, and how this affected their behaviour, was not uniform. While most officers expressed frustration at the way the standards limited the scope for 'common sense', there was little evidence of anything we might call resistance. Given the relentless inevitability of the computerised records, there was little they could do other than work with it.

> Barry attends a report of a domestic dispute with a second officer. They enter the address, switching on their BWCs as they do so and separate the couple to speak to them in different rooms. The couple have been drinking, though not obviously to excess. They have argued and a neighbour has called the police as the dispute escalated. There is no apparent evidence of violence and there have been no complaints alleging this. Barry and his colleague seek to resolve the dispute by separating the couple. Are there other places one of them can stay for the night? They don't want to have to arrest anyone and would rather resolve this with a cooling-off period. The negotiation is moving towards a resolution. The woman will spend the night at the neighbour's. The officers are almost ready to leave when the woman makes a small remark. He did strike her earlier in the evening. Suddenly, everything has changed. That statement is recorded on the BWC. There is now no leeway. The male is arrested.[20]

[18] Response, Westmarch, February 2018.
[19] Response, Arlesdale Green, February 2018.
[20] Response, Westmarch, February 2018.

Whether or not we agree with their preferred solution in response to this report of a domestic dispute, the officers spent time negotiating a way around the assumption that an arrest should be made. They were ultimately frustrated in this endeavour. The woman's statement that she had been struck meant that they then must treat the case very differently. The officers were not convinced but, since the statement had been recorded, they would not be able to ignore it or work around it. In this instance, the officers' options were constrained not just by policies and by anticipated reports. The BWC, that almost all officers turn on when attending domestic abuse or violence calls, was a further factor. Their actions and decisions would be open to subsequent review, not just on the basis of the reports they submitted. In some distant future, should anything happen, their decisions would be visible and the evidence audible.

The idea that police officers play a role in *constructing* the criminal population[21] here starts to mutate. Through new technologies, and particularly those associated with recording incidents and actions taken, and while the police themselves still play a role in determining both what is a crime and who is the perpetrator, this construction is increasingly taking place in the Radio Control Rooms.[22] Rather than responding to incidents and determining whether crimes have occurred, Response officers in particular are essentially tasked to process crimes and criminals that have been determined remotely, prior to an officer arriving on the scene. Increasingly, every action can also be reviewed using not just the officer's submitted reports, but also their BWC footage.

# III.  Recording

## A.  Body-worn Cameras

While it is a comparatively new technology, the BWC has quickly become ubiquitous. The research evidence of their effect on officer behaviour and on interactions with citizens is also growing.[23] This evidence tends to ask questions, such as whether cameras have reduced the use of force[24] or resulted in a reduction of

[21] M McConville et al, *The Case for the Prosecution: Police Suspects and the Construction of Criminality* (London, Routledge, 1993).

[22] A Black and K Lumsden, 'Precautionary Policing and Dispositives of Risk in a Police Force Control Room in Domestic Abuse Incidents: an Ethnography of Call Handlers, Dispatchers and Response Officers' (2020) 30(1) *Policing and Society* 65.

[23] For a recent review of this research, see C Lum et al, 'Research on Body-worn Cameras: What we Know, What we Need to Know' (2019) 18 *Criminology and Public Policy* 93.

[24] For example, WM Kozlicki et al, 'When No One is Watching: Evaluating the Impact of Body-worn Cameras on Use of Force Incidents' (2019) *Policing and Society*, doi: 10.1080/10439463.2019.1576672; B Ariel et al, 'Report: Increases in Police Use of Force in the Presence of Body Worn Cameras are Driven by Officer Discretion: a Protocol Based Subgroup Analysis of Ten Randomised Experiments' (2016) 12 *Journal of Experimental Criminology* 453.

complaints against officers.[25] Other research asks about officer attitudes towards the technology.[26] Observing officers in the two police forces, while BWCs were being rolled out in each, afforded us the opportunity to note the way officers have adopted and adapted to the cameras and their use.[27] What we are interested in here are the ways in which BWCs can affect the approach officers take to using their powers. We should note that, for the most part, we observed officers using BWCs and, therefore, cannot say much about the conduct of officers not carrying them. However, their effects were remarked upon, and not just by officers. During a stop and search, a young man pointed at the camera and remarked: 'This has ruined it for you, hasn't it?'[28] While this is too simple an evaluation, we have observed officers coming to terms with the equipment, its use on the street and at scenes, and some of the consequences of recording and not recording.

The decision to turn on a camera was mandatory in particular circumstances, such as when conducting a stop and search or attending a domestic incident, in both of the police forces we observed. However, remembering to turn on the equipment was something officers struggled with at first. One officer explained that she frequently forgot to switch it on during a Grade One response. As she 'piled out of the car, it is the last thing on my mind'. Her colleague would remember to do it and think that he had done it. Only later would he realise that he had not, what with everything else he was trying to keep in mind. Both officers worked at a station which had signs above the urinals in the men's toilets saying: 'Are you recording? Your footage could secure a conviction or stop a complaint in its tracks. Turn it on – there's no excuse'.[29] A common problem was then the failure to turn the camera off at the end of an incident. Officers could sometimes wait for some time while their camera was downloaded at the end of the shift as they wondered what indiscretions they might have caught by mistake. This was generally a source of amusement, but one officer reported being asked by the CPS to edit his BWC footage. They didn't want to watch the 90 minutes he had recorded. They just wanted 10 minutes of the most salient points. The officer refused to do so because, should it ever become a discussion in court, it should be for the CPS to make the judgements about what is shown and what is not.[30]

---

[25] For example, B Ariel et al, 'The Effect of Body-worn Cameras on Use of Force and Citizens' Complaints against the Police: a Randomized Controlled Trial' (2015) 31 *Journal of Qualitative Criminology* 509; WG Jennings et al, 'Evaluating the Impact of Police Officer Body-worn Cameras (BWCs) on Response-to-Resistance and Serious External Complaints: Evidence from the Orlando Police Department (OPD) Experience Utilizing a Randomized Controlled Experiment' (2015) 43 *Journal of Criminal Justice* 480.

[26] For example, M Goetschel and JM Peha, 'Police Perceptions of Body-worn Cameras' (2017) 42 *American Journal of Criminal Justice* 698.

[27] M Rowe et al, 'Body-worn Cameras and the Law of Unintended Consequences: Some Questions Arising from Emergent Practices' (2018) 12 *Policing* 83.

[28] Territorial Support, Knapford, September 2015.

[29] Neighbourhood, Dale, January 2018. We assume this was not a recommendation that officers should be recording in the men's toilets.

[30] Response, Westmarch, January 2017.

As officers became familiar with the equipment, we observed that they began to use it in more situations. An officer, whose camera was still charging up, felt the absence of it. What if someone were to jump off a bridge? The coroner would want to see the evidence.[31] Another switched the camera on to record the faces of individuals as they walked past a location associated with drug dealing.[32] A Territorial Support team recorded the details of an operation to execute a search warrant on an address. They recorded everything from the moment they entered the housing estate because, in the past, they had been attacked while doing similar jobs in the same area.[33] One officer took still images and recorded statements on his BWC in order to avoid a trip to Custody or the need to arrange for a VA. The job he was engaged with was a shoplifting case that was 'going nowhere'. This officer recognised that it was not official policy, indeed that it breached policies, but considered it a sensible approach and an efficient use of his time.[34]

What is evident, and not just from our observations, is that officers have a good deal of discretion in the way they use their cameras.[35] Questions and suspicions might be raised, by supervisors and the researchers, about the absence of footage in some circumstances, perhaps particularly where the policies suggested it was mandatory. For example, an officer who routinely used his camera most of the time did not record the search of a car in which he recovered a crowbar.[36] On another occasion, and just before stopping a 'gang' of young men, officers conferred: 'are we having BWCs on?' Our fieldnotes indicate the answer was 'yes', but it later transpired that the cameras remained turned off for what was an illegal search that was not recorded by any means.[37] However, the decision not to record was not always simply an act of concealment. Officers often considered whether they should or should not switch their BWCs on as they approached incidents, playing out different scenarios. For example, one officer decided not to switch his on as he approached a Grade Two domestic violence call. He did not want to record any allegations made because that would force his hand. Later in the same shift, he did the same again at another Grade Two domestic. In neither case were there visible injuries, although in the first case there was visible evidence of criminal damage. Both offences were 'cuffed'.[38] This observation indicated that there remained some wriggle room on the frontline, despite the technological modes of monitoring officer discretion and recording offences. This undermined the NCRS and the force policy of positive action on domestic violence. Whether

[31] Neighbourhood, Withered Heath, September 2017.

[32] Night-time Economy Team, Brandham, October 2015.

[33] Territorial Support, Peel Godred, July 2016.

[34] Neighbourhood, Abbey, April 2016.

[35] BC Newell and R Greidanus, 'Officer Discretion and the Choice to Record: Officer Attitudes towards Body-worn Camera Activation' (2018) 96 *North Carolina Law Review* 1525.

[36] Neighbourhood, Withered Heath, March 2018.

[37] Response [Redacted] 2017.

[38] Response [Redacted] 2016.

or not this officer's judgements were sound ones, they illuminate the continuing scope for horizontal fragmentation of BWC policies, despite the increasing potential for surveillance. It also suggests a degree of resistance, if at the level of individual officers rather than as a facet of 'police culture'.

Some officers were clear that the cameras have affected their conduct. They were aware when they were switched on and remarked upon the way they affected the dynamics in exchanges with the public. Officers noted that they were less likely to conduct stops without grounds.[39] They became more scripted in their spoken interactions and, in turn, the public were less likely to engage with them.[40] The result, they argued, was that less intelligence was passed on during an encounter while cameras were on.[41] But, for most officers, the benefits of a camera outweighed these negatives. In particular, complaints against them were more readily dealt with. After searching one male, the Inspector had a complaint passed on that same evening. As they returned to the station for a break and to update their records, the officers downloaded their recording of the incident. By the end of the shift, the Inspector had reviewed it, dismissed the complaint and informed the complainant that there was nothing in the officers' conduct that warranted further investigation.[42] This aspect of BWCs has been much remarked upon in the literature.[43]

Less remarked upon is the use of footage to reconstruct what happened at an incident. It is common to see officers watching recordings before writing a statement, and we have already noted some examples of this. For example, we described the care that one officer took while writing up her decision to deploy her Taser. She quickly reviewed her BWC footage as she crafted her statement.[44] This might appear to be a common sense way of using the technology. However, it does raise questions about the extent to which existing rules of criminal evidence, in particular those relating to witness testimony, remain appropriate for dealing with new forms of real and testimonial evidence. The common law rules on hearsay and against narrative, and statutory provisions on aides memoires and the video recording of testimony,[45] are likely to need revisiting as BWV starts to become used more extensively as an integral part of the case for either prosecution or defence.

Our observations suggest that BWCs have affected officer behaviours and the ways in which they act and interact. However, as officers become more familiar with the technology and begin to use it in different ways, the impacts cannot be reduced to simple questions about the use of force or complaints. Recordings became a source of further entertainment back at the station, a new way of

---

[39] Territorial Support, Knapford, September 2015.
[40] Rowe et al, 'Body-worn Cameras and the Law of Unintended Consequences'.
[41] Territorial Support, Knapford, January 2016.
[42] Territorial Support, Knapford, May 2015.
[43] See fnn 23–27 at the start of this section.
[44] Response, Ffarquhar Road, September 2015.
[45] Criminal Justice Act 2003; Youth Justice and Criminal Evidence Act 1999.

telling the stories that are an important feature of policing.[46] They became the focus of discussion. After executing a search warrant, a Territorial Support team reviewed the use of a new piece of kit, a powerful saw, used to take a front door off its hinges. To get through in under 30 seconds was impressive. More important was that, by using the saw at an angle, they hadn't broken the blade, unlike colleagues on a second team who had used it incorrectly.[47] They were used to gather evidence in domestic violence cases, but were equally turned off when officers felt some things should not be recorded. At a very distressing suicide, the officer did not record the scene because he would not want it to be shown in front of family and friends at the Coroner's Court, despite the evidential value.[48] Thus, as a relatively new piece of kit, it became something that officers used in different ways to make their job easier as well as to demonstrate the legitimacy of their conduct. In that sense, the BWC became another piece of kit that was available to help get the job done, but it was one used more frequently and with more imagination than most of the hardware hanging from an officer's belt.

## B. Tablets and Other Mobile Devices

During the course of our observations, the technology available to officers developed significantly. At the start, a minority of vehicles were equipped with mobile data terminals (MDT). These were mainly in use within Territorial Support and Traffic units and allowed officers to check car registration details. They were capable of more, but this was their main function. However, to be of real value, they required a second officer (or, on accession, an observer) to enter registration details and to flick through the details of registered driver, insurance, and MOT. Even rarer were vehicles kitted out with Automatic Number Plate Recognition (ANPR). While this equipment had some use, officers found it to be a source of countless 'hits', most of them of dubious value. Instead, officers preferred to tune in to a dedicated radio channel for ANPR, relaying information from the static cameras located across the two forces, and other traffic intelligence. By the end of our observations, officers were all equipped with mobile devices, providing access to various police systems and databases. Most had been issued with laptops and still more were using handheld tablets, allowing them to access intelligence, to enter key information relevant to most common types of incident and to complete reports while outside the police station. Ericson and Haggerty noted

---

[46] M van Hulst, 'Storytelling at the Police Station: the Canteen Culture Revisited' (2013) 53 *British Journal of Criminology* 624; PAJ Waddington, 'Police (Canteen) Sub-culture: An Appreciation' (1999) 29 *British Journal of Criminology* 287; E Turner and M Rowe, 'Police Culture, Talk and Action: Exploring Narratives in Ethnographic Data' (2017) 4–5 *European Journal of Policing Studies* 52.
[47] Neighbourhood, Peel Godred, July 2016.
[48] Response, Bywater, November 2016.

the enthusiasm with which police forces embraced technology as a solution to the problems of communication and sharing information.[49] Austerity added a further dynamic. It appeared to enable greater flexibility in the deployment of officers, making local information easily available to officers otherwise unfamiliar with a place.

However, there remained some signs of resistance to these new technologies. This resistance was generally passive. A refusal to use a mobile device to write reports or to update progress on case logs while waiting in a hospital waiting room was not the act of a technophobe. The same officer was using his own mobile phone to browse eBay.[50] There were also some practical difficulties. Laptops were not easy to use in the front seat of a patrol car and the screens were small, making it hard to read some of the text. If officers were to use them while on the road, they had to pull over, sometimes stopping for a coffee. Many officers preferred to return to the station for anything requiring more than a quick query.[51] The emergence of tablets received a similarly mixed reception.

> Jim likes his tablet – throughout the whole shift, he pulls up incidents on his tablet – he thinks it provides better quality intelligence than given over radio. He regularly uses it to do vehicle checks. He only uses paper or goes back into the station if it runs low on batteries or if the software is unreliable.[52]

> Tibs doesn't even bother taking his tablet out. He says it never works and it is easier to write on paper or go back to the station. 'You can never connect and it's not user-friendly.' It is also less sociable than radioing in requests or receiving information over the airwaves – the latter gives you a chance to have a chat and even have a laugh with the call handler.[53]

The variation in uptake undermined the potential of any new technology. Some officers could not wait to try out new kit and to see what they could do with it. Others were deeply sceptical and could find any number of reasons not to make use of it. Two officers, confronting similar cases of a car failing to stop for the police, approached the problem very differently. One took a seat at a computer in the nearest police station, not his own base, and spent some time trawling through ANPR looking for the make of car and the partial plate he had glimpsed.[54] The other had never used ANPR and was unsure whether he would get permission to

---

[49] R Ericson and K Haggerty, *Policing the Risk Society* (Oxford, Oxford University Press, 1997). We would note, however, that this enthusiasm was not accompanied by the parallel paper records that they noted. More and more work was scanned on to the system. Witness signatures were taken on touch sensitive screens. Paper-based DASH forms were replaced by an electronic version, automatically populated with information from the previous DASH form submitted for the individual.

[50] Response, Ravenhill, August 2018.

[51] Response, Westmarch, February 2018.

[52] Response, Weathertop, January 2018.

[53] Response, Eriador, October 2017.

[54] Response, Hackerbeck, June 2015.

try it. He also believed that every search cost money and he couldn't justify such expenditure in this case.[55]

## C. Intelligence

The capacity to access intelligence was significantly enhanced by MDT, laptops, and tablets. However, what we observed was the very limited use of what we might understand to be intelligence (that is, information that has been processed and analysed to develop something that is actionable).[56] We noted, in Chapter 5, how limited the information passed out at formal briefings at the start of a shift tended to be. It was little more than information about incidents that had occurred since the officers had last been on duty. There might be attention drawn to wanted individuals, with little indication of where to look for them, or to a spate of burglaries in a particular area, but no indication of any suspects or modus operandi.[57] Officers might 'float about' in such areas during quieter moments in a shift, but they then tended to drive around in a rather purposeless manner.[58]

In Neighbourhood teams, officers often received no briefing at all. Split shift patterns and variable start times meant that few officers started at the same time. To bring officers together at any point during a shift would entail bringing some back into the station. Instead, officers adopted different ways of updating themselves and colleagues. In one team, it was the responsibility of the PCSOs to trawl through the reports and incidents that had come in to identify any points of interest.

> While we are waiting to go, the PCSOs are clearing the notices from the intelligence database that have come in overnight. There was a fire in a skip at a Burger King – 25 kids reported causing trouble. And fireworks were set off towards Frankie and Benny's. 'That's a restaurant' the PCSO adds. 'Thanks for clarifying that. Not someone's house then!' 'If it were a house, it could also be a hate crime!' Other reports include a suspected cannabis farm. The PCSO takes this information and plans his day, walking to [Housing Estate] via the cannabis farm and then back by way of the Burger King towards lunchtime. Final call last night was from someone reporting a man who is either unwell or very drunk, claiming to be the IRA. Nobody wants that job.[59]

---

[55] Response, Ffarquhar Road, September 2015.
[56] JG Carter et al, 'Implementing Intelligence-led Policing: An Application of Loose-coupling Theory (2014) 42 *Journal of Criminal Justice* 433; JG Carter and SW Phillips, 'Intelligence-led Policing and Forces of Organisational Change in the USA' (2015) 25 *Policing and Society* 333; A James, 'Forward to the Past: Reinventing Intelligence-led Policing in Britain' (2014) 15 *Police Practice and Research* 75; JH Ratcliffe, *Intelligence-led Policing*, 2nd edn (London, Routledge, 2016); C Sanders and C Condon, 'Crime Analysis and Cognitive Effects: the Practice of Policing through Flows of Data' (2017) 18 *Global Crime* 237.
[57] Response, Trollshaws, September 2016.
[58] Response, Hackerbeck, October 2016.
[59] Neighbourhood, Arlesdale, September 2014.

On more proactive teams, officers were engaged in making the connections themselves. One group of Traffic officers spent the first hour or two of each shift checking reports of stolen vehicles, of vehicles failing to stop for police cars and of reports of gang activity. They were looking for patterns and for vehicles to target. On one shift, they identified a high-performance vehicle they believed to be in the use of a group of men who, reports suggested, were looking for opportunities to shoot members of a rival group. They did this intelligence work themselves without input from analysts or other experts. They then spent four hours hunting the vehicle in a coordinated effort with dog handlers ready nearby.[60] Another proactive officer, in Territorial Support, did much the same as the PCSO in Neighbourhood. But he wrote everything down in a file that he had been keeping for years. The act of writing helped him remember things and make connections to previous reports he had noted. Over his four years in the role, the file had grown to an impressive size.[61]

While on patrol and outside the police station, officers did have increasingly ready access to the intelligence databases through their tablets and other devices. However, they tended to access information rather than intelligence. They would most commonly check car number plates, address details or the intelligence records of individuals. The promise of tablets highlighting local priorities or crime hotspots to focus the attention of officers unfamiliar with the area proved to be a distant promise during the period of our observations and one that would have been practically difficult in singly-crewed cars. The ready availability of largely undigested information then had other consequences. All records of contact with the police are available in an individual's intelligence record. And all such contact infers patterns when simply reviewed in their raw format. We have noted that, in stop and account interactions, officers would often open with the question, 'are you known to the police?' Every stop and search, whether anything was found or not, will appear on a record. The more such encounters there are, the more the officers' suspicions are aroused. For most of our observed officers, there was, as we noted at the end of Chapter 8, no smoke without fire.[62]

Furthermore, through patrol work in particular, officers without any specific training in intelligence-gathering, were actively contributing to the information available to their colleagues. If an address was identified on the system as being used by suspected drug dealers, a car parked outside it might have its number plate recorded in that information 'package', absent any other intelligence that the vehicle was connected to that address or that its occupants were involved in any criminality.[63] Indeed, 'markers' on properties were frequently out of date,

---

[60] Dog Team, Midgewater, May 2019.

[61] Territorial Support, Ettenmoor, December 2017.

[62] M Rowe and T Søgaard, '"Playing the Man, not the Ball": Targeting Organised Criminals, Intelligence and the Problems with Pulling Levers' (2020) *Policing and Society* available at doi.org/10.1080/10439463.2019.1603226.

[63] Response, Hackerbeck, October 2016.

with suspects having moved house unknown to the police. Technological developments in policing therefore played a proactive role in raising suspicion on an individual level and also in constructing criminal communities and organisations. It had the potential to exaggerate social connections between individuals into criminal connections, and created confirmation bias. Furthermore, as police numbers dwindled due to austerity, and more officers found themselves patrolling unfamiliar areas and relying on such information, it could gain disproportionate significance.

## IV. Technology and Discretion

It would be overstating the case if we were to suggest that the uptake of technology was somehow itself a matter of officer discretion. Most of the systems we have referred to in this chapter were ones that all officers had to use. As Ericson and Haggerty found,[64] even those officers reluctant to use computers were forced to engage with them once annual leave and shift patterns were all arranged through a force management system. These systems structured the work of officers in ways that affected what they did and the decisions they took. They made the work of officers on the street, once remote and largely invisible, open to scrutiny and supervision in ways that some suggest has 'severely circumscribed' their discretion.[65] Officers can avoid responding to particular jobs by claiming to be already engaged in another, or in completing reports,[66] but it is harder to operate entirely out of sight. Police cars are now tracked, so that Radio Control Room staff can know which officers are nearest to a reported incident. Sergeants scrutinise reports and progress as it happens in the live computer record. All subsequent forms and tick boxes must be completed or their omission will be flagged to be pursued at a later date. Even a slight 'kiss' on the kerb of a road sets off an alarm that must be handled in a prescribed manner. The failure to do so results in suspension from driving for a period while it is resolved. When it came to the input of 'intelligence' on police databases, there was no supervision of what could and could not be added to the system, but analysts (who we did not observe) were tasked with grading the value of this information, hopefully mitigating the extent to which chance connections could draw innocent people into the unnecessary use of police powers.

However, we must be careful not to exaggerate the influence of these systems on the work of officers. We did not observe the emergence of the 'abstract police' that Terpstra et al have identified.[67] In most instances, the technology enabled officers to work in different and generally more convenient ways. Not all officers

---

[64] Ericson and Haggerty, *Policing the Risk Society*.
[65] Ericson and Haggerty, *Policing the Risk Society* 36.
[66] Neighbourhood, Abbey, June 2016.
[67] J Terpstra et al, 'The Abstract Police: a Conceptual Exploration of Unintended Changes of Police Organisations' (2019) 92 *Police Journal* 339.

engaged with these possibilities, preferring to work as they had always done, returning to the station for social reasons and not working remotely in the search for efficiency. For those that embraced the new kit, it generally enabled them to make the decisions they wanted to make. We have noted the P tensions 'at the boundaries, where forms direct attention and require the gathering of unnecessary information, or where the Radio Control Room and the NCRS predefine a situation. But these tensions are not the product simply of technology. The influence of the Radio Control Room in defining jobs by the way they pass them on has long been acknowledged.[68] But these tensions are not the product simply of technology. The need to complete particular forms shapes the actions of officers, even when that form is on paper. That the system demands the information and automatically checks on compliance does add another dimension, but the fears of surveillance that accompanied much of the new technology was often overstated, and none more so than in response to the roll-out of BWCs.[69] Officers' concerns that their actions could now be watched were soon allayed. The volume of material that each officer could generate in a shift ensured that no sensible Sergeant could possibly review it all. However, the footage could be – and was – reviewed in particular incidents or in the case of complaints. That the new technologies enabled closer supervision is clear. But the extent to which it constrained discretion in the way officers sometimes suggested, and as Ericson and Haggerty indicate, is less clear.

---

[68] P Manning, *Symbolic Communication* (Cambridge, MA, MIT Press, 1988); P Manning, 'Producing Drama: Symbolic Communication and the Police' (1982) 5 *Symbolic Interaction* 223; P Manning, 'Sign-work' (1986) 39 *Human Relations* 283; Black and Lumsden, 'Precautionary Policing and Dispositives of Risk'.

[69] Goetschel and Peha, 'Police Perceptions of Body-worn Cameras'; JE Gaub et al, 'Officer Perceptions of Body-worn Cameras Before and After Deployment: a Study of Three Departments' (2016) 19 *Police Quarterly* 275.

# 10

## Uniform Change? Revisiting Policing, Regulation, and the Law

### I. Our Argument So Far

This book has put forward a number of central arguments based on our observations of the use of discretion by frontline police officers, particularly but not exclusively in relation to their street powers. From our fieldwork, we have identified a number of themes, experienced by both researchers over six years 'in the field' across two forces, numerous officer roles, 38 different stations, and nearly 80 primary participants. These themes feed into the development of our arguments about how street powers are used by officers, how the use of these powers affects the legitimacy of individual officers, the force, and the institution of the police as a whole, and finally the extent to which police discretion here is restricted, controlled, or managed by the criminal law, Codes of Practice, and – in a broad sense of the word – policy.

First, we have identified the way in which the criminal law as a determinant of police action varies significantly between individual officers but, most dramatically, between roles. Our findings concurred with those of Waddington,[1] that individual officers struggle to enforce 'the law', partially, because they are not equipped to do so. To expect an officer to be able to dynamically apply an accurate and up-to-date knowledge of the laws across a range of different areas in high-pressure and often split-second decisions is unrealistic. Instead, what an officer on the street does is apply their interpretation of a handful of offences that their attention has been brought to by training packages or supervisors. And increasingly this interpretation is led by the Radio Control Room. Either way, this interpretation is sometimes wrong or inappropriate, and many relevant criminal offences are not identified.

Second, we have shown that even where the officer is clear that an offence has been – or is about to be – committed, the action they take against the suspect still varies. Neighbourhood officers and those in Territorial Support seemed to possess a great deal of discretion to: (a) take only informal action, or turn a blind eye to, quite serious or blatant offences; and (b) take formal action against very

---

[1] P Waddington, *Policing Citizens: Authority and Rights* (London, UCL Press, 1999).

minor or inconsequential offences. In these proactive roles, the criminal law did take the form of a resource for,[2] rather than a determinant of, police action. In contrast, and particularly as austerity began to bite, officers operating in Response roles experienced their discretion – once they had agreed to respond to a call – as curtailed by National Crime Recording Standard (NCRS) and force policies on, for example, positive action. Response officers were not using the law as a resource, but were instead expected to identify crimes that corresponded with the report or complaint that was called in. A Response officer who, for example, responded to a 999 call from a wife who said that her husband had hit her, would be 'fighting against the system' if she did not record it as assault or an Offences Against the Person Act crime and respond to it as such. The operation of the NCRS here brought officers back to the basic law they learned in training and put pressure on them to apply and enforce it.

Third, when we look at the use of proactive police powers, which are normally considered necessary as part of the officer's role to detect or deter crime, the criminal law played only a vague and underlying role in how the officer utilised those powers. Officers used stop and account and stop checks in the same manner, as an excuse to stop individuals or vehicles they deemed to be acting suspiciously or to fit a certain 'type'. Sometimes this was based on intelligence-led or contextual factors, centred around a particular crime (for example, burglary or possession of prohibited drugs with intent to supply) but often it was simply based on the officer's feeling that something wasn't quite right. Searches were nominally based on an attempt to find a particular prohibited item (most usually under the Misuse of Drugs Act 1971), but searches for drugs were carried out by officers who were actually hoping to find weapons, or large amounts of currency. The extent to which coercive police powers were connected to suspicion of a particular crime, therefore, varied widely between proactive policing and Response policing. Further, the extent to which these largely proactive powers are restrained by the law is very limited. Apparent restrictions, such as 'reasonable suspicion' for searches, and necessity for arrest, have little effect on curtailing the use of these powers. For stop and account and stop checks, there was no real legal check on the use of these powers. Codes of Practice were more likely to be at the forefront of an officer's mind, but again the extent to which these were applied varied, and effective guidance on stop and account and stop checks was virtually non-existent.

Fourth, we have identified how the use of police powers varies between individuals and between police roles, and that the ways powers are used change over time. Officers recounted how they changed their use of their powers as they moved between different roles or different stations. Moreover, even in the space of six years, we were able to identify a change in the way the same officer, in the same role and under the same supervision, used their powers. The difference between the ways in which officers in different roles used their powers and the temporal

---

[2] R Ericson, *Reproducing Order: A Study of Police Patrol Work* (University of Toronto Press, 1982) 11.

change was closely connected to practical and structural reforms (during our fieldwork, these were largely driven by austerity), technology, new force policies, national guidance, and directives from supervisors at a local level. These policies or directives included requiring officers to wear and to use body-worn cameras (BWCs) in a way which further affected changes to police behaviour.

Finally, we have seen that systemic and technological changes, intended to ensure consistency and to reduce discrimination and complaints, have in effect only increased the accountability of frontline officers to their superiors rather than to the public. To a certain extent they have also curtailed the discretion that officers have, when responding to incidents already crimed by NCRS, and in their broader interactions with suspects, victims, and complainants. At times, this resulted in the utilisation of powers (usually arrest) that failed to satisfy the suspect, the victim, or the officer. This raises serious concerns about how these changes affect police legitimacy across communities over a longer period of time.

In this final chapter, we consider the implications of our conclusions for debates about the extent to which we can or should regulate police street powers. This is linked to our observations about the extent to which it is possible to change police behaviour. Obviously, if we cannot change police behaviour, then debates about regulation run the risk of becoming academic exercises. As we have seen, for many researchers of the police, it is 'police culture' that prevents significant changes to police behaviour and the more proportionate use of police powers. In contrast, our evidence pointed in a different direction: policy, guidance, and directions – enforced by local supervision and the fear of censure – were observed to change even apparently entrenched behaviour of police officers. This change could be rapid and could be evidenced quantitatively across the force through recorded outcomes. However, *attitudes* were more difficult to change than *behaviours* and, partly as a result of this, change was not uniform. Neither was it likely to be permanent, unless policy and supervision remained consistent over time.

## II. Revisiting the Legal Regulation of Policing

Over the six years of fieldwork, we noted quite significant changes in terms of the use of police street powers at an individual level but also within and across police stations. These changes related primarily to the use of stops, searches, and arrests. Indeed, the pace of change during the period of the fieldwork at times became a problem in terms of being able to follow what was happening on observations or when analysing our data. This problem was exacerbated because changes were happening at different rates between stations or teams of officers, or were understood or applied differently by different officers. Policies, directives, guidance, structural changes, and new technology appeared to be imposed upon certain shifts or roles but not others, and these variations were then exacerbated by their different application between the two observed forces.

On occasion, the researchers argued with each other about what the actual policy or accepted practice was, before the penny dropped that actually this was not the important feature of what was being observed. Police officers also talked about changes that had occurred prior to our research, harking back to a golden age with higher officer numbers and more Custody Suites, a time when they socialised together more and had a canteen and licensed bar in the station. Structural and behavioural change was both observed and spoken about in a way that appeared to make it an integral challenge and a fundamental part of the job.

Some of the variations in the way changes were received, adapted, and adopted might be interpreted as resistance. Worden and McLean have argued that 'police departments are no exceptions to the rule that organizations tend to resist change'.[3] This tendency might, in part, explain some of the horizontal and vertical fragmentation of policy we observed. Some teams undermined efforts to brigade Response officers together in centralised teams by recreating tea and locker facilities in satellite stations.[4] Others maintained the levels of stop and search in the face of pressures to reduce those numbers.[5] Elsewhere, supervisors persisted in the use of performance targets long after the force had dispensed with them as a management tool.[6] The adoption of body-worn video was reluctant, slow and patchy in some Response teams.[7] However, this resistance to change was fragmented and largely a passive phenomenon, clinging to old habits, rather than anything we would identify as organisational resistance at the street level.[8] It might be characterised more as the inevitable interpretation and misinterpretation of policies that is a constant problem in public administration.[9] There was explicit and very public opposition to changes, such as to stop and search, in particular from police representative bodies and some senior officers. However, and as we have underlined throughout this book, there has been change, and quite significant change with respect to stop and search.

With a specific focus on how officers used their street powers, it is useful here to re-engage with the arguments discussed in Chapter 3 about the extent to which the law is able to regulate the behaviour and actions of police officers. As we have seen, while there is some dispute about whether or not the police are primarily

---

[3] R Worden and S McLean, *Mirage of Police Reform: Procedural Justice and Police Legitimacy* (Oakland, CA, University of California Press, 2017) 40.

[4] Response, Arlesdale Green, February 2018.

[5] Territorial Support, Peel Godred, July 2018.

[6] Traffic, Knapford, July 2014.

[7] Response, Rivendell, August 2017.

[8] P Manning, *Police Work: the Social Organization of Policing*, 2nd edn (Prospect Heights, IL, Waveland Press, 1997)

[9] JL Pressman and A Wildavsky, *Implementation: How Great Expectations in Washington are Dashed in Oakland; or, Why it's Amazing that Federal Programs Work at all, this being a Saga of the Economic Development Administration as Told by Two Sympathetic Observers Who Seek to Build Morals on a Foundation*, 3rd edn (Berkeley, University of California Press, 1984); M Hill and P Hupe, *Implementing Public Policy*, 3rd edn (London, Sage, 2014); M Rowe, 'Discretion and Inconsistency: Implementing the Social Fund' (2002) 22 *Public Money and Management* 19.

the enforcers of law, the consensus seems to be that changes to the regulation of police powers through legislation or case law tend to have, at best, a modest direct impact upon frontline police behaviour (although a greater impact upon discretion post-arrest). It is difficult here to be certain about the way in which the key major statutory changes to the regulation of frontline police powers impacted on officers. Our fieldwork started long after both the Police and Criminal Evidence Act 1984 (PACE) and the Human Rights Act 1998 (HRA 1998) had been introduced and so, while we were able to hear retrospectively what long-serving officers felt had been the impact of the introduction of the HRA 1998, and we were able to see both PACE and the HRA 1998 in action, we were not able to observe to what extent significant changes occurred as a result of their introduction. In terms of common law regulation, as we noted in Chapter 3, case law has tended to entrench and defend police powers rather than curtail them. This was also true during our project. A major case (*Hayes* on arrest necessity)[10] was reported shortly before we undertook our fieldwork, but this largely supported police practice. Nevertheless, at one force, a desk-based training package was introduced following the case to try to clarify the situation, which did have an effect on the understanding of some officers. Combined with previous research on PACE and the HRA 1998, it is clear that significant legal changes will be followed by national guidance and force-wide training packages to try to help officers to remain compliant. Many officers will be aware of the overarching reason for these changes, but others were unaware or uninterested in their legal context.

When we spoke with officers about their use of street powers they would, on occasion, refer directly to PACE or the HRA 1998, but they did not generally have knowledge of how this legislation operates (for example, in relation to different statutory provisions). Instead, reference to legislation tended to be mediated through Codes of Practice (on which they seemed more fluent), practical training packages, special briefings on legal changes, and instructions from supervisors. Phrases like 'arrest necessity', and 'reasonable suspicion' were typically used without their statutory context and, as we have seen, often officers' understanding of these concepts diverged from their primary source. The legal regulation and obligations of frontline officers were constantly at work, but only in a diffused and often altered form. So, when officers talked about the regulation of their pre-interview powers, they only rarely made reference to legislation or case law, instead referring to guidance, training, or – most commonly – 'policy'. It was this understanding of 'policy' that was the main driver of change when it came to street powers. Officers would often explain what 'policy used to be', or that 'there's a new policy' when they explained why they were operating differently. They were often unclear as to whether this 'policy' was an instruction of settled practice from the force (as Grimshaw and Jefferson would understand it),[11] national guidance

---

[10] See Chapter 7.

[11] R Grimshaw and T Jefferson, *Interpreting Police Work: Policy and Practice in Forms of Beat Policing* (London, Allen & Unwin, 1987).

from the College of Policing or the Home Office, training packages, or simply an instruction from an Inspector, a Sergeant, or even another Constable acting in a supervisory role for a shift.

We are unequivocal in our position that changing policy – as understood in this wide form of supervised instruction – does broadly lead to significant changes in the behaviour of frontline officers. However, it does not always change police behaviour in the way that was originally intended and it does not change behaviour uniformly. Furthermore, change brought about in this way is unlikely to be permanent; a progression towards more ethical or proportionate use of street powers is not like travelling along a one-way street. Even during our research, reversals of what appeared to be long-term trends occurred as a result of what appeared to be fairly minor factors. At one force, a critical HMICFRS inspection, combined with a new cadre of recruits, all of whom needed to complete a stop search in order to pass probation, corresponded with a dramatic spike in statistics of the number of reported searches, which had been declining steadily over the preceding years (see Chapter 6).

## III.  What Sarge Says: Supervision and Monitoring

Grimshaw and Jefferson argue that, on operational issues, policy led by the Chief Constable is unlikely to achieve its aims.[12] Our evidence suggested a more complex picture. We found consistent evidence that policy, as it was understood by frontline officers, was a major driving force behind changes to an officer's use of their street powers. In this sense, our conclusions were more akin to those recently coming out of studies and evaluations of frontline police in the United States, which suggest that introducing or reforming state-wide policies and procedures can have a positive impact upon police behaviour.[13] Worden and McLean note that some officers are more receptive to change than others,[14] while in the UK, Bradford and Quinton indicate that officers are more likely to identify with the aims, and buy-in to policies and procedures that they consider to be fair and legitimate.[15] Reforms perceived by officers to enhance their ability to 'fight crime' were much less likely to be resisted.[16]

Falk-Moore argues that, to comprehend the 'rules of the game' in a semi-autonomous social field, you need to understand the 'working social context' in

---

[12] Grimshaw and Jefferson, *Interpreting Police Work*.

[13] Worden and McLean, *Mirage of Police Reform* 191.

[14] Worden and McLean, *Mirage of Police Reform* 181.

[15] B Bradford and P Quinton, 'Self-Legitimacy, Police Culture and Support for Democratic Policing in and English Constabulary' (2014) 54 *British Journal of Criminology* 46.

[16] A Myhill and B Bradford, 'Can Police Enhance Public Confidence by Improving Quality of Service? Results from Two Surveys in England and Wales' (2012) 22 *Policing and Society* 397.

which they are made.[17] The source of the rules, whether it be law or non-legal norms and practices, is less significant than the extent to which they are 'socially enforceable' *within* the field.[18] This is a good way of interpreting what we observed happening on a day-to-day basis. Policy would only have a significant impact upon frontline officers where this was effectively supervised. It is not merely the case that an awareness of rank permeates the police force[19] and that the lower ranking officers are aware of the leadership structure and their duty to follow orders. Effective supervision of policy sometimes came from briefings given by an Inspector based at, and present in, the station. More usually, it came from the day-to-day desk-based management of an officer's shift from their Sergeant, about which there is currently insufficient research. The important factors behind this conclusion were both the physical presence of the supervising officer in the station during the shift, and their ability to question Constables about each job they attended. The impact of technologically-mediated methods of supervision must also be considered. Monitoring of officers over the radio and on screen can facilitate supervision of individual decisions that, previously, would have taken place largely out of sight. As Engel has argued, the most effective supervisors of frontline officers – in terms of regulating behaviour – were those who were most 'active'.[20] Immediate supervisors can affect some types of officer behaviour, but the different orientations and styles of supervision can determine the extent to which they can effect change.[21] With ratios of Sergeant to Constable as high as 1:33,[22] it is not surprising that we find horizontal fragmentation of policy at the frontline.

According to HMIC, the Sergeant is 'a pivotal figure in delivering corporate aims and vision and, through these, the quality of service to the public', and they should be 'leaders, coaches, mentors and custodians of excellence in service delivery'.[23] The generic 'Patrol Sergeant' profile states that their role is 'To ensure and enable their staff to patrol the area for which they are responsible, in order to prevent crime and disorder, and to respond to calls from the public'.[24] According to the College of Policing's role description, 'Sergeants are the first level of line

[17] S Falk-Moore, 'Law and Social Change: The Semi-Autonomous Social Field as an Appropriate Subject of Study' (1973) 7 *Law and Society Review* 719, 743.

[18] Falk-Moore, 'Law and Social Change' 744–45.

[19] C Davis, 'Rank Matters: Police Leadership and the Authority of Rank' (2018) *Policing and Society* DOI: 10.1080/10439463.2018.1555250.

[20] R Engel, 'Patrol Officer Supervision in the Community Policing Era' (2002) 30 *American Journal of Criminal Justice* 51, 62.

[21] Worden and McLean, *Mirage of Police Reform* 16; Engel, 'Patrol Officer Supervision'.

[22] Her Majesty's Inspectorate of Constabulary, *Serving Neighbourhoods and Individuals: A Thematic Report on Neighbourhood Policing and Developing Citizen Focus Policing* (London, HMIC, 2008) 14.4.

[23] Her Majesty's Inspectorate of Constabulary, *Leading from the Frontline: Thematic Inspection of Frontline Supervision and Leadership, at the Rank of Sergeant in the Police Service of England and Wales* (London, HMIC, 2008).

[24] HMIC, *Leading from the Frontline* 2.3.

management in policing and as such carry an important role in ensuring effective daily supervision, guidance and support of officers and staff',[25] which was broadly in line with how Sergeants perceived their role during our fieldwork. Importantly, for our purposes, 'Sergeants are empowered, indeed obligated, to suggest and promote changes',[26] placing them front and centre when it comes to ensuring that force policy is enacted on the street.

**Figure 10.1**  Percentage of time spent on tasks as reported by respondents

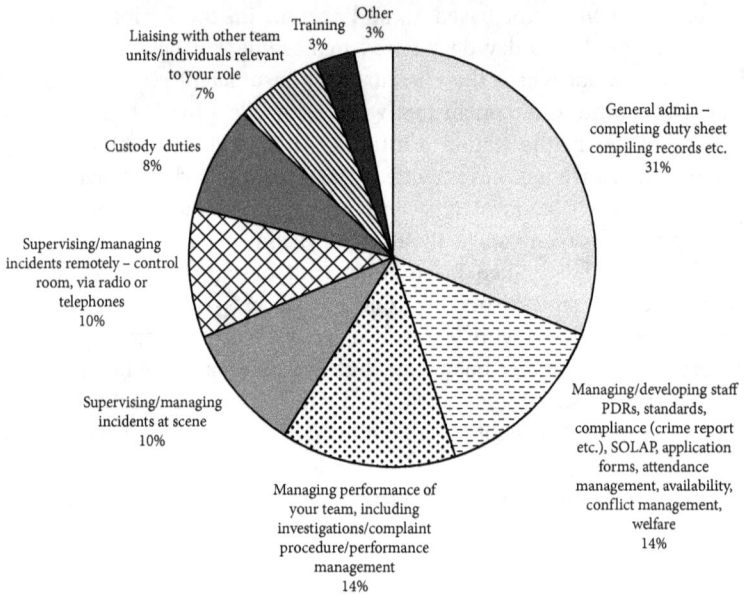

*Source*: HMIC *Leading from the Frontline* 6.6. Figure 6.1 in source.

Reflecting HMIC's research (see Figure 10.1),[27] we observed Sergeants at both forces to be largely desk-based during the shift, although sometimes they would attend serious incidents or those requiring specific skills,[28] or where they considered Constable numbers were too low during a shift.[29] Their job would revolve around managing their team of Constables and managing a list of 'jobs' that the team had accrued, which normally also involved managing jobs left over from previous shifts and ensuring that other jobs were picked up by later shifts. This supervisory function was facilitated by technological developments enabling Sergeants to see

[25] See profdev.college.police.uk/professional-profile/police-sergeant/.
[26] HMIC, *Leading from the Frontline* 6.5.
[27] HMIC, *Leading from the Frontline* 6.6.
[28] For example, one Sergeant was skilled at picking locks and would attend suspected suicides and sudden deaths to assist their Constables in gaining access to a building (Response, Bywater, November 2016).
[29] Neighbourhood, Dunland, June 2018.

officer reports as a shift progressed. As we saw in Chapter 9, the Sergeant could see – almost in real time – which jobs were being dealt with by which Constable and advise on how best to proceed, either by further investigation or by trying to identify a way to 'close' the job that would be acceptable both to their own line managers and to the complainant or victim. Sergeants might visit the room in which the Constables were working to ask how a particular job was progressing or would radio through for updates while the Constable was out of the station. Response officers, in particular, were more often subject to 'micro-management', in contrast to Neighbourhood officers who were often more experienced and considered to work better with greater freedom.[30] The presence of the Sergeant was, therefore, always felt. What 'Sarge' wanted, disliked, or was ambivalent to, was regularly referred to by officers explaining their prioritising or operational decisions. Further, officers were aware that different Sergeants had different priorities, and so the use of their powers or their decision on how to proceed with a job could change from one shift to the next depending on who they were reporting to.

The operation of police discretion by frontline officers has rightly been characterised as 'low visibility'.[31] Reflecting the 1987 findings of Chatterton,[32] Sergeants spent the vast majority of their time at their desk when the frontline officer was making key decisions away from the station. The frontline officer may be sitting in their car, deciding which job to respond to, standing in the living room of a house, deciding whether or not to arrest a husband accused of domestic violence, or on the street, determining whether the excuse given by the youth was sufficient to allay their suspicions that they might be carrying drugs and needed to be searched. However, there was a significant difference in the extent to which these discretionary decisions were supervised, depending on the officer's role. Proactive officers, particularly those in Neighbourhood or Traffic, received little in the way of 'direct'[33] supervision either on the beat or at the site of an incident.[34] In contrast, Response officers in particular, were being pre-managed from the station and Radio Control Room in the form of categorisation of incidents and expectations of disposal in line with force policies. In either case, much of what the officer did remained hidden from the Sergeant – a decision to turn a blind eye to someone they saw speeding, or smoking cannabis, would be invisible. Sometimes the explanation for the use of a power provided to a Sergeant did not tally with the actual situation. On rare occasions officers would also go out of their way to hide their practices, for example by omitting information in their Personal Note Book, advising witnesses to avoid making certain allegations, not recording stop and searches, or ensuring that BWCs were switched off.

---

[30] Neighbourhood, Dunland, June 2018.
[31] J Goldstein, 'Police Discretion' (1960) 69 *Yale Law Journal* 543, 552.
[32] M Chatterton, 'Misuse of Sergeants' (1987) 3 *Policing* 106.
[33] C Currie, 'First-Line Supervision: The Role of the Sergeant Part One' (1988) 61 *Police Journal* 312.
[34] Although for Territorial Support units a Sergeant was sometimes present in the van.

But as we saw in the previous chapter, such activity always carried with it some risk, with police vehicles and radios tracked, and BWC footage remaining on record to be potentially viewed by a supervisor at a later date. And even if the officer's own BWC was not switched on, there was a chance that another officer's footage might capture the incident. There was the risk that colleagues might reveal information that undermined an officer's explanation, or even that an unknown plain-clothed or off-duty officer may be present.[35] Furthermore, officers were always mindful that a member of the public might make a complaint. The freedom to apply the 'Ways and Means Act', even for officers in proactive roles, was therefore not unfettered, and officers were usually only likely to ride roughshod over regulations and policies in high-crime areas where complaints were unlikely and when they believed their colleagues and their Sergeant would support them.

The key to all this is that legal restrictions, regulations, and guidance only controlled or changed frontline officer behaviour and use of street powers where it was understood by the officer to be 'policy' that could be enforced directly by their supervisor. It was the efficacy of the supervisory relationship, normally between the Constable and their Sergeant, and mediated through technological modes of communication and monitoring, that gave law, codes of practice, policy, or guidance their teeth. This was through pre-incident policies around disposal, categorisation of incidents by the Radio Control Room, and what Currie describes as *indirect supervision*, including 'post-facto discussions about the handling of an incident with the attending officer',[36] supported by potentially intrusive in-shift monitoring. Ultimately, whether direct or indirect, it was aversion to the threat of censure or sanction which buttressed these types of 'discussion' that explains the speed with which officers or teams could change their behaviour. As McConville et al rightly point out, career self-preservation remains high on an officer's list of priorities when it comes to what does and does not regulate their behaviour on the street.[37] But it is also important here to not overlook the importance of censure. A Sergeant who disagreed with how a Constable had acted could let it be known in very subtle terms that they would have preferred a different course of action to have been taken. This was not usually a direction to do things differently in the future, but a Sergeant informally questioning the wisdom of the officer would have an impact. Being called into Sarge's office (as opposed to going to report on 'successful' jobs) was something Constables preferred to avoid, with its potential for personal and professional embarrassment.

---

[35] On one observation an officer stop and accounted someone who turned out to be the 'Night Silver' – in other words the senior officer responsible for the Night shift for the entire division. The senior officer had been checking out a suspected burglary and was male, wearing a black North-Face jacket, and driving a 'hot hatch' (Response, Eriador, October 2017).

[36] Currie, 'First Line Supervision Part 1' 329.

[37] M McConville et al, *The Case for the Prosecution: Police Suspects and the Construction of Criminality* (London, Routledge, 1993) 182–84.

The manner in which direct supervision occurred also meant that rather than simply applying law, guidance, or force/divisional policy, Sergeants were taking an active role in both interpreting and constructing policy for officers.[38] Policy did cascade down from the senior ranks but, like a waterfall, its path was neither direct nor unchanging. At each level that policy was communicated there came the opportunity for its message to be changed. An Inspector or Sergeant could of course find and read policy in its original form, but in many cases they relied upon an interpretation of it by their line manager: 'what the policy is looking to achieve is this …' Where policy was nuanced and gave a number of alternatives, the tendency was that the further down the chain of command, the narrower the focus became, honing in on the approach with the lowest risk to the force. Risk remained the 'dominant discourse among officers'.[39] When it came to a Constable's interpretation of policy, this was usually dependent on how the Sergeant understood it and wanted it to be applied in practice. Again, this tended to be a low-risk interpretation of the policy. In practical terms, the Constable would be answerable in almost all cases to the Sergeant on shift at the time; the path of least resistance when it came to following policy was to follow the Sergeant's understanding and interpretation of this policy. The best example of this came from the way that the force policy of 'positive action' to remove a suspected domestic violence perpetrator from the home was constructed by Sergeants and applied by Constables to mean a policy of mandatory arrest in these circumstances (see Chapter 7). 'Policy' therefore ceased to be merely a force directive, and instead was reconstructed locally.

# IV. 'Police Culture' and Uniform Change

The implications of the construction of policy at a shift-by-shift and station-by-station level are that different versions of the same policy will be in play at the same time, and that settled working practice becomes difficult to establish. This may also be exacerbated by the Constable's own interpretation in practice of the Sergeant's policy. In the station the officer can always ask their colleagues or their Sergeant (and were usually not shy about doing this), but on a particular job, this support network was not readily available, or officers preferred not to give the impression of needing their hands held. As a result, in high-pressure decision-making, often towards the end of a long shift, different Constables might interpret and apply the same policy in different ways. For the effectiveness of policy, therefore, there is

---

[38] M Lipsky, *Street-Level Bureaucracy: Dilemmas of the Individual in Public Services* (New York, Russell Sage, 1980); S Maynard-Moody and M Musheno, 'State Agent or Citizen Agent: Two Narratives of Discretion' (2000) 10 *Journal of Public Administration Research and Theory* 329.

[39] K Bullock and P Johnson, 'The Impact of the Human Rights Act 1998 on Policing in England and Wales' (2012) 52 *British Journal of Criminology* 630, 640.

both good and bad news: policy has the potential to effect change both fundamentally and rapidly. However, in the short- and medium-term at least, change is not uniform. Nor, in many cases, is the change what was intended. The layers of interpretation, combined with the layers of risk-management that seem to be inherent in the middle-ranks of the police service, mean that often what policy intends, and what policy delivers, are very different.

As we have noted, vertical fragmentation of policy means that it changes as it cascades down from the senior management team through the middle ranks. This is then exacerbated by horizontal fragmentation at all observed levels. Worden and McLean note that in the United States,

> many efforts to change the way that street-level policing is performed are subject to a process of interpretation by the officers whose behavior is the target of the change, a process known in the study of organizations as 'sensemaking'. Officers' interpretations will not always conform with those of police executives.[40]

This was also reflected in our data. Horizontally, Sergeants were engaging in their own 'sense-making' of the policy and applying their own priorities, before instructing and supervising their officers based on this interpretation. The impact of this could be seen from officers reporting that they were sometimes minded to apply their powers differently depending on whether a particular Sergeant was on duty. And at the lowest rank there was a further element of horizontal fragmentation as Constables applied the same version of the policy differently as a result of both personal interpretation and understanding of the policy. When we consider both horizontal and vertical fragmentation, alongside the differing individual approaches to police work and discretion that we have considered throughout this book, we can see not only the inconsistent and sometimes unpredictable effects of policy decisions, but also once again the limitations of explaining police action by reference to an overarching 'police culture'. In terms of the long-standing but now considerably-nuanced debates about the extent to which the police possess an organisational or occupational 'culture', we contend that the disparate ways in which policy affects behaviours of frontline officers is further evidence that police organisational 'culture' or 'sub-culture' exists neither as an identifiable deterministic phenomenon nor as a helpful explanatory tool.

From our observations at least, 'police culture' cannot be seen simply as a barrier to change. Individual responses to policy varied among both supervisors and Constables. Overall, some policies were undoubtedly more popular than others but there was certainly no palpable and uniform resistance to change at an organisational level. Officers would discuss how a specific policy may not be working, and more experienced officers would on occasion be seen to influence newer recruits. But disagreements about the efficacy of policy were also common, and newer recruits were often able to explain to more experienced officers why, maybe,

---

[40] Worden and McLean, *Mirage of Police Reform* 14.

they should look at a new practice or development more positively. Examples from the previous chapters have shown how some individual officers resisted policy changes, but it was more common for these to be implemented even where the Constable fundamentally disagreed with the change. A supervisor who chose to resist a policy change was a more formidable hurdle than any 'cultural' resistance. That said, in terms of attempting to achieve uniform and consistent change, the *lack* of a coherent 'police culture' is as much a barrier to policy-based change as it is an opportunity.

There is one important caveat to this. For while, as a form of inhibitory rules,[41] an effectively-supervised policy can change police *practice*, it is much less clear to what extent *attitudes* amongst officers change. One of the few common features we saw across all officers was a desire to use the researcher as a sounding board for their complaints about many features of police work, which usually focused on lack of resources, shift patterns, lack of support from senior officers, paperwork, and some policies. To reiterate, officers did not share the same views about new policies, but there were many experienced officers who expressed a deeply entrenched preference for the former policy and hoped the new policy would be changed. This reflects Waddington's work, which highlights the difference between what police officers do and what they think.[42] It should also act as a warning that policy-led 'progressive' changes to police practice may only last as long as their effective supervision. Having established the power of (reconstructed local-level) policy to change the way that frontline officers utilise their discretion, we now consider the implications this has for reforming the way in which street powers are used, as set out in the preceding chapters.

## V. Reform to Police Stops

In Chapter 6, we considered how the street power of the vehicle stop check and the de facto power of stop and account were of fundamental importance to proactive policing tactics and to the triggering of the more formal powers of stop and search and of arrest. The relatively unfettered proactive discretion to carry out these stops meant that there was little or no accountability for the disproportionate use of these powers against young (usually working class) men in contrast to other demographics. Finally, we noted how we had observed a marked decrease in the number of stop and searches carried out by frontline officers during our research, as a result of changes to national policies, increased scrutiny of decisions, and pressures on time arising from austerity. As we have previously indicated, there is nothing to suggest that the changes we observed with regard to stop and search, and to a lesser extent stop and account/stop check, are irreversible, and during the

---

[41] D Smith and J Gray, *Police and People in London: the PSI Report* (Aldershot, Gower, 1985).
[42] Waddington, *Policing Citizens*.

course of writing this book, we noted with interest that the number of stop and searches in both forces rose again, in response to policy changes that followed pressure from central government.

However, despite the changes to how frontline officers in the observed forces were using stop and account, stop check, and stop and search, disproportionality remained in terms of the use of the powers against young males. Further, although both forces performed relatively well in national comparisons, people from ethnic minority populations were still over twice as likely to be subjected to a stop and search. Chapter 6 demonstrated: (a) how most searches escalate from an initial stop and account/stop check; but (b) that the vast majority of stops do not result in a search. Given this relationship, and what we have seen about the way in which officers come to a decision about when to question an individual or stop a vehicle, a conversation needs to be had about whether we should return to recording stop and accounts. We need to also consider whether we should be recording stop checks and whether we need to amend PACE, Code A in terms of detailing grounds on which vehicles can be stopped. In the case of stop checks, the bureaucratic burden will be only a marginal increase on the current requirement that a search of the database for a vehicle registration number check needs to be recorded and the officer's identification and location be given. Adding the grounds for the check might not represent an unduly onerous addition.

In terms of stop and account, we do, however, need to be realistic about the extent to which this recording could mitigate the current concerns. Not all stops would be recorded, especially as such a change would require a legally-workable definition of stop and account that would exclude many of the more routine public-police encounters. Where stops which were interpreted by the member of the public to fall under the definition of stop and account were not recorded, this could further challenge the legitimacy of the police. Conversely, where stops were recorded, members of the public stopped without further action would be more inconvenienced due to the delay of completing forms. Additionally, this more formal process may be interpreted by the individual as more oppressive than a less formal conversation, again raising questions of legitimacy. Nevertheless, our research suggests that, even assuming the sorts of vertical and horizontal fragmentation of policy we have identified, these changes to stop check and stop and account would lead to a reduction in the number of stops, and in particular a reduction in the number of stops made for purely frivolous grounds or as part of a 'fishing expedition'. The observed, and much written about, antipathy towards bureaucratic 'paperwork' by frontline officers will also inevitably act as a disincentive for any but the most necessary stops.

However, if we were to legally formalise stop checks or stop and account, it would also be important to ensure that stops are not deemed to be 'unsuccessful' if they do not then lead to a search, arrest, or an OSCO. This could in turn raise the spectre of the misuse of these more coercive powers, as officers may feel pressured to conduct, for example, a search, in order to record a 'successful' stop. We should also bear in mind that the inevitable reduction in stops which would follow the introduction of a formal recording procedure would further accelerate the move-ment of police officers from proactively identifying and trying to deter crime to officers increasingly being purely responsive to – and in many cases reduced to the mere recorders of – crime. It may be that recording all stop and accounts in particular, would be a disproportionate response to the problem of groundless, unnecessary, and discriminatory stops, and a response that does not remedy the problem.

Nevertheless, the likely advantage of increased regulation in this manner would be that fewer members of the public are stopped and, if we are genuinely concerned about the legitimacy of the police in deprived and high-crime areas, then a recogni-tion of the fundamentally coercive nature of both stop and account and stop check needs to be where we begin. Recording stops would, for a start, provide us with data about the use of the two powers, the effectiveness of these powers in terms of detecting crime, and any discrimination in their use. At present, these stops are almost completely shielded from the eyes of supervisors, with a wide varia-tion in the use of the powers between frontline officers. The practical concerns about the amount of time that recording stops will take, based on the evidence from the post-MacPherson experiment that a significant amount of police hours would be lost (see Chapter 6), could be alleviated by the use of BWCs to record details in real time for later capture on a computer record or, as we noted above, the addition of data to existing recording requirements for traffic stops. Given the entrenched and seemingly intractable problems of age and gender discrimination in stop and account, and the persistently high levels of racial disparity in many parts of the country in relation to stop and search, to do nothing does not seem a viable option.

## VI.  Best Use of Arrest

In Chapter 7, we detailed the findings of our fieldwork on the use of arrest, iden-tifying the way in which the legal tests set out in PACE, section 24 were regularly misunderstood, misapplied, and subsumed by policy and practical pressures. This leads not only to unlawful arrests but also to a discounting of alternatives that may provide an appropriate criminal justice response for offenders. Based on this data, and our more general arguments about supervision and police reform, there are two potential ways in which the police could look to mitigate the problem of unlawful arrest and a failure to consider alternatives. First, attention needs to be given in police training, staff development, and supervision, to ensure that officers are more likely to consider arrest necessity rather than just arrest reasons. If we can read anything into the hierarchy of statutory provisions, the PACE framework currently places necessity (section 24(4)) before arrest reasons (section 24(5)). Unfortunately, in reality the former is forgotten by officers. Further, the impact of *Hayes* has exacerbated this problem, making necessity totally subservient to section 24(5) and effectively neutering section 24(4) considerations for all except ongoing investigations where the suspect has already engaged positively with the police. This has, we believe, frustrated parliament's intent. In the absence of an appeal court decision overruling *Hayes*, an amendment of section 24 to clarify that arresting officers must only arrest once alternatives have been discounted will probably be required to remedy the malfunctioning statutory frame-work. Whether such a change to the law occurs or not, this principle should be disseminated to frontline officers through national and force-level guidance and training.

A second potential solution is through the use of voluntary attendance at a police station (VA), which enables formal action to be taken against suspects with-out triggering many of the procedural and practical barriers identified above and without raising the European Convention on Human Rights (ECHR), Article 5 concerns that would be triggered by arrest and subsequent detention. Our research suggests the increased use of VA be encouraged, which we believe would reduce the number of unlawful arrests and detentions, and at the same time reduce the risk of those who pose a continuing threat to the public not being pursued through the criminal justice system. The barriers to VA identified by officers included paperwork, a lack of specialist VA suites, timing issues, and delays in chasing up suspects who did not attend. The first three problems are also replicated, to a certain extent, in decisions to arrest, and can be overcome by diverting resources to make VA easier.

We are not claiming that VA is a silver bullet that will solve all the problems we have identified, particularly around discrimination. We acknowledge that VA, in many cases, will be impracticable and can sometimes be as resource-draining as an arrest. On its own, incentivising VA may not significantly reduce the number of crimes that are ignored or cuffed by officers. Further, in terms of improving the rights of suspects, the 'voluntary' aspect of VA is not an unproblematic concept. As we saw in Chapter 6 on stop and account, genuine consent on the part of the suspect cannot be established due to the imbalance of power resulting from the inferred threat of arrest or other sanction.[43] There are also practical concerns about VA relating to the fact that it is not always made clear to the suspect that they are free to leave,[44] to the lack of regulation of the length of interviews, and finally the take-up of legal advice.[45] However this has already been the subject of amendments to PACE, Code C, which in 2018 looked to put interviews following Voluntary Attendance under the same regulatory framework as those of arrested persons.[46] Nevertheless, these concerns over VA (which were not an aspect of the current research) do not change the fact that it is preferable, in terms of suspect treatment and the ECHR, Article 5 right to liberty, to the lengthy, unpleasant, and

---

[43] D Dixon et al, 'Consent and the Legal Regulation of Policing' (1990) 17 *Journal of Law and Society* 345.

[44] I McKenzie et al, 'Helping the Police with their Inquiries: The Necessity Principle and Voluntary Attendance at the Police Station' (1990) *Criminal Law Review* 22.

[45] Dixon et al, 'Consent and the Legal Regulation of Policing' 356.

[46] PACE, Code C 3.21(b), 3.21A, 3.21B, 3.22A.

coerced procedure of arrest and custody. Our research suggested that officers were always likely to choose 'the path of least resistance' when exercising their discretion, and that force policies, interpreted by supervisors, can change the working practices of officers. A combination of practical and policy inducements directed towards reducing paperwork and waiting and travelling times for VA has the potential to fundamentally change how arrest without warrant is viewed by front-line officers and how it affects suspects.

# VII.  Professionalisation

These proposed reforms to the powers of police stops and arrests, however, are limited, and on their own do not solve the wider problems of the over-policing of certain communities or inconsistency in use of police powers. Neither, by themselves, will they solve the problem of police illegitimacy in some communities (although we would hope they improve perceived legitimacy). Before concluding this book we should consider the extent to which the ongoing and significant reforms to police education and training, through the process commonly referred to as *police professionalisation*, may impact upon police discretion. Throughout the period of our observations, officers referred to debates about the education and training of police officers. Policies for a 'professional framework for the training of police officers and staff', the Policing Education Qualifications Framework (PEQF), was most commonly associated with the proposals for degree-level entry.[47] This was a misunderstanding of the broader ambition to develop staff at all ranks to operate as professionals on a par with doctors. Much of the discussion in the police station revolved around a simplistic debate about the nature of policing, whether it was a craft or, as the College was suggesting, a profession. What is meant by either term is not clear, but each term draws upon implied ideals.

Those arguing that policing is a craft draw upon the idea of the skilled artisan in a workshop, turning a lathe or fashioning clay, blowing glass or working with a loom. These skills are learned over time, apprenticed to a master. They are physical and tactile skills, not just intellectual ones. But there is a good deal of learning as well. To be an artisan is to be able to feel the qualities of a material, to work with the specifics of a particular piece of wood or clay or wool and to produce something of beauty with skill and care.[48] It is analogous to many aspects of policing, a

---

[47] College of Policing, *Policing Education Qualifications Framework* (2017) available at www.college. police.uk/What-we-do/Learning/Policing-Education-Qualifications-Framework/Pages/Policing-Education-Qualifications-Framework.aspx; BBC, 'All Police Officers "Should Have Degrees", Says College of Policing' (November 2015) available at www.bbc.co.uk/news/uk-34805856; E Williams, 'Professionalising the Police by Degrees: A Worthwhile Direction?' (2015) *Policing Insight*, 7 October.

[48] R Sennett, *The Craftsman* (London, Penguin Books, 2008).

point made by a number of commentators in the US in the 1960s and 1970s.[49] For example, Wilson argued:

> The patrolman is neither a bureaucrat nor a professional, but a member of a *craft*. As with most crafts, his has no body of generalized, written knowledge nor a set of detailed prescriptions as to how to behave – it has, in short, neither theory nor rules. Learning in the craft is by apprenticeship, but on the job and not in the academy. The principal group from which the apprentice wins (or fails to win) respect are his colleagues on the job, not fellow members of a discipline or attentive supervisors.[50]

Wilson was concerned to distinguish policing as a craft in contrast to a profession as narrowly defined in classic sociological terms.[51] While we have noted the importance of rules, in the form of the law and what we broadly term policies, and the looming presence of supervision, particularly in the form of the Sergeant, we also recognise the craft as described by Wilson. We each observed experienced officers who approached complex or tense situations in an assured manner, calmly assessing the evidence or the risks. Possessing an understanding of the law and policies, they nevertheless sought to work with what was in front of them and to make something of it.[52]

Professionalisation emerged in the US context as a defensive response to political interference.[53] Bittner argued for 'informed, deliberating and technically efficient professionals' educated at 'institutions of higher learning',[54] while Skolnick saw it as a solution to the problem of officers using discretion out of sight of supervision.[55] In contrast, in the UK, current debates appear very differently. The College of Policing has connected the idea of professionalisation to

---

[49] E Bittner, 'The Police on Skid Row: A Study of Peace-Keeping' (1967) 32(5) *American Sociological Review* 699; E Bittner, 'Police Discretion in Emergency Apprehension of Mentally Ill Persons' (1967) 14(3) *Social Problems* 278; JH Skolnick, *Justice without Trial: Law Enforcement in Democratic Society* (New York, John Wiley & Sons, 1967).

[50] JQ Wilson, *Varieties of Police Behaviour: the Management of Law and Order in Eight Communities* (Cambridge MA, Harvard University Press, 1968) 283.

[51] AM Carr-Saunders and PA Wilson, *The Professions* (Oxford, Clarendon Press, 1933); T Parsons, *The Social System* (New York, Free Press, 1951); RH Tawney, *The Acquisitive Society* (New York, Harcourt Bruce, 1921); J Evetts, 'Sociological Analysis of Professionalism: Past, Present and Future' (2011) 10 *Comparative Sociology* 1.

[52] M Rowe et al, 'Learning and Practicing Police Craft' (2016) 5 *Journal of Organizational Ethnography* 276.

[53] P Ashenhurst, 'The Goal: a Police Profession' (1959) 49 *The Journal of Criminal Law, Criminology, and Police Science* 605; SO White, 'A Perspective on Police Professionalization' (1972) 7 *Law & Society Review* 61.

[54] E Bittner, *The Functions of the Police in Modern Society* (Rockville, MD, National Institute of Mental Health, 1970) 121.

[55] JH Skolnick, *Justice without Trial: Law Enforcement in Democratic Society* (New York, John Wiley & Sons, 1967). See also, on Canada, MA Martin, *Urban Policing in Canada: Anatomy of an Aging Craft* (Montreal, McGill-Queen's University Press, 1995). And on Australia, T Green and A Gates, 'Understanding the Process of Professionalisation in the Police Organisation' (2014) 87 *Police Journal* 75.

those classic definitions of the medical or legal professions.[56] The emphasis on the emerging body of knowledge and of what works, most commonly associated with the idea of evidence-based policing,[57] is a significant element of this claim to professional status. Rather than being a defence mechanism, protecting discretion from political interference as was the case in the US in the 1960s, this model of professionalisation appears to be more like an external imposition. While it is unclear how the PEQF[58] and professionalisation[59] will develop in the coming years, it represents an attempt to change the frontline by intervening in training, in guidance and policy, and in the continuing development of officers. We have in these pages noted the shortcomings of many current police training and development programmes, and reform is certainly required. But, we would suggest that without wider reform to supervisory structures and practices, professionalisation is likely to be frustrated by the same processes of vertical and horizontal fragmentation we have identified, playing out differently between different officers, from one team to another, and from one force to the next.

## VIII. Prognosis

We finish this book with a number of concluding remarks and some thoughts on the foreseeable future of frontline policing in England and Wales. As we saw in Chapter 2, ethnographers of police are almost hardwired to seek out 'culture' when they enter the field. However, while we observed many of the behaviours and patterns that have been subsumed under the label of 'culture', we were struck by the variety and variability of these patterns over time and across police stations, shifts, and duties. We have had the comparative luxury of spending six years with two forces and so, perhaps, this element of variability has been more apparent. It has certainly allowed us to observe the effect of efforts to change police behaviours with respect to key street powers. In highlighting the importance of change, whether driven by austerity, by technology, or efforts to bring police practice into line with legal requirements or political desires, we hope we add to the debate about police powers and discretion. However, if change is a constant, we

[56] A Marshall, 'Police Work is Changing, so Officers Must Get the Recognition They Deserve' *The Guardian* (29 September 2015) www.theguardian.com/public-leaders-network/2015/sep/29/police-officers-crime-qualifications.
[57] L Sherman, 'A Tipping Point for "Totally Evidenced Policing": Ten Ideas for Building an Evidence-based Police Agency' (2015) 25 *International Criminal Justice Review* 11; H Gundhus, 'Experience or Knowledge? Perspectives on New Knowledge Regimes and Control of Police Professionalism' (2012) 7 *Policing* 178.
[58] Not least because one police force took the College of Policing to judicial review over it. See Lincolnshire Police (2019), 'PEQF – judicial review action launched' www.lincs.police.uk/news-campaigns/news/2019/peqf-judicial-review-action-launched/.
[59] S Holdaway, 'The Re-professionalization of the Police in England and Wales' (2017) 17(5) *Criminology and Criminal Justice* 588.

should also note that, at the conclusion of this book, we have not reached any kind of end point. As we also noted in Chapter 2, the more time we spent in the field, the more we realised that we needed to stay to observe the changes as they unfolded.

The starting point for our prognosis for the regulation of police powers is that the practices of frontline police officers, however entrenched, can be changed. If we believe that a police power is being utilised in an ineffective, disproportionate, or illegitimate way, we suggest that there is opportunity to change both the manner in which this power is used and the regularity with which it is used. If we wish, for example, for fewer black men to be stop and searched, or for fewer young people to be arrested, then through force policy and effective supervision, an impact upon overall levels of disproportionality can be achieved. Furthermore, it is possible to achieve behavioural changes of this nature over a relatively short space of time; we do not need to wait for a new generation of officers to come through or for new legislation to pass through Parliament and then to bed in.

However, this claim comes with two important caveats. First, while this type of policy-driven change can affect the *behaviour* of officers, we are not claiming that it also necessarily changes *attitudes*. So for example, while there was a fall in the numbers of stop and searches of black men in the period 2014–2017, the levels of disproportionate use against them remained stubbornly high. Therefore, it is unlikely to take much of a policy shift in the other direction for behaviour to revert to what it was before. Only through a sustained period of *consistent* and *effectively-supervised* policy change might we start to see attitudes and behaviours starting to converge over the long term. It is possible that this explains the currently-entrenched nature of PACE protections in detention.

Second, we need to acknowledge that policy-driven change will not be uniform. The extent to which change demanded by law or national policy cascades down to frontline officers and is implemented in a recognisable form is dependent on effective supervision at the level of the Inspector and, most importantly, Sergeant. Change is not a simple and mechanical process. Changes to law or to policies at a national level are filtered through the interpretive lenses of senior officers in many police forces, and we have emphasised the significance of the immediate supervision of frontline officers in this process of interpretation, transmission, and frustration. So, while we have observed changes, we have noted the vertical fragmentation that characterises those changes as policy cascades down through the various police ranks and layers of supervision. It should come as no surprise that new policies often play out differently across different stations, shifts, teams, and officers, nor that complicated legislative requirements, such as those imposed by the HRA 1998, are applied inconsistently. Given the problems this can lead to, in terms of both legitimacy amongst communities and the risk of litigation, this fragmentation needs to be better understood. In particular, we need to better understand the role and influence of the Sergeant in the supervision of frontline officers, an area that is currently under-researched.

The problem of horizontal fragmentation in the understanding of rules across frontline officers is a more difficult problem to confront. Officers in different teams, on different shifts, at different points in their careers, and with different personalities and understandings of what is 'good' policing, will continue to interpret and apply the same policies and laws differently. It is clear that there is a serious problem relating to the effectiveness of educational packages put together to introduce law or policy changes, or to skill officers in the use of new technologies or systems. More research is needed into how to make officer training, and in particular mentoring and on-going development and education packages, more accessible and effective. It is possible that the increasingly intrusive and technologically-based monitoring and accountability of frontline officers to their superiors, might mitigate the problem of horizontal fragmentation of law and policy, but we should be careful not to overstate the extent to which this type of accountability can and should constrain officer behaviour.

However, in focusing on the understandings, interpretations and behaviours of frontline officers, and on efforts to change these, we also need to reflect on what this perspective can overlook. Those officers in proactive roles, notably our Territorial Support teams, were often tasked to disrupt organised crime and gangs. They were expected to stop and search people and were deployed to areas on the basis of intelligence about conflict between groups. Briefings then further directed their attention to the sorts of people they should be paying attention to. We should not be surprised that those officers then disproportionately attend to young men and to young black men.[60] Changing the influence of intelligence systems, and the confirmation bias inherent in this approach to policing those communities most affected by gangs and crime, is a broader discussion, one that is emerging in recent reports as we write.[61] To focus on the behaviour and attitudes of frontline officers, or on their problematic 'culture', is to miss the context and the structural influences on any officer's decisions and actions.

In this book we have detailed the growth in the way that new technologies have the potential to hold frontline officers accountable to their superiors through tracking geographical movement, monitoring the registering of crimes and disposals, and recording face-to-face engagements with members of the public through BWCs. Our account suggests that these developments increased the levels of micro-management and accountability that officers perceive. As a result, the developments have, to varying degrees, had an effect in reducing the

[60] NJ Sekhon, 'Redistributive Policing' (2012) 101 *Journal of Criminal Law and Criminology* 1171; M Rowe and T Søgaard, '"Playing the Man, not the Ball": Targeting Organised Criminals, Intelligence and the Problems with Pulling Levers' (forthcoming) *Policing and Society* https://doi.org/10.1080/10439463.2019.1603226.

[61] P Williams, *Being Matrixed: the (Over)Policing of Gang Suspects in London* (London, StopWatch, 2018); P Williams and B Clarke, *Dangerous Associations: Joint Enterprise, Gangs and Racism* (Manchester, Centre for Crime and Justice Studies, 2016).

invocation discretion[62] that officers possess when they are deciding whether or not to use formal police powers against an individual suspected of committing a criminal offence. While this type of technological monitoring has the potential to improve consistency in frontline police responses to certain problems (for example domestic violence), and the potential to improve the conduct of officers during arrests or stop searches, we have grave doubts as to whether such developments are able to improve the legitimacy of the police amongst the public. Such monitoring and recording will not, for example, prevent the power of stop and search from falling disproportionately on young men, the working class, or ethnic minorities. The entrenched problems here are not predominantly *how* stops and searches are carried out, but the regularity with which unsuccessful stop and searches occur. When it comes to positive action to prevent domestic violence, again the increasingly intrusive monitoring does not appear to us to reduce the risk of harm; instead we saw the policy leading to violent men being returned to the household within hours of arrest, and to young men being forced onto the streets late at night with no accommodation. In many of these cases the policy being implemented was seen as illegitimate not only by the perpetrator, but also by both complainant and officer. The creeping levels of micro-management and accountability here have the potential to *reduce* the legitimacy of the police response amongst the policed as much as they have to improve it.

Moreover, even if technological methods of monitoring and in-house accountability are reducing invocation discretion amongst officers, or moderating police conduct during interactions with the public, this will not in and of itself reduce complaints that the police service applies its powers disproportionately, particularly against young black men. As we have explained, police 'discretion' is a multi-faceted construct. The traditional view of police discretion, particularly in early legal studies of the police, took a rather narrow focus on how officers apply the criminal law and work within procedural rules when choosing whether to invoke the law or apply a street power in any given situation. As we have shown, new monitoring and recording procedures have the potential to exert significant influence over how officers utilise their powers. But this limited definition of discretion only scratches the surface.

We need to develop a better understanding of the context of these decisions, the wider temporal and geographical background, as well as those factors driving an officer's career. We need to consider the effect of different police roles, the progression of the shift, the available resources, new technologies, and – of course – the role of supervision. All these factors have been relatively underexplored in the study of police powers. If we truly wish to reduce disproportionality in police responses to alleged or suspected criminality, and increase consistency in the application of the law across society, we must consider how and

---

[62] J Goldstein 'Police Discretion Not to Invoke the Criminal Process: Low-Visibility Decisions in the Administration of Justice' (Yale, Faculty Scholarship Series, 2426, 1960).

when the opportunity to utilise discretion about enforcing street powers comes into play. For proactive officer roles, such as Territorial Support, the decision to turn left out of the police station towards Crime-Ridden Estate, rather than right towards Gentrified Suburbia, has a fundamental influence on how, and against whom, powers will be used later in the shift. For Response officers, the decision to choose the pub fight ahead of the domestic violence incident plays a similar role. These decisions, which we might argue form an essential part of the craft of policing, are currently less constrained by the law, policies, technologies, or supervision. Only through an understanding of this wider context in which discretion is exercised, which has more in common with social science than with traditional legal understandings, can we understand how these decisions can play a direct role in when and where stops and searches or arrests are made, and against whom.

The question we need to ask is how and why we want to change the way in which frontline officers utilise their powers. Our research, and much of that which has gone before, has been clear that the law alone cannot achieve any significant change, and that policies and rules will only change policing so far as they are *interpreted* accurately and consistently (both vertically and horizontally), are *supervised* effectively, and are *achievable* with the time and resources available to the officer. If we are serious about directing change to achieve legal goals or national or force-level policies relating to specific offences or police powers, we must also be serious about paying attention to the wider issues of training and staff development, supervisory styles, shift patterns, technologies, and resourcing.

At the time of writing, we appear to be at the end of a cycle of diminishing financial resources and political support for the police service and at the start of a new cycle of increased funding and another 'law and order' political agenda from central government. These political pressures and increased resources have the potential to result in relatively quick increases in stop and searches and arrests across forces. We would note, however, that decisions made during austerity, such as the closure of police stations, may mean that expansion is not so simple a task. The potential for the revival of the much-diminished Neighbourhood role is one that we would welcome. But this is a revival that will take time, both to re-establish relationships and to rebuild trust. We can only hope for patience in this endeavour. Without such patience, as increasing resources find themselves (either through senior officer strategic decision-making or frontline use of discretion) focused on 'high crime' communities, the problems of disproportionate application of coercive police powers upon some communities will continue, and the number of people subjected to inappropriate or unnecessary use of these powers will increase.

We are, therefore, left in a peculiar situation that, while frontline policing is continually evolving and, as we have seen, can change quite dramatically, the problems of disproportionality against ethnic minorities, young males, and working class communities appear entrenched. While the 'law and order' model of policing continues to dominate politics, and while proactive policing remains focused on high-crime areas, it is difficult to foresee how the disproportionate use of police street powers will be resolved. But this does not mean that we cannot mitigate these problems and try to establish a police service that is not only fairer and more proportionate in its response to crime, but is also seen as more legitimate by the communities it is policing. Ultimately, throwing money at the police service, without long-term consideration or planning about how, for example, the extra officers will be deployed, where they will be stationed, or how officers will be supported in the appropriate application of their street powers, will not solve the entrenched problems; neither, on its own, will changes to the law or to the PACE Codes of Practice. But reforming the police is not particularly hampered by resistance from something as coherent as a unified 'police culture'. There is no reason why a longer-term funding model for the police and a focus on the strategic development of police training, mentoring, and – most importantly – day-to-day supervision will not start to yield results. But only by understanding the context in which police powers are utilised, not only geographically across different stations and forces, but across the time it takes for a policy to be rolled out, a shift to run its course, or an officer's career to develop, can we hope to make substantial, consistent, and enduring improvements to the legitimacy of the police in our communities.

# BIBLIOGRAPHY

ACPO, *Guidance on Policing Cannabis – Use of Cannabis Warnings* (London, ACPO, January 2007).

Agar, M, 'Culture: Can You Take it Anywhere?' (2006) 5 *International Journal of Qualitative Methods* 1.

Allen, DA, 'Police Supervision on the Street: an Analysis of Supervisor/Officer Interaction during the Shift' (1982) 10 *Journal of Criminal Justice* 91.

Ariel, B, Farrar, WA, and Sutherland, A, 'The Effect of Body-worn Cameras on Use of Force and Citizens' Complaints against the Police: a Randomized Controlled Trial' (2015) 31 *Journal of Qualitative Criminology* 509.

Ariel, B, Sutherland, A, Henstock, D, Yound, J, Drover, P, Sykes, J and Henderson, R, 'Report: Increases in Police Use of Force in the Presence of Body Worn Cameras are Driven by Officer Discretion: a Protocol Based Subgroup Analysis of Ten Randomised Experiments' (2016) 12 *Journal of Experimental Criminology* 453.

Ashenhurst, P, 'The Goal: a Police Profession' (1959) 49 *The Journal of Criminal Law, Criminology, and Police Science* 605.

Atkinson, P, *The Ethnographic Imagination: Textual Constructions of Reality* (London, Routledge, 1994).

—— 'Ethnography and Craft Knowledge' (2013) XI *Qualitative Sociology Review* 56.

Atkinson, P and Hammersley, M, 'Ethnography and Participant Observation' in N Denzin and Y Lincoln (eds), *Handbook of Qualitative Research* (Thousand Oaks, Sage, 1994) 248–61.

Austin, R, 'The New Powers of Arrest: Plus ça Change: More of the Same or Major Change?' (2007) *Criminal Law Review* 439.

Bacon, M, *Taking Care of Business: Police Detectives, Drug Law Enforcement and Proactive Investigation* (Oxford, Clarendon, 2016).

Banakar, R and Travers, M, *Theory and Method in Socio-legal Research* (London, Hart Publishing, 2005) 70.

Banton, M, *The Policeman in the Community* (London, Tavistock, 1964).

Barker, T, *Police Ethics: Crisis in Law Enforcement* (Springfield IL, Charles C Thomas, 2011).

Beetham, D, *Legitimation of Power* (London, Macmillan, 1991).

—— *Bureaucracy* (Buckingham, Open University Press, 1996).

—— 'Revisiting Legitimacy, Twenty Years on' in J Tankebe and A Liebling (eds), *Legitimacy and Criminal Justice* (Oxford, Oxford University Press, 2013) 326–52.

Bittner, E, 'The Police on Skid Row: A Study of Peacekeeping' (1967) 32 *American Sociological Review* 699.

—— *The Functions of the Police in Modern Society* (University of Minnesota, National Institute of Mental Health, Center for Studies of Crime and Delinquency, 1970).

—— 'Florence Nightingale in Pursuit of Willie Sutton: A Theory of the Police' in H Jacob (ed), *The Potential for Reform of Criminal Justice* (Beverley Hills, CA, Sage, 1974) 17–44.

—— (ed), *Aspects of Police Work* (Boston, Northeastern University Press, 1990).

Black, A and Lumsden, K, 'Precautionary Policing and Dispositives of Risk in a Police Force Control Room in Domestic Abuse Incidents: An Ethnography of Call Handlers, Dispatchers and Response Officers' (2020) 30(1) *Policing and Society* 65.

Black, D, 'The Social Organization of Arrest' (1971) 23 *Stanford Law Review* 1087.

Bohannan, P, 'Ethnography and Comparison in Legal Anthropology' in L Nader (ed), *Law in Culture and Society* (Chicago, Aldine, 1969) 401–18.

Borneman, J and Masco, J, 'Anthropology and the Security State' (2015) 117 *American Anthropologist* 781.

Bottoms, A and Tankebe, J, 'Beyond Procedural Justice: a Dialogic Approach to Legitimacy in Criminal Justice' (2012) 103 *The Journal of Criminal Law and Criminology* 119.

Bowling, B, Parmar, A and Phillips, C, 'Policing Minority Ethnic Communities' in T Newburn (ed), *Handbook of Policing*, 2nd edn (London, Willan Publishing, 2008) 611–41.

Bowling, B and Phillips, C, 'Disproportionate and Discriminatory: Reviewing the Evidence on Police Stop and Search' (2007) 70 *The Modern Law Review* 936.

—— *Racism, Crime and Justice* (Harlow, Pearson Education, 2002).

Boyne, G and Walker, R, 'Strategy Content and Public Service Organizations' (2004) 14 *Journal of Public Administration Research and Theory* 231.

Bradford, B, *Stop and Search and Police Legitimacy* (London, Routledge, 2017).

Bradford, B and Quinton, P, 'Self-Legitimacy, Police Culture and Support for Democratic Policing in and English Constabulary' (2014) 54 *British Journal of Criminology* 1023.

Brief, AP, Aldag, RJ and Walden, RA, 'Correlates of Supervisory Style among Policemen' (1976) 3 *Journal of Criminal Justice and Behaviour* 263.

Brightman, R, 'Forget Culture: Replacement, Transcendence, Relexification' (1985) 10 *Cultural Anthropology* 509.

Brogden, M, *On the Mersey Beat: Policing Liverpool between the Wars* (Oxford, Oxford University Press, 1991).

Brogden, M, Jefferson, T and Walklate, S, *Introducing Police Work* (London, Unwin Hyman, 1988).

Brown, D, *PACE Ten Years On: A Review of the Research: Home Office Research Study 155* (London, HMSO, 1997).

Brown, MK, *Working the Street: Police Discretion and the Dilemmas of Reform* (New York, Russell Sage Foundation, 1988).

Bullock, K and Johnson, P, 'The Impact of the Human Rights Act 1998 on Policing in England and Wales' (2012) 52 *British Journal of Criminology* 630.

Burns, S (ed), *Ethnographies of Law and Social Control* (London, Elsevier, 2005) 1.

Buvik, K 'The Hole in the Doughnut: a Study of Police Discretion in a Nightlife Setting' (2016) 26 *Policing and Society* 771.

Cain, M, *Society and the Policeman's Role* (London, Routledge and Kegan Paul, 1973).

Callaghan, D, *Seeing Through a Bourdieusian Lens: a Field-level Perspective of Anti-bullying Interventions in a UK Police Force* (Liverpool, unpublished PhD thesis, University of Liverpool, 2019).

Campbell, E, 'Towards a Sociological Theory of Discretion; (1999) 27 *International Journal of the Sociology of Law* 79.

Cape, E, 'PACE Now and Then: Twenty-One Years of "Rebalancing"' in E Cape and R Young (eds), *Regulating Policing: The Police and Criminal Evidence Act 1984 Past, Present and Future* (London, Bloomsbury, 2008) 191–220.

—— 'Arrest: Power of Summary Arrest – Reasonable Grounds for Believing that Necessary to Arrest Person in Question' (2012) *Criminal Law Review* 35.

Carr-Saunders, AM and Wilson PA, *The Professions* (Oxford, Clarendon, 1933).

Carter, JG and Phillips, SW, 'Intelligence-led Policing and Forces of Organisational Change in the USA' (2015) 25 *Policing and Society* 333.

Carter, JG, Phillips, SW and Gayadeen, SM, 'Implementing Intelligence-led Policing: an Application of Loose-coupling Theory' (2014) 42 *Journal of Criminal Justice* 433.

Cassan, D, 'Police Socialisation in France and in England: How do They Stand Towards the Community Policing Model?' (2010) 16 *Cahiers Politiestudies* 243.

Chan, JB, *Changing Police Culture: Policing in a Multicultural Society* (Cambridge, Cambridge University Press, 1997).

Charman, S, *Police Socialisation, Identity and Culture: Becoming Blue* (London, Palgrave Macmillam, 2017).

Chatterton, M, 'The Supervision of Patrol Work under the Fixed Points System' in S Holdaway (ed), *The British Police* (London, Edward Arnold, 1979) 83–101.

—— 'Frontline Supervision in the British Police Service' in G Gaskell and R Benewick (eds), *The Crowd in Contemporary Britain* (London, Sage, 1987) 123–54.

Chatterton, M, 'Misuse of Sergeants' (1987) 3 *Policing* 106.

Chiesa, M and Hobbs, S, 'Making Sense of Social Research: How Useful is the Hawthorne Effect?' (2006) 38 *European Journal of Social Psychology* 67.

Choongh, S, 'Policing the Dross: A Social Disciplinary Model of Policing' (1998) 38(4) *British Journal of Criminology* 623.

Clifford, J and Marcus, G, *Writing Culture: the Poetics and Politics of Ethnography* (Berkeley, University of California Press, 1986).

Coicaud, JM, 'Crime, Justice, and Legitimacy: a Brief Theoretical Inquiry' in J Tankebe and A Liebling (eds), *Legitimacy and Criminal Justice* (Oxford, Oxford University Press, 2013) 37–59.

College of Policing, *Code of Ethics* (Ryton, College of Policing, 2014).

—— *Leadership Review: Recommendations for Delivering Leadership at All Levels* (London, College of Policing, 2015).

Cooper, F, 'Masculinities, Post-Racialism and the Gates Controversy: The False Equivalence between Officer and Civilian' (2011) 11 *Nevada Law Journal* 1.

Cotterrell, R, *Law's Community: Legal Theory in Sociological Perspective* (Oxford, Clarendon, 1996).

—— *Law, Culture and Society: Legal Ideas in the Mirror of Social Theory* (Aldershot, Ashgate, 2006).

Currie, C, 'First-Line Supervision: The Role of the Sergeant Part One' (1988) 61 *Police Journal* 312.

Curtis, I, *The Use of Targets in Policing* (2015) www.policesupers.com/wp-content/uploads/2015/12/Review_Targets_2015.pdf.

Dai, M, Frank, J and Sun, I, 'Procedural Justice During Police-Citizen Encounters: the Effects of Process-based Policing on Citizen Compliance and Demeanor (2011) 39 *Journal of Criminal Justice* 159.

Darian-Smith, E, 'Ethnographies of Law' in A Sarat (ed), *The Blackwell Companion to Law and Society* (Oxford, Blackwell, 2004) 545–68.

Davis, C, 'Rank Matters: Police Leadership and the Authority of Rank' (2018) *Policing and Society* doi: 10.1080/10439463.2018.1555250.

Davis, K, *Discretionary Justice: A Preliminary Inquiry* (New Orleans, Louisiana State University Press, 1969).

—— *Police Discretion* (St Paul, MN, West Publishing Co, 1975).

Day, P and Klein, R, *Accountabilities – Five Public Services* (London, Tavistock, 1987).

Delsol, R, 'Effectiveness' in R Delsol and M Shiner (eds), *Stop and Search: Anatomy of a Police Power* (London, Palgrave Macmillan, 2015) 79–101.

Dixon, D, *Law in Policing: Legal Regulation and Police Practices* (Oxford, Clarendon, 1997).

—— 'Changing Law, Changing Policing' in M Mitchell and J Casey (eds), *Police Management and Leadership* (Sydney, Federation Press, 2007) 23–36.

Dixon, D, Coleman, C and Bottomley, K, 'Consent and the Legal Regulation of Policing' (1990) 17 *Journal of Law and Society* 245.

Donner, C, Maskaly, J, Fridell, L and Jennings, WG, 'Policing and Procedural Justice: a State-of-the-art Review' (2015) 28 *Policing* 153.

Drummond, H, *The Art of Decision-Making: Mirrors of Imagination, Masks of Fate* (Chichester, John Wiley & Sons, 2001).

Duster, T, 'Comparative Perspectives and Competing Explanations: Taking on the Newly Configured Reductionist Challenge to Sociology' (2006) 71 *American Sociological Review* 1.

Dworkin, R, *Taking Rights Seriously* (Cambridge, MA, Harvard University Press, 1977).

Engel, RS, *How Police Supervisory Styles Influence Patrol Officer Behavior* (Washington, Office of Justice Programs, 2001).

—— 'The Supervisory Styles of Patrol Sergeants and Lieutenants' (2001) 29 *Journal of Criminal Justice* 341.

—— 'Patrol Officer Supervision in the Community Policing Era' (2002) 30 *Journal of Criminal Justice* 51.

Engel, RS and Patterson, S, 'Leading by Example: the Untapped Resource of Frontline Police Supervisors' in JM Brown (ed), *The Future of Policing* (London, Routledge, 2014) 428–44.

Ericson, R, *Reproducing Order: A Study of Police Patrol Work* (Toronto, University of Toronto Press, 1982) 11.

—— 'Rules in Policing: Five Perspectives' (2007) 11 *Theoretical Criminology* 367.

Ericson, R and Haggerty, K, *Policing the Risk Society* (Oxford, Oxford University Press, 1997).

Evans, G, 'Practising Participant Observation: An Anthropologist's Account' (2012) 1 *Journal of Organizational Ethnography* 96.

Evetts, J, 'Sociological Analysis of Professionalism: Past, Present and Future' (2011) 10 *Comparative Sociology* 1.

Ewing, K, *Bonfire of the Liberties: New Labour, Human Rights, and the Rule of Law* (Oxford, Oxford University Press, 2010).

Falk-Moore, S, 'Law and Social Change: The Semi-autonomous Social Field as an Appropriate Subject of Study' (1973) 7 *Law and Society Review* 719.

—— *Law as Process: An Anthropological Approach* (London, Routledge, 1978).

Fassin, D, *Enforcing Order: An Ethnography of Urban Policing* (Cambridge, Polity, 2013).

Fenwick, H, 'Marginalising Human Rights, Breach of the Peace, "Kettling", the Human Rights Act and Public Protest' (2009) 4 *Public Law* 737.

Ferdinand, J, Pearson, G, Rowe, M and Worthington, F, 'A Different Kind of Ethics' (2007) 8 *Ethnography* 521.

Ferrill, J, *Buzzwords, Bureaucracy and Badges: an Ethnographic Exploration of How Versions of Wellbeing are Constructed through Social Ideology Projects in a UK Police Organisation* (Loughborough, unpublished PhD Thesis, Loughborough University, 2018).

Fielding, N, *Joining Forces: Police Training, Socialization and Occupational Competence* (London, Routledge, 1988).

Fletcher, GP, 'Some Unwise Reflections about Discretion' (1984) 47 *Law and Contemporary Problems* 269.

Galligan, D, *Discretionary Powers: A Legal Study of Official Discretion* (Oxford, Clarendon, 1986).

Gau JM, 'Consent Searches as a Threat to Procedural Justice and Police Legitimacy: an Analysis of Consent Requests during Traffic Stops' (2012) 24 *Criminal Justice Policy* Review 759.

—— 'Procedural Justice, Police Legitimacy, and Legal Cynicism: a Test for Mediation Effects' (2015) 16 *Police Practice and Research* 402.

Gaub, JE, Choate, DE, Todak, N, Katz, CM and White, MD, 'Officer Perceptions of Body-worn Cameras Before and After Deployment: a Study of Three Departments' (2016) 19 *Police Quarterly* 275.

Gayadeen, SM and Phillips, SW, 'Donut Time: the Use of Humour across the Police Work Environment' (2016) 5 *Journal of Organizational Ethnography* 44.

Geertz, C, *The Interpretation of Cultures* (London, Hutchinson, 1973).

Goetschel, M and Peha, JM, 'Police Perceptions of Body-worn Cameras' (2017) 42 *American Journal of Criminal Justice* 698.

Goffman, E, *The Presentation of Self in Everyday Life* (Harmondsworth, Penguin, 1971).

Goldsmith, A, 'Taking Police Culture Seriously: Police Discretion and the Limits of Law' (1990) 1 *Policing and Society* 91.

Goldstein, H, *Policing a Free Society* (1977) University of Wisconsin Legal Studies Research Paper No 1349.

Goldstein, J, 'Police Discretion Not to Invoke the Criminal Process: Low-Visibility Decisions in the Administration of Justice' (Yale, Faculty Scholarship Series, 2426, 1960).

—— 'Police Discretion' (1960) 69 *Yale Law Journal* 543.

Green, T and Gates, A, 'Understanding the Process of Professionalisation in the Police Organisation' (2014) 87 *Police Journal* 75.

Grimshaw, R and Jefferson, T, *Interpreting Police Work: Policy and Practice in Forms of Beat Policing* (London, Allen & Unwin, 1987).

Gundhus, H, 'Experience or Knowledge? Perspectives on New Knowledge Regimes and Control of Police Professionalism' (2012) 7 *Policing* 178.

Gupta, A and Ferguson, J, 'Beyond "Culture": Space, Identity, and the Politics of Difference' (1992) 7 *Cultural Anthropology* 6.

Haas, NE, van Craen, M, Skogan, WG and Fleitas, DM, 'Explaining Officer Compliance: the Importance of Procedural Justice and Trust inside a Police Organization' (2015) 15 *Criminology and Criminal Justice* 442.

Hall, S, Roberts, B, Clarke, J, Jefferson, T and Critcher, C, *Policing the Crisis: Mugging, the State and Law and Order* (London, Macmillan, 1978).

Harfield, C, 'Paradigm not Procedure: Current Challenges to Police Cultural Incorporation of Human Rights in England and Wales' (2009) 4 *The Journal of Law and Social Justice* 91.

Hart, HLA, *The Concept of Law* (Oxford, Clarendon, 1993).

Hawkins, K, 'The Use of Legal Discretion: Perspectives from Law and Social Sciences' in K Hawkins (ed), *The Uses of Discretion* (Oxford, Oxford University Press, 1992) 11–46.

Her Majesty's Inspector of Constabulary, *Leading from the Frontline: Thematic Inspection* (London, HMIC, 2008).

—— *Increasing Efficiency in the Police Service: the Role of Collaboration* (London, HMIC, 2012).

—— *PEEL: Police Efficiency 2015* (London, HMIC, 2015).

Herbert, S, 'Police Culture Reconsidered' (1998) 36 *Criminology* 343.

Herzfeld, M, *The Social Production of Indifference: Exploring the Symbolic Roots of Western Bureaucracy* (Chicago, University of Chicago Press, 1993).

Hewitt, P, *The Abuse of Power – Civil Liberties in the United Kingdom* (London, Martin Robertson, 1982).

Hill, M and Hupe, P, *Implementing Public Policy*, 3rd edn (London, Sage, 2014).

Holdaway, S, *Inside the British Police* (Oxford, Basil Blackwell, 1983).

—— 'Discovering Structure: Studies of the British *Police* Occupational Culture' in M Weatheritt (ed), *Police Research: Some Future Prospects* (Avebury, Police Foundation, 1989) 55–76.

—— 'Constructing and Sustaining "Race" within the Police Workforce' (1997) 48 *British Journal of Sociology* 19.

Home Office/College of Policing, *Best Use of Stop and Search Scheme* (2014) assets.publishing.service. gov.uk/government/uploads/system/uploads/attachment_data/file/346922/Best_Use_of_Stop_ and_Search_Scheme_v3.0_v2.pdf.

Hough, M, 'Procedural Justice and Professional Policing in Times of Austerity' (2013) 13 *Criminology and Criminal Justice* 181.

Hough, M, Jackson, J, Bradford, B, Myhill, A and Quinton, P, 'Procedural Justice, Trust, and Institutional Legitimacy' (2010) 4 *Policing* 203.

House of Commons, *Police Grant Report England and Wales 2016/17*, HCWS426, Written Questions and Answers and Written Statements HCWS426, 17 December 2015 www.parliament.uk/business/ publications/written-questions-answers-statements/written-statement/Commons/2015-12-17/ HCWS426/.

Hoyle, C, *Negotiating Domestic Violence: Police, Criminal Justice and Victims* (Oxford, Oxford University Press, 1998).

Jackson, J and Bradford, B, 'What is Trust and Confidence in the Police?' (2010) 4 *Policing* 241.

Jackson, J, Bradford, B, Hough, M, Myhill, A, Quinton, P and Tyler, Tom R, 'Why Do People Comply with the Law? Legitimacy and the Influence of Legal Institutions' (2012) 52(6) *The British Journal of Criminology* 1051.

James, A, 'Forward to the Past: Reinventing Intelligence-led Policing in Britain' (2014) 15 *Police Practice and Research* 75.

James, M and Pearson, G, 'Public Order and the Rebalancing of Football Fans' Rights: Legal Problems with Pre-emptive Policing Strategies and Banning Orders' (2015) 3 *Public Law* 458.

Jennings, WG, Lynch, MD and Fridell, L, 'Evaluating the Impact of Police Officer Body-worn Cameras (BWCs) on Response-to-Resistance and Serious External Complaints: Evidence from the Orlando Police Department (OPD) Experience Utilizing a Randomized Controlled Experiment' (2015) 43 *Journal of Criminal Justice* 480.

Jowell, J and Oliver, D, *The Changing Constitution* (Oxford, Clarendon, 1994).

Kadish, S, 'Legal Norm and Discretion in the Police and Sentencing Processes' (1961) 75 *Harvard Law Review* 904.

Kennedy, DM, 'Pulling Levers: Chronic Offenders, High-crime Settings, and a Theory of Prevention' (1997) 31 *Valparaiso University Law Review* 449.

Kerman, HC, 'Reflections on Social and Psychological Processes of Legitimization and Delegitimization' in JT Jost and B Major (eds), *The Psychology of Legitimacy: Emerging Perspectives on Ideology, Justice and Intergroup Relations* (Cambridge, Cambridge University Press, 2001) 54–73.

Kidder, R, 'Exploring Legal Culture in Law-Avoidance Societies' in J Starr and M Goodale (eds), *Practicing Ethnography in Law: New Dialogues, Enduring Methods* (Houndmills, Palgrave-MacMillan, 2002) 87–107.

Kozlicki, WM, Makin, DD and Willits, D, 'When No One is Watching: Evaluating the Impact of Body-worn Cameras on Use of Force Incidents' (2019) *Policing and Society* doi: 10.1080/10439463.2019.1576672.

Kyle, D, 'Correcting Miscarriages of Justice: The Role of the Criminal Cases Review Commission' (2004) 52 *Drake Law Review* 657.

Lacey, N, Wells, C and Quick, O, *Reconstructing Criminal Law*, 4th edn (Cambridge, Cambridge University Press, 2010).

LaFave, WR, 'Police and Nonenforcement of the Law – Part I' (1962) *Wisconsin Law Review* 104.

—— 'Police and Nonenforcement of the Law – Part II' (1962) *Wisconsin Law Review* 179.

—— *Arrest: The Decision to take a Suspect into Custody. The Report of the American Bar Foundation's Survey of the Administration of Criminal Justice in the United States* (Boston, Little Brown, 1965).

Lave, J and Wenger, E, *Situated Learning: Legitimate Peripheral Participation* (Cambridge, Cambridge University Press, 1991).

Ley, D, 'Interpretive Social Research in the Inner City' in J Eyles (ed), *Research in Human Geography: Introductions and Investigations* (Oxford, Blackwell, 1988) 121–38.

Lipsky, M, *Street-Level Bureaucracy: Dilemmas of the Individual in Public Services* (New York, Russell Sage, 1980).

Loftus, B, *Police Culture in a Changing World* (Oxford, Oxford University Press, 2009).

Long, J, 'Keeping PACE? Some Front Line Policing Perspectives' in E Cape and R Young (eds), *Regulating Policing* (Oxford, Hart Publishing, 2008) 91–120.

Lum, C, Stoltz, M, Koper, CS and Scherer, JA, 'Research on Body-worn Cameras: What we Know, What we Need to Know' (2019) 18 *Criminology and Public Policy* 93.

Lumsden, K and Black, A, 'Austerity Policing, Emotional Labour and Boundaries of Police Work: An Ethnography of a Police Force Control Room in England' (2018) 58 *British Journal of Criminology* 615.

Lustgarten, L, *The Governance of the Police* (London, Sweet and Maxwell, 1986).

Lamb, M, 'A Culture of Human Rights: Transforming Policing in Northern Ireland' (2008) 2 *Policing* 386.

Macpherson, W, *The Stephen Lawrence Inquiry* (London, HM Stationery Office, 1999).

Maguire, M, 'Criminal Statistics and the Recording of Crime' in M Maguire, R Morgan and R Rainer (eds), *The Oxford Handbook of Criminology*, 5th edn (Oxford, Oxford University Press, 2012) 206–44.

Maguire, M and Norris, C, *The Conduct of Criminal Investigations Royal Commission on Criminal Justice Research Study #5* (London, HMSO, 1991).

Maguire, M and Norris, C, 'Police Investigations: Practice and Malpractice' (1994) 21 *Journal of Law and Society* 72.

Maguire, M and McVie, S, 'Crime Data and Criminal Statistics: a Critical Reflection' in A Liebling, S Maruna and L McAra, *The Oxford Handbook of Criminology*, 6th edn (Oxford, Oxford University Press, 2017) 163–89.

Manning, P, 'Producing Drama: Symbolic Communication and the Police' (1982) 5 *Symbolic Interaction* 223.

—— 'Signwork' (1986) 39 *Human Relations* 283.

—— *Symbolic Communication* (Cambridge, MA, MIT Press, 1988).

—— *Police Work: the Social Organization of Policing*, 2nd edn (Prospect Heights, IL, Waveland Press, 1997).

Marcus, G, *Ethnography through Thick and Thin* (Princeton, Princeton University Press, 1998).

Marcus, G and Fischer, M, *Anthropology as Cultural Critique: An Experimental Monument in the Human Sciences* (Chicago, University of Chicago Press, 2014).

Martin, MA, *Urban Policing in Canada: Anatomy of an Aging Craft* (Montreal and Kingston: McGill-Queen's University Press, 1995).

Maskaly, J and Jennings, W, 'A Question of Style: Replicating and Extending Engel's Supervisory Styles with New Agencies and New Measures' (2016) 39 *Policing* 620.

Maynard-Moody, S and Musheno, M, 'State Agent or Citizen Agent: Two Narratives of Discretion' (2000) 10 *Journal of Public Administration Research and Theory* 329.

Mazerolle, L, Bennett, S, Davis, J, Sargeant, E and Manning, M, 'Procedural Justice and Police Legitimacy: A Systematic Review of the Research Evidence' (2013) 9 *Journal of Experimental Criminology* 245.

McBarnet, D, 'Arrest: The Legal Context of Policing' in S Holdaway (ed), *The British Police* (London, Edward Arnold, 1978) 24–40.

—— 'False Dichotomies in Criminal Justice Research' in J Baldwin and A Bottomley (eds), *Criminal Justice* (London, Martin Robertson, 1978) 23–34.

—— *Conviction: The Law, the State and the Construction of Justice* (London, Palgrave MacMillan, 1981) 156.

—— 'Pre-trial Procedures and the Construction of Conviction' (1983) 23 *Sociological Review Monograph on the Sociology of Law* 172.

McClure, J, *Spike Island: Portrait of a Police Division* (London, Macmillan, 1980).

McConville, M, Sanders, A and Leng, R, *The Case for the Prosecution: Police Suspects and the Construction of Criminality* (London, Routledge, 1993).

McGregor, J, 'From the State of Nature to Mayberry: The Nature of Police Discretion' in J Kleinig (ed), *Handled with Discretion: Ethical Issues in Police Decision Making* (Lanham, MD, Rowman & Littlefield, 1996) 47–64.

McKenzie, I, Morgan, R and Reiner, R, 'Helping the Police with their Inquiries: The Necessity Principle and Voluntary Attendance at the Police Station' (1990) *Criminal Law Review* 22.

Medina, J, Robinson, A and Myhill, A, 'Cheaper, Faster, Better: Expectations and Achievements in Police Risk Assessment of Domestic Abuse' (2016) 10 *Policing* 341.

Miller, J and D'Souza, A, 'Indirect Effects of Police Searches on Community Attitudes?' (2016) 56 *British Journal of Criminology* 456.

Miner, H, 'Body Ritual among the Nacirema' (1956) 58 *American Anthropologist* 503.

Moore, M, *Creating Public Value: Strategic Management in Government* (Cambridge, MA, Harvard University Press, 1995).

Muir, WK, *Police: Streetcorner Politicians* (Chicago, University of Chicago Press, 1977).

Munday, R, 'The Royal Commission on Criminal Procedure' (1981) 40 *The Cambridge Law Journal* 193.

Murphy, K, 'Does Procedural Justice Matter to Youth? Comparing Adults' and Youths' Willingness to Collaborate with Police (2015) 25 *Policing and Society* 53.

Murphy, K, Mazerolle, L and Bennett, S, 'Promoting Trust in Police: Findings from a Randomised Experimental Field Trial of Procedural Justice Policing (2014) 24 *Policing and Society* 405.

Mutsaers, P, *A Public Anthropology of Policing: Law Enforcement and Migrants in the Netherlands* (Tilburg, Tilburg University, 2015).

Myhill, A, and Bradford, B, 'Can Police Enhance Public Confidence by Improving Quality of Service? Results from Two Surveys in England and Wales' (2012) 22 *Policing & Society* 397.

Myhill, A and Johnson, K, 'Police use of Discretion in Response to Domestic Violence' (2015) 61 *Criminology and Criminal Justice* 3.

Nader, L, 'Moving On – Comprehending Anthropologies of Law' in J Starr and M Goodale (eds), *Practicing Ethnography in Law* (London, Palgrave MacMillan, 2002) 190, 191.

Newell, BC and Greidanus, R, 'Officer Discretion and the Choice to Record: Officer Attitudes towards Body-worn Camera Activation' (2018) 96 *North Carolina Law Review* 1525.

Newman, J, *Modernising Governance* (London, Sage, 2001).

Neyroud, P and Beckley, A, *Policing, Ethics and Human Rights* (Cullompton, Willan Publishing, 2001).

Nickels, EL, 'A Note on the Status of Discretion in Police Research' (2007) 35 *Journal of Criminal Justice* 570.

Norris, C, 'Avoiding Trouble: The Patrol Officer's Perception of Encounters with the Public' in M Weatheritt (ed), *Police Research: Some Future Prospects* (Avebury, Police Foundation, 1989) 89–106.

O'Neil, M and Loftus, B, 'Policing and the Surveillance of the Marginal: Everyday Contexts of Social Control' (2013) 17 *Theoretical Criminology* 437.

Oliver, D, *Government in the UK – the Search for Accountability, Effectiveness and Citizenship* (Milton Keynes, Open University Press, 1991).

Ormerod, D, and Birch, D, 'The Evolution of the Discretionary Exclusion of Evidence' (2004) *Criminal Law Review* 767.

Parsons, T, *The Social System* (New York, Free Press, 1951).

Pearson, G, 'Talking a Good Fight: Authenticity and Distance in the Ethnographer's Craft', foreword to D Hobbs and T May (eds), *Interpreting the Field: Accounts of Ethnography* (Oxford, Clarendon, 1993) viii–xx.

Pearson, G, Rowe, M and Turner, E, 'Policy, Practicalities, and PACE s 24: Police Understanding and Subsuming of Necessity in Decision-Making on Arrest' (2018) 45 *Journal of Law and Society* 282.

Pepinsky, H, 'Better Living Through Police Discretion' (1984) 47 *Law and Contemporary Problems* 249.

Phillips, C and Brown, D, *Entry into the Criminal Justice System: A Survey of Police Arrests and Their Outcomes* (London, HMSO, 1998).

Power, M, *The Audit Explosion* (London, Demos, 1994).

Pressman, JL and Wildavsky, A, *Implementation: How Great Expectations in Washington are Dashed in Oakland; or, Why it's Amazing that Federal Programs Work at all, this being a Saga of the Economic Development Administration as Told by Two Sympathetic Observers Who Seek to Build Morals on a Foundation*, 3rd edn (Berkeley, University of California Press, 1984).

Public Administration Select Committee, *Caught Red-handed: Why we Can't Count on Police Recorded Crime Statistics* (London, House of Commons, HC760, 2014).

Quinton, P, McNeill, A, and Buckland, A, *Searching for Cannabis: Are Grounds for Search Associated with Outcomes?* (Ruyton, College of Policing, 2017).

Quinton, P, Tiratelli, M and Bradford, B, *Does More Stop and Search Mean Less Crime? Analysis of Metropolitan Police Service Panel Data, 2004–14* (London, College of Policing, 2017).

Quirk, H, 'Identifying Miscarriages of Justice: Why Innocence in the UK Is Not the Answer' (2007) 70 *The Modern Law Review* 759.

Ramshaw, P, 'On the Beat: Variations in the Patrolling Styles of the Police Officer' (2012) 1 *Journal of Organizational* Ethnography 213.

Ratcliffe, JH, *Intelligence-led Policing*, 2nd edn (London, Routledge, 2016).

Reid, K, 'Race Issues and Stop and Search: Looking behind the Statistics' (2009) 73 *Journal of Criminal Law* 183.

Reiman, J, 'Is Police Discretion Justified in a Free Society' in J Kleinig (ed), *Handled With Discretion: Ethical Issues in Police Decision Making* (London, Rowman & Littlefield. 1996) 71–84.

Reiner, R, *The Politics of the Police*, 4th edn (Oxford, Oxford University Press, 2014).

Reuss-Ianni, E, *Two Cultures of Policing: Street Cops and Management Cops* (London, Transaction Books, 1983).

Riccucci, NM, van Ryzin, GG and Lavena, CF, 'Representative Bureaucracy in Policing: does it Increase Perceived Legitimacy?' (2014) 24 *Journal of Public Administration Research and Theory* 537.

Rosaldo, R, *Culture and Trust: The Remaking of Social Analysis* (Boston, Beacon Press, 1989).

Rose, D, *In the Name of the Law* (London, Jonathan Cape, 1996).

Rowe, M, 'Discretion and Inconsistency: Implementing the Social Fund' (2002) 22 *Public Money and Management* 19.

—— *Policing, Race and Racism* (Devon, Willan, 2004).

Rowe, M, Pearson, G and Turner, E, 'Body-worn Cameras and the Law of Unintended Consequences: some Questions Arising from Emergent Practices' (2018) 12 *Policing* 83.

Rowe, M and Søgaard, T, '"Playing the Man, not the Ball": Targeting Organised Criminals, Intelligence and the Problems with Pulling Levers' (forthcoming) *Policing and Society* doi.org/10.1080/104394 63.2019.1603226.

Rowe, M, Turner, E and Pearson, G, 'Learning and Practicing Police Craft' (2016) 5 *Journal of Organizational Ethnography* 276.

Royal Commission of Criminal Procedure, *The Investigation and Prosecution of Criminal Offences in England and Wales: The Law and Procedure* (London, HMSO, 1981, Cmnd 8092).

Ryle, J, *Collected Papers*, vol 1 (London, Hutchinson, 1971).

Sacks, H, 'Notes on Police Assessment of Moral Character' in D Sudnow (ed), *Studies in Social Interaction* (New York, The Free Press, 1972) 280–93.

Sanders, A, 'Reconciling the Apparently Different Goals of Criminal Justice and Regulation: the "Freedom Perspective"' in H Quirk, T Seddon and G Smith (eds), *Regulation and Criminal Justice: Innovations in Policy and Research* (Cambridge, Cambridge University Press, 2010) 42–71.

Sanders, A and Young, R, 'Police Powers' in T Newburn (ed), *Handbook of Policing*, 2nd edn (Cullompton, Willan Publishing, 2008) 281–312.

Sanders, A, Young, R and Burton, M, *Criminal Justice*, 4th edn (Oxford, Oxford University Press, 2010).

Sanders, C and Condon, C, 'Crime Analysis and Cognitive Effects: the Practice of Policing through Flows of Data' (2017) 18 *Global Crime* 237.

Scarman, Lord, *The Brixton Disorders 10–12 April 1981: Report of an Inquiry* (London, HMSO, 1981).

Sekhon, NJ, 'Redistributive Policing' (2912) 101 *Journal of Criminal Law and Criminology* 1171.

Sellitz, C, Wrightsman, L and Cook, S, *Research Methods in Social Relations* (London, Methien, 1965) 201–202.

Sennett, R, *The Craftsman* (London, Penguin, 2008).

Shearing, C and Ericson, R, 'Culture as Figurative Action' (1991) 42 *British Journal of Sociology* 481.

Sherman, L, 'A Tipping Point for "Totally Evidenced Policing": Ten Ideas for Building an Evidence-based Police Agency' (2015) 25 *International Criminal Justice Review* 11.

Shouhami, A, 'Constructing Tales of the Field: Uncovering the Culture of Fieldwork in Police Ethnography' (forthcoming) *Policing and Society* doi.org/10.1080/10439463.2019.1628230.

Shull, FA, Delbecq, AL and Cummings, LL, *Organizational Decision Making* (New York, McGraw-Hill, 1970).

Simey, M, *Democracy Rediscovered: A Study in Police Accountability* (Liverpool, Liverpool University Press, 1988).

Simon, D, *In Doubt: the Psychology of the Criminal Justice Process* (Cambridge, MA, Harvard University Press, 2012).

Simon, H, *Administrative Behavior: a Study of Decision-Making Processes in Administrative Organizations* (New York, Free Press, 1957).

Skinns, L, *Police Custody: Governance, Legitimacy and Reform in the Criminal Justice Process* (London, Routledge, 2011).

—— *Police Powers and Citizen Rights: Discretionary Decision Making in Police Detention* (London, Routledge, 2019).

Sklansky, DA, 'Seeing Blue: Police Reform, Occupational Culture, and Cognitive Burn-in' in M O'Neill, M Marks and A-M Singh (eds), *Police Occupational Culture: New Debates and Directions* (London, Elsevier, 2007) 19–45.

Skogan, WG, van Craen, M and Hennessy, C, 'Training Police for Procedural Justice' (2015) 11 *Journal of Experimental Criminology* 319.

Skolnick, J, *Justice without Trial: Law Enforcement in Democratic Society*, 2nd edn (London, MacMillan, 1986).

—— 'Enduring Issues of Police Culture and Demographics' (2008) 18 *Policing and Society* 35.

Smith, D and Gray, J, *Police and People in London: the PSI Report* (Aldershot, Gower, 1985).

Starmer, K, *European Human Rights Law: The Human Rights Act 1998 and the European Convention on Human Rights* (London, Legal Action Group, 1989).

Stenson, K and Waddington, P, 'MacPherson, Police Stops and Institutional Racism' in M Rowe (ed), *Policing Beyond MacPherson: Issues in Policing, Race and Society* (London, Routledge, 2013) 128–47.

Stewart, J, *The Rebuilding of Public Accountability* (London, European Policy Forum, 1992).

Stott, C, Hoggett, J and Pearson, G, 'Keeping the Peace: Social Identity, Procedural Justice and the Policing of Football Crowds' (2012) 52 *British Journal of Criminology* 381.

Sunshine, J and Tyler, TR, 'The Role of Procedural Justice and Legitimacy in Shaping Public Support for Policing' (2003) 37 *Law and Society Review* 513.

Tawney, RH, *The Acquisitive Society* (New York, Harcourt Bruce, 1921).

Terpstra, J, Fyfe, NR and Salet, R, 'The Abstract Police: a Conceptual Exploration of Unintended Changes of Police Organisations' (2019) 92 *Police Journal* 339.

Theobald, NA, and Haider-Markel, DP, 'Race, Bureaucracy, and Symbolic Representation: Interactions between Citizens and Police' (2009) 19 *Journal of Public Administration Research and Theory* 409.

Tiratelli, M, Quinton, P and Bradford, B, 'Does Stop and Search Deter Crime? Evidence from Ten Years of London-Wide Data' (2018) 58 *British Journal of Criminology* 1212.

Turner, E, 'PCCs, Neo-liberal Hegemony and Democratic Policing' (2014) 13 *Safer Communities* 13.

Turner, E, Medina, J and Grown, G, 'Dashing Hopes? The Predictive Accuracy of Domestic Abuse Risk Assessment by Police' (2019) 59(5) *British Journal of Criminology* 1013.

Turner, E and Rowe, M, 'Police Culture, Talk and Action: Exploring Narratives in Ethnographic Data' (2017) 4–5 *European Journal of Policing Studies* 52.

Tyler, T, 'A Psychological Perspective on the Legitimacy of Institutions' in JT Jost and B Major (eds), *The Psychology of Legitimacy: Emerging Perspectives on Ideology, Justice and Intergroup Relations* (Cambridge, Cambridge University Press, 2001) 416–36.

Tyler, T, *Why People Obey the Law* (Princeton, Princeton University Press, 2006).

Uhrig, N, *Black, Asian and Minority Ethnic Disproportionality in the Criminal Justice System in England and Wales* (London, Ministry of Justice, 2016).

van Hulst, M, 'Storytelling at the Police Station: the Canteen Culture Revisited' (2013) 53 *British Journal of Criminology* 624.

van Maanen, J, 'Police Socialization: A Longitudinal Examination of Job Attitudes in an Urban Police Department' (1975) 20 *Administrative Science Quarterly* 207.

—— 'Observations on the Making of Policemen' in P Manning and J van Maanen (eds), *Policing: a View from the Street* (Santa Monica, CA, Goodyear, 1978) 292–308.

—— 'Beyond Account: The Personal Impact of Police Shootings' (1980) 452 *The Annals of the American Academy of Political and Social Science* 145.

—— 'The Boss: First-line Supervision in an American Police Agency' in M Punch (ed), *Control in the Police Organization* (Boston, MA, MIT Press, 1983) 275–317.

—— 'Making Rank: Becoming an American Police Sergeant' (1984) 13 *Urban Life* 155.

—— *Tales of the Field: On Writing Ethnography* (Chicago, University of Chicago Press, 1988).

—— 'Ethnography as Work: Some Rules of Engagement' (2011) 48 *Journal of Management Studies* 218.

Waddington, P, *Liberty and Order: Policing Public Order in a Capital City* (London, UCL Press, 1994).

—— 'Police (Canteen) Sub-culture. An Appreciation' (1998) 39 *British Journal of Criminology* 287.

—— *Policing Citizens: Authority and Rights* (London, UCL Press, 1999).

Waddington, P, Stenson, K and Don, D, 'In Proportion: Race, and Police Stop and Search' (2004) 44 *British Journal of Criminology* 1.

Waddington, P, Williams, K, Wright, M and Newburn, T, 'Dissension in Public Evaluations of the Police' (2015) 25 *Policing and Society* 212.

Walker, S, *Taming the System: The Control of Discretion in Criminal Justice 1950–1990* (Oxford, Oxford University Press, 1993).

Watson, T, 'Ethnography, Reality, and Truth: The Vital Need for Studies of "How Things Work" in Organizations and Management' (2011) 48 *Journal of Management Studies* 202.

Weir, S and Beetham, D, *Political Power and Democratic Control in Britain* (London, Routledge, 1998).

Wenger, E, *Communities of Practice: Learning, Meaning and Identity* (Cambridge, Cambridge University Press, 1999).

Westmarland, L, *Gender and Policing: Sex, Power, and Police Culture* (Cullompton, Willan, 2001).

—— 'Police Cultures' in T Newburn (ed), *Handbook of Policing*, 2nd edn (Cullompton, Willan, 2008) 253–80.

White, MD, Mulvey, P and Dario, LM, 'Exploring Procedural Justice, Legitimacy, and Willingness to Cooperate with Police across Offender Types' (2016) 43 *Criminal Justice and Behavior* 343.

White, SO, 'A Perspective on Police Professionalization' (1972) 7 *Law & Society Review* 61.

Williams, P, *Being Matrixed: the (Over)Policing of Gang Suspects in London* (London, StopWatch, 2018).

Williams, P and Clarke, B, *Dangerous Associations: Joint Enterprise, Gangs and Racism* (Manchester, Centre for Crime and Justice Studies, 2016).

Willis, P and Trondman, M, 'Manifesto for Ethnography' (2000) 1 *Ethnography* 5.

Wilson, D, Ashton, J and Sharp, D, *What Everyone in Britain Should Know About the Police* (London, Blackstone, 2001).

Wilson, JQ, *Varieties of Police Behaviour: The Management of Law and Order in Eight Communities* (Cambridge, MA, Harvard University Press, 1968).

Worden, R, 'Situational and Attitudinal Explanations of Police Behavior: A Theoretical Reappraisal and Empirical Assessment' (1989) 23 *Law and Society Review* 667.

Worden, R and McLean, S, *Mirage of Police Reform: Procedural Justice and Police Legitimacy* (Oakland, CA, University of California Press, 2017).

Wycoff, MA and Skogan, WG, 'The Effects of a Community Policing Management Style on Officers' Attitudes' (1994) 40 *Crime and Delinquency* 371.

Zander, M, *Zander on PACE: The Police and Criminal Evidence Act*, 6th edn (London, Sweet and Maxwell, 2013).

Zelditch, M, 'Theories of Legitimacy' in JT Jost and B Major (eds), *The Psychology of Legitimacy: Emerging Perspectives on Ideology, Justice and Intergroup Relations* (Cambridge, Cambridge University Press, 2001) 33–53.

# INDEX